Praise for Jonathan Maberry and

Vampire Universe

"A book to sink your teeth into . . . An A to Z listing of the frighteningly long of tooth." —*Philadelphia Inquirer*

Zombie CSU

"Fascinating! An indispensable tool for anyone contemplating tackling a festering corpse onslaught." —*Fearzone.com*

"Candid, eye-opening, cutting-edge, startling . . . the existence of zombies may not be so far-fetched after all." —*Rue Morgue*

Bad Moon Rising

"One of the best supernatural thrillers of recent years."
—**John Connolly, author of *The Reapers***

Dead Man's Song

"Maberry takes us on another chilling roller-coaster ride through the cursed town of Pine Deep. You might want to keep the night light on for this one. Really." —**Laura Schrock, Emmy Award–winning writer/producer**

"A fabulously written novel that grips you from its first line to its last. Jonathan Maberry's writing runs from dark and beautiful to sharp and thought-provoking, and his books should be on everyone's must-read list." —**Yvonne Navarro, author of *Mirror Me***

"What began as a classic ghost story evolves with *Dead Man's Song* into something more of a classic monster tale. Ignore the curse of the second book of the trilogy. *Dead Man's Song* keeps the reader rapt and moves quickly, leaving the audience hungry for the final chapter in the saga."
—**Dreadcentral.com**

Ghost Road Blues
Winner of the Stoker Award for Best First Novel

"Jonathan Maberry rushes headlong toward the front of the pack, proving that he has the chops to craft stories at once intimate, epic, real, and horrific." **—Bentley Little, author of *The Academy***

"Every so often, you discover an author whose writing is so lyrical that it transcends mere storytelling. Jonathan Maberry is just such an author." **—Tess Gerritsen, *New York Times* best-selling author of *The Keepsake***

"Maberry knows that true horror lies in the dark, hidden places in the human heart and to take this journey with him is genuinely chilling." **—T.J. MacGregor, author of *Running Time***

"I read as much horror fiction as I can get my hands on, and it's been a *long* time since I've read anything that I've enjoyed as much as *Ghost Road Blues*." **—Stephen Susco, screenwriter of *The Grudge***

"Maberry will scare the bejibbers out of you!" **—John Lutz, *New York Times* best-selling author of *Night Kills***

"Maberry takes his reader to new and chilling places. If you read horror, you can't miss this book." **—H. R. Knight, author of *What Rough Beast***

"*Ghost Road Blues* is a hell of a book—complex, sprawling, and spooky . . . with strong characters and a setting that's pure Americana Halloween hell. A satisfying chunk of creepy, visceral horror storytelling—I'd recommend this to anyone who loves the works of Stephen King." **—Jemiah Jefferson, author of *A Drop of Scarlet***

"Reading Maberry is like listening to the blues in a graveyard at the stroke of midnight—the dead surround you, your pounding heart keeps steady rhythm with the dark, melodic prose, and the scares just keep coming. You find yourself wondering if it's the wind howling through the cold, foreboding landscape of gray-slate tombstones or whether it's Howlin' Wolf's scratchy voice singing '*Evil.*' "

—Fred Wiehe, author of *Strange Days*

"Get ready to be totally hooked, because it's all here: incredible atmosphere, characters you truly care about, and a level of pure suspense that gets higher with every page. Jonathan Maberry is writing as well as anyone in the business right now, and I'll be counting the days until his next book." **—Steve Hamilton, Edgar Award–winning author of *Night Work***

BOOKS BY JONATHAN MABERRY

NOVELS

Assassin's Code * Bad Moon Rising * Bits & Pieces * Broken Lands: A Rot & Ruin novel *
Code Zero * Dark of Night (with Rachael Lavin) * Dead Man's Song * Dead of Night *
Deep Silence * Dogs of War * Dust & Decay * Extinction Machine * Fall of Night *
Fire & Ash * Flesh & Bone * Ghost Road Blues * Ghostwalkers: A Deadlands novel *
Glimpse * Ink * Kill Switch * King of Plagues * Lost Roads: A Rot & Ruin novel * Mars One *
Patient Zero * Predator One * Rage * Rot & Ruin * Still of Night (with Rachael Lavin) *
The Dragon Factory * The Orphan Army—The Nightsiders, Book 1 * The Unlearnable Truths
* The Wolfman * V-Wars * Vault of Shadows—The Nightsiders, Book 2 *
Watch Over Me * World of Eli * X-Files Origins: Devil's Advocate

SHORT STORY COLLECTIONS

A Little Bronze Book of Cautionary Tales * Beneath the Skin * Darkness on the Edge of Town
* Hungry Tales * Joe Ledger: Special Ops * Strange Worlds * The Sam Hunter Case Files *
Whistling Past the Graveyard * Wind Through the Fence

GRAPHIC NOVELS

Age of Heroes: Black Panther * Black Panther: DoomWar * Black Panther: Klaws of the Black
Panther * Black Panther: Power * Captain America: Hail Hydra * Marvel Universe vs.
The Avengers * Marvel Universe vs the Punisher * Marvel Universe vs Wolverine * Marvel
Zombies Return * Pandemica * Punisher: Naked Kills * Road of the Dead: Highway to Hell *
Rot & Ruin: Warrior Smart * V-Wars: All of Us Monsters * V-Wars: Crimson Queen *
V-Wars: God of Death * V-Wars: The Collection * Wolverine: Flies to the Spider

ANTHOLOGIES (as editor)

Aliens: Bug Hunt * Don't Turn Out the Lights: A Tribute to Scary Stories to Tell in the Dark *
Hardboiled Horror * Joe Ledger: Unstoppable (co-edited with Bryan Thomas Schmidt) *
New Scary Stories to Tell in the Dark * Nights of the Living Dead (co-edited with George A.
Romero) * Out of Tune, Volume I * Out of Tune, Volume II * Scary Out There: Baker Street
Irregulars (co-edited with Michael Ventrella) * The Game's Afoot (co-edited with Michael
Ventrella) * The X-Files: Secret Agendas * The X-Files: The Truth Is Out There * The X-Files:
Trust No One * V-Wars * V-Wars: Blood and Fire * V-Wars: Night Terrors * V-Wars:
Shockwaves

NONFICTION BOOKS

Vampire Universe * The Cryptopedia (with David Kramer) * Zombie CSU: The Forensic
Science of the Living Dead * They Bite! (with David Kramer) * Wanted Undead or Alive (with
Janice Gable Bashman) * Ultimate Jujutsu: Principles and Practices * Ultimate Sparring:
Principles and Practices * The Martial Arts Student Handbook * Judo and You

THEY BITE!

**Endless
Cravings
of
Supernatural
Predators**

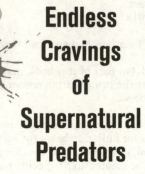

Jonathan Maberry
and
David F. Kramer

CITADEL PRESS
Kensingon Publishing Corp.
www.kensingtonbooks.com

CITADEL PRESS BOOKS are published by

Kensington Publishing Corp.
119 West 40th Street
New York, NY 10018

All Kensington titles, imprints, and distributed lines are available at special quantity discounts for bulk purchases for sales promotions, premiums, fund-raising, educational, or institutional use. Special book excerpts or customized printings can also be created to fit specific needs. For details, write or phone the office of the Kensington sales manager: Kensington Publishing Corp., 119 West 40th Street, New York, NY 10018, attn: Sales Department; phone 1-800-221-2647.

ISBN: 978-0-8065-4143-3

First printing: September 2009

10 9 8 7 6 5 4 3 2

Printed in the United States of America

Library of Congress Control Number: 2009923872

Electronic edition:

ISBN: 978-0-8065-3216-5 (e-book)

This one is for Fran and Randy Kirsch—because you've always believed. And—as always—for Sara Jo.

—JM

Dedicated to things that stalk and stir in the darkness and places that are dank and stinking; to things that slink and creep; that crawl and dig; that wait and devise; that plot and plan; that prey on the lost, wayward and unknowing; to those that call out like lost children in the night to attract their victims; that rend and tear; that trick and deceive; that feed upon the essence of the living; that lurk and hunt.

—DFK

CONTENTS

ACKNOWLEDGMENTS

Thanks to . . .

Our intern Katy Diana for endless hours of help, research, and nit-picking. Thanks also to guest sidebar writers Patti Kerr, Ruth Heil, and Janice Gable Bashman. Thanks to the Horror Writers Association, the World Horror Conference, Dragon*Con, Zombie Fest, HorrorFind, MonsterMania, International Thriller Writers, Mystery Writers of America, Doran Townsend, Tony Timpone of *Fangoria*, Monica Keubler of *Rue Morgue*, the Australian Horror Writers Association, and to all of the filmmakers, authors, artists, comic creators, and pop-culture gurus who shared their knowledge and insights with us.

INTRODUCTION: THE NATURE OF THE BEAST

Hell Hags by Andy Jones

They're out there. In the shadows. Moving out of sight in the darkness, or darting away from the corner of our eye. And yet we can feel them watching us with hungry eyes . . . supernatural predators that haunt our nightmares and even creep into our waking lives. What are they? What do they want? Where do they come from? Are they real or figments of our collective imagination?

These predators appear in all cultures and in many forms, from the seemingly beautiful and seductive to the hideous and repellent. We've always believed in monsters and they appear in all myths, all religions, and all kinds of folklore. Our holy books are as full of them as are epic poems and campfire tales. They fly on leathery wings or slither through the grass; they stalk the countryside on twisted goat legs or lope along through shadowy ruins on great clawed feet. But they're all monsters, and they all want to take a bite.

Science has, in fact, been able to explain away many of the monsters in which we once believed—or if not explained away, at least provided rationale for the beliefs we had (or in some cases, still have). SIDS (sudden infant death syndrome) seems to be a clear explanation for legends of invisible beings that come in the night to steal the breath and life from a healthy child. The same holds for the Old Hag concept, which involves a person (usually a man) waking up, terrified, utterly paralyzed, with a crushing weight on his chest. In some cases the victim claimed to have seen a gnarled old crone hunched over him, sucking out his life's breath. The Old Hag legend is common throughout the world and until very recently it was an inexplicable mystery that was so strange and persistent that it lent great credence to a belief in the supernatural. Now, of course, we know about the medical phenomenon called Sleep Paralysis, which consists of a period of inability to perform voluntary movements either at sleep onset (called hypnogogic or predormital form) or upon awakening (called hypnopompic or postdormital form).[1]

1. Kryger, Meir H., Thomas Roth, William C. Dement, *Principles and Practice of Sleep Medicine*, 2nd Edition. Philadelphia: W. B. Saunders Company, 1994

We now know that many of the mass deaths once thought to be the work of Nosferatu ("plague carrier"),[2] were actually disease pathogens. Many of the legends of vampires—many of which were invisible spirits—can be traced to improper burial practices that resulted in the spread of bacteria from putrefying corpses.

Other monsters have been dissolved by our understanding of porphyry, catalepsy, catatonia, psychosis, rabies, bipolar disorder, autism, mental retardation, genetic disorders . . . well, the list goes on and on. Science frequently shines a light that dispels the darkness.

Frequently . . . but not always.

Some monsters defy science to explain them away. There are still reported sightings of Bigfoot, lake monsters, the Jersey Devil, and many other creatures. There is an enduring and pervasive belief in ghosts, poltergeists, and demons. Many of the world's major religions preach a belief in gods, monsters, angels, devils, risen corpses, and other beings and events that do not fall easily into the pages of scientific journals, things that can be neither proved nor disproved by measuring or laboratory testing.

Switch on your cable TV and skim through the channels for history and science and you see dozens of programs about unexplained creatures. El Chupacabra, Nessie, the Yeti, the Mothman, Bloody Mary, La Llorona, the Hobbits,[3] Champ . . . they all get airtime in specials that promise to unlock the secrets of these unknown beings. Sadly, none of these shows ever do what they promise. Instead they collect the facts, they interview the witnesses, they have scientific analysis done on what few pieces of physical evidence can be collected, and then they wrap up with a cryptic statement like, "we don't know whether these creatures are out there . . . but the belief remains." Or words to that effect. Science wants to disprove it or explain it, but in an unnerving number of cases, it can't. Makes you wonder, doesn't it? Makes

2. In his novel *Dracula*, Bram Stoker incorrectly defines *Nosferatu* as meaning "undead".

3. See the entry on the Ebu Gogo, a dwarfish race of predatory humans (*Homo floresiensis*) whose remains were discovered in Indonesia in 2003 by anthropologists Peter Brown, Michael Morwood, and their colleagues.

you want to check to see if the windows are locked, the curtains drawn, and the doors bolted. Sure, there are no monsters. But, just to be on the safe side . . .

The same holds true with visitors from beyond. Hundreds of people each year claim to see UFOs, and thousands swear they've been taken aboard alien craft and subjected to painful and humiliating tests. Predators, it seems, not only come in all shapes and sizes, but they may come from other worlds as well as our own.

Find a comfortable chair for that thought to sit in.

They Bite! is an exploration of these predators. In these pages we'll poke our heads into some dark caves, go creeping through dusty attics, prowl the dank passageways of deserted ruins, dive beneath the waves of troubled seas, and generally poke our noses into places they don't belong.

This volume is a stand-alone book on these creatures, but it also fits into the growing library of books on the occult and paranormal we've been writing for Citadel Press. Some of these creatures were discussed in *Vampire Universe: The Dark World of Supernatural Beings That Haunt Us, Hunt Us, and Hunger for Us* (2006), but in that volume the focus was mainly on the folklore and legends of vampires and werewolves in all their shapes and guises around the world and throughout history. A year later we explored thirteen different aspects of "the larger world" in *The Cryptopedia: A Dictionary of the Weird, Strange & Downright Bizarre.*[4] Those books are pathways to *They Bite!*

In the book you're holding we'll not only meet a whole new batch of biting, clawing, devouring supernatural predators, but we'll follow them as they break free of folktales and myth and escape into the equally magical world of storytelling. It is through storytelling that we get to confront these monsters (in a way that doesn't actually result in dismemberment or exsanguination) and get to explore the myths in a countless number of ways. We learn more about the mind-set of our ancestors who either invented these creatures or recorded them. In either case, storytelling allows us an empathic microscope through which we can understand how

---

4. Winner of the 2007 Bram Stoker Award for Outstanding Achievement in Nonfiction.

our ancestors tried to make sense of the known world and their own place in the drama of life and how they struggled to put shape and sense to the unseen world.

They Bite! is your guidebook into the weird. Grab a torch, load your pistol with silver bullets, stuff garlic in your pockets, string that magic charm around your neck, and follow us. We know the way.

THEY BITE!

**Endless
Cravings
of
Supernatural
Predators**

THEY THIRST
Vampires in All Their Guises

The Dark Side by Mahmood Alkhaja

MORE THAN BLOOD

No supernatural predator has gotten as much press or inspired as many stories as the vampire. In many ways they are the quintessential supernatural predator, because they are practiced and deliberate. Most vampires are thinking monsters[1] who use their longevity to acquire insight, improve hunting skills, gain practical experience, hone their self-control, and cultivate their appetites. Their long lives also give them time to refine their cruelties so that they not only hunt for sustenance but also feed off the pain and misery they cause.

Vampire legends can be found in the myths and religions of all nations. Vampire legends are found among the earliest stories of the Assyrians, Hebrews, Romans, and ancient Greeks. These monsters have a great many aspects, and the stereotypical image of an Eastern European nobleman in a tuxedo and opera cloak is not one that is in keeping with the creatures of legend. Some vampires are human; some are not. Some vampires drink blood; many do not. Some vampires are shape-shifters; others appear in a single form. Some vampires are resurrected corpses, others are quite alive. Vampires also cross the identity line with ghosts, demons, werewolves, witches, and other beings in ways that make classification a real challenge.

STORY AND MYTH

What most people know about vampires comes from pop culture—movies, comics, novels, TV. The vampires of folklore and ancient myth are often quite different from the popular versions with which we're all so familiar; they're so different that even labeling them all as "vampire" gets tricky. It's tough to even make a short list of "Things We Know About Vampires" because most of what we know has been filtered through storytelling and embellished by screenwriters and novelists. It's okay that they did that—storytellers are supposed to keep things fresh and interesting—but if the story is based on folklore, then it tends to muddy the view of the source material.

1. There are some fangy dimwits and we'll get to those as well.

On Mining Folklore for Modern Horror

Vampirella by Joshua Hale Fialkov

"Most of my work plays into the primordial nature of folklore and the roots of horror. For something like *Vampirella*, for example, there's this biblical scope that goes into horror that's really a lot of where the character grew from, even if she was originally established as more of an occult figure. So, you get to play with the idea of the fallen angel, the rapture, plagues . . . all these grand, great things that shape so much of our lives. We sometimes forget that books like *Frankenstein*, *Dracula*, and so on are about people. Not about monsters. In fact, what makes the villains of these stories so monstrous is their humanity."
—Joshua Hale Fialkov writes *Vampirella* for Harris Comics and is the Harvey Award–nominated creator of *Elk's Run* (Random House).

On Folklore into Fiction

"So many of my novels and short stories have been inspired by folklore, either things I've run across in research or bits I've invented for the stories themselves. In *Baltimore or The Steadfast Soldier and the Vampire*, a novel I cowrote with *Hellboy* creator Mike Mignola, there are three long stories told by characters in the book, each of which is a bit of wild, tangled folklore. One concerns a man cursed by a demon-bear so that each night, when he sleeps, he transforms, a demon-bear slipping off the man's human skin to kill everyone around him. The end of that particular story is purposefully built to echo the ending of many folkloric tales. Another, about a lake demon called El Cuero, takes bits and pieces of South American folklore and weaves it into something pretty hideous. Mining folklore for modern storytelling offers endless possibilities. Endless."
—Christopher Golden is the award-winning, best-selling author of *The Myth Hunters*, *Wildwood Road*, and *Mind the Gap* with Tim Lebbon.

Bram Stoker created much of what most people "know" about vampires. Although *Dracula* does have some basis in vampire folklore, Stoker takes great license in his presentation of vampire powers and defenses. But Stoker was a novelist, not a historian or cultural anthropologist. He took bits and pieces of lore, picked what he thought sounded most interesting, and made up the rest. Even with the folklore he used, he was often mistaken. Case in point is the word *nosferatu*, which has always been linked with vampirism. Stoker either misunderstood its meaning or simply didn't know it and gave a new one for his novel. He translated the word to mean either "undead" or "not dead," but the term is a relatively modern word derived from an old Slavonic expression, *nosufur-atu*, which in turn was drawn from the Greek term *nosophoros*, or "plague carrier." Historically, the nosferatu was an invisible evil presence that spread disease and was widely believed to be an intelligent and malevolent driving force behind the great plagues of Europe.

Stoker's error may come from the fact that many of the world's most dangerous vampires do not take a physical form, but instead exist as a presence of evil that brings sickness, misery, and death. Like vampires that take blood, the *nosferatu* take health and vitality. In both cases death ensues. These two supernatural predators have become inextricably linked, their crimes overlapping so that it became common to believe that vampires, apart from drinking blood, also have the ability to spread disease, and in a number of the cases we'll discuss they actually are capable of both. A number of films and movies have run with this theme, notably Werner Herzog's underappreciated 1988 *Nosferatu the Vampyre*, which is a remake of F. W. Murnau's 1922 silent film, *Nosferatu: A Symphony of Horror.*

Ask the next hundred random people you meet to describe a vampire's powers and limitations and they'll pretty much say the same thing: vampires are pale, nonbreathing corpses who cast no reflection, cannot enter a house without being invited, cannot cross running water; they can be warded off by holy objects and garlic, and can only be killed by a stake through the heart. This is

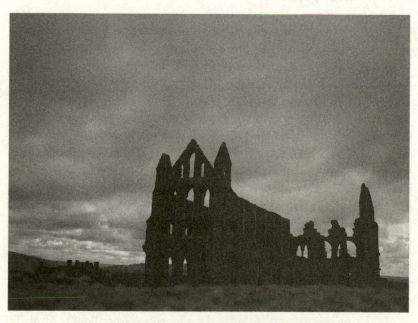

Whitby Abbey, from *Dracula* by Francine Kirsch

On Folklore and Modern Storytelling

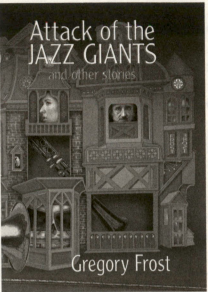

Gregory Frost

"*The Tain*²—the tales of Cu Chulainn—he says, comes from Irish folklore, and I wrote two books spinning off that and the fragments of other related tales that remain. The characters in my version include the grotesque Morrigu, which have been linked to the Welsh character of Morgan le Fey—which suggests that certain archetypes transform as they move through time, sort of the way an ancient pagan goddess is absorbed into Catholic theology and becomes St. Brigid. Likewise the ancient Celtic god Cernunos, often shown seated cross-legged and with antlers or horns, is the likely prototype for the most common portrayals of the devil. I've also worked with Gullah folklore for the story, 'The Prowl,'³ tracing the Angolan folktale monster, the platyi, to Charleston, South Carolina, where it evolves into the 'plateye prowl' with vampires a number of times, most recently in 'So Coldly Sweet, So Deadly Fair,'⁴ a story about Dr. Van Helsing's

2. Ace Fantasy Books, 1986.
3. *Mojo: Conjure Stories*, Nalo Hopkinson, ed., Warner Books, April 2003.
4. *Weird Tales*, April 2006.

first encounter with the undead, and 'Ill Met in Ilium,'[5] where vampires take over Troy while the Greeks are laying siege to the city; and some Japanese folklore (tengu, kitsune, kaidan stories) in short fiction and now in the Shadowbridge novels, which are the culmination of my fascination with such material."
—Gregory Frost, the acclaimed author of the Shadowbridge novels[6] has often dipped into the well of folkloric tales as the source material for new stories.

---

canon law as far as vampires go . . . except that it *isn't*. Most of this so-called common knowledge is actually faulty, because it's been run through the filter of pop culture, which changed it substantially from its older folkloric roots. From an entertainment standpoint, this is great, because it keeps monster storytelling from getting stale; but for a vampire slayer researching ways of destroying the undead, this is misinformation that will get him (or her) killed.

We can probably make a solid argument that virtually all beliefs have been similarly filtered. Granted, in centuries past, we didn't have horror authors like Bram Stoker or Stephen King retelling the old vampire tales. Or did we? We've had storytellers throughout history who told classic tales of monsters and perhaps embellished them for effect or edited them to fit local beliefs or current doctrine. This is what storytellers do, and this is why stories endure. The Scottish fairy story of Tam Lin, for example, exists in hundreds of forms in folktale, song, story, novel, and film. When dealing with the fantastical, the very nature of the material provides a marvelous elasticity. Novelists, poets, and screenwriters have taken a lot of perfectly acceptable liberties with the vampire over the years by changing this, modifying that, completely fabricating the other—all in an attempt to create a fresh slant or a novel twist.

When writers began telling tales of vampirism in a way that was purely fictional as opposed to recounting folktales that were

---

5. *The Secret History of Vampires*, Daw Books, 2008.
6. *Shadowbridge* and *Lord Tophet*, both published by Random House in 2008.

intended to be believed as true, they took the position that these monsters were in direct opposition to the Church and established new "traditions" to retell the stories of vampires in relation to purely Christian concepts. Once a concept was established through a popular piece of fiction or a landmark film, there was often a pretty quick transfer to our shared body of vampire knowledge. We

---

On Modern Vampire and Werewolf Storytelling

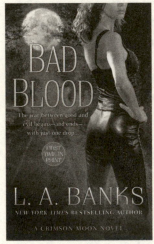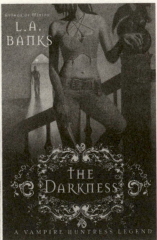

L. A. Banks, photo by Keith Major

"You can make anything new by updating the context . . . like, what would happen to a fight between the supernatural and the natural in an age where humans have advanced technology? I've explored that in the Vampire Huntress series and am doing it again in the Crimson Moon novels. Think about it: How would a werewolf respond to an assault rifle filled with silver bullets or a den getting hit with an F-18 fighter jet's payload? Might be a different outcome than a guy with a crossbow back in the day. Same deal with our advances in forensics. Or one could show how for all the so-called scientific advances, we still don't know jack. There are still plenty of ways to spin a good supernatural tale that will keep the subject matter fresh."   —L. A. Banks

see something in a vampire flick and we accept that it's so because the writer did his homework.

For example, the inability to face a crucifix was invented for fiction but was presented with such deftness that it appeared as if the writers were using established folklore practices as backstory in much the same way that Michael Crichton used established genetic science as backstory for his dinosaur novels. When other writers played off the same concept, it served to reinforce the belief. This has continued since the publication of *Dracula*, and it's clear that the general populace was accepting the newly created methods, powers, and limitations of the vampire as a new kind of gospel.

On the other hand, many of these new paradigms do have ties, however tenuous, to folklore. Take the use of the crucifix in vampire fiction. Stoker wrote that vampires cannot bear the sight or touch of consecrated items such as holy water, the crucifix, the eucharist, and similar apotropes.[7] In movies the cross itself is not only a protection but also an actual method of destruction, as shown in the 1960 Hammer Films classic, *The Brides of Dracula*, in which a real holy cross isn't even used—Van Helsing turns the vanes of a windmill so that their shadow falls across a fleeing vampire and that alone destroys him. In 1958's *Horror of Dracula*, candlesticks are used to form a cross and, combined with the rays of the sun, turn the Count to dust. This suggests that any "cross" was fatal to vampires. If you don't think too carefully about that, it seems reasonable; but stop for a moment and look around you and see how many times lines intersect at right angles. By that reasoning a man in a checkered suit would be a mass-slaughterer of vampires. And don't even get us started on hot cross buns. In folklore the best weapons aren't religious symbols but charms made specifically for the purpose of protection. Local tradition and ritual are often crucial in these matters.

Stoker also states that vampires can't enter a church or sacred ground. Most of them are buried in cemeteries, many of which are part of church grounds, which makes the ground sacred by definition. And during most burials a cleric of some kind prays over the

7. Any object that wards off evil.

On Using Folklore

Simon Clark,
photo by Sandy Auden

"Rather than taking a chunk of folklore and bolting it whole to a story, what I tend to do is digest the myth or legend for years before it resurfaces as a story idea. In *Vampyrrhic* (Hodder & Stoughton, 1999), a novel about Norse vampire-like creatures, I wove in a piece of folklore that always fascinated me. When Christianity arrived in Britain some fifteen hundred years ago there's a story that the pagan gods were defeated by the Christian priests, yet the old gods weren't destroyed but retreated into the rivers and lakes. I think the hook for me is this notion of those ancient pagan deities biding their time in their watery hiding places and brooding about their loss of status. In *Vampyrrhic* Viking gods unleash their undead warriors on the living because they crave revenge at any cost. Just to add to the frisson for me is the fact I live in a town called Doncaster, which is named after the River Don. The Don were a powerful clan of Celtic goddesses. Sometime I look at the river and I can't help my imagination going with that flow."
—Simon Clark's novels include the *Night of the Triffids* (Hodder Headline, 2001), the authorized sequel to John Wyndham's sci-fi classic, *The Day of the Triffids*.

---

deceased. That further consecrates the ground. And, as we'll discover in this chapter, there are vampires who even attend church.

Nearly all vampire movies and books use a vampire's inability to cast a reflection as a nice trick for establishing that a person is actually a vampire. But this is another bit of information that isn't found in vampire folktales . . . except in China. Oddly, the Chiang-Shih of China *does* possess most of the qualities ascribed to the vampires in *Dracula*. Running water, garlic, mirrors, shape-shifting; all of it affects them. But this vampire is an anomaly and by no means the standard.

As for a vampire's inability to cross running water, few vampires have that restriction, and there are several vampires who actually live in water. If that was the case, then Dracula would not have been able to take a ship to England. In the 1966 Hammer Films flick *Dracula Prince of Darkness*, the titular count falls through a break in a patch of ice and the rushing water beneath kills him. However, that would not have worked against any of the European vampires who could easily cross bodies of water. Besides, there is running water everywhere, from rainwater runoff to sewers, indoor plumbing, and underground streams. The Kappa of Japan and the Animalitos of Spain are water-dwelling demon-vampires, as are the Green Ogresses of France.

Sunlight has little actual power against true vampires (again with the exception of the Chiang-Shih). Even in the novel *Dracula* the count was able to move around in sunlight, though his powers were diminished. The idea that sunlight is fatal to vampires was concocted by film director Friedrich Wilhelm Murnau as a way of disposing of his Dracula-pastiche vampire, Count Orlock, in the 1922 silent classic *Nosferatu*. Since then it has been accepted as gospel in vampire stories, but in folklore most vampires can exist

---

Folklore in Horror Fiction

"Folklore played a vital role in my first published short story, 'The Mirror.' One Victorian-era Halloween custom involved a young lady eating an apple in front of a mirror at midnight on Halloween. The face of her future husband would appear in the glass. I combined that with an element from Bram Stoker's *Dracula* to create the story. Either element by itself may have been enough to carry the story, but combining the two folklores (one historical, one fictional) made for a more compelling tale."

—Eric Christ's short fiction has appeared in *Shadowed Realms*, *Nocturnal Ooze*, BloodlustUK.com, and the charity e-anthologies *Shadow Box* and *Black Box*.

during daylight hours. The Upierczi of Poland, for example, rises at noon and hunts until midnight. The Bruja of Spain lives a normal life by day and only becomes a vampire at night, as do the Soucouyan of Dominica and the Loogaroo of Haiti, along with many others.

In most vampire fiction the monsters don't cast shadows, won't have a reflection in a mirror, and won't appear on film. Bram Stoker is also responsible for this. For the most part the lack of a shadow or reflection does not appear in folklore.

In almost every vampire story the creatures have exaggerated canines. Folkloric vampires seldom have fangs of any kind beyond ordinary human teeth. In fact most of them use their normal teeth to tear through flesh. Their teeth are not hollow like soda straws (an element that pops up every now and then in movies). Once the flesh is torn they suck blood the way you'd slurp barbecue sauce off hot wings.

Vampire fiction also insists that no vampire can enter a house uninvited, however this is not something found in legend. That's Stoker again . . . otherwise Dracula would have slaughtered the Harkers and everyone else ten minutes after he landed in England. In folklore special precautions usually have to be taken to keep a vampire out. Various rites, spells, or herbs are employed by different cultures to bar a vampire from entering. In the absence of those protections, the vampire can enter freely and of his own will.

Their hearts don't beat, nor do they breathe, right? This varies. Some vampires are corpses that rise to attack the living, so there's no organic function of any kind happening. However, most of the world's vampires are alive to some degree, so circulation and respiration are probably happening even if at a reduced level. Also, vampires talk, and speech requires exhaled air causing the vocal cords to vibrate.

In movies vampires shy away from garlic, but in folklore the vampires actually fear it; and this is something seen in virtually all of the world's vampire legends. Garlic is a blood purifier and is believed to cleanse the blood of supernatural impurities. Throughout Europe garlic plays a big role in the ritual of exorcism, which is the standard method of vampire disposal. In this ritual, after a vampire's grave has been opened, garlic is stuffed into the mon-

On Supernatural Predators

American Wasteland by R. D. Hall

"With pop-culture reimagining of these monsters there's a fine line between respecting the original legends and twisting them into something that continues to relate to our modern sensibilities. That's the real trick: figuring out how to make the old folklore relate. We all have cell phones now. It's hard to isolate us and make us afraid. If Little Red Riding Hood had a cell phone, the Big Bad Wolf wouldn't stand a chance."
—R. D. Hall writes the comic *American Wasteland: Blood and Diesel* (Arcana Studio) with art by Mark Kidwell.

ster's mouth, then its head is cut off and turned backward so that it looks downward to hell. The body is then tied or pinned and reburied. Or, if there's some doubt as to whether the vampire is truly destroyed, the vampire slayers might douse it with water and flick a Bic. Garlic can also be used to bar entry to a house by making a paste out of it and smearing window frames and doorjambs.

The stake-through-the-heart business is tricky because it does appear in folktales of vampires from all over the world, but it is not used to kill the undead. Despite the quick, clean "dustings" shown on *Buffy the Vampire Slayer*, or the bloody stakings in so many vampire films, the stake was not a weapon used to actually destroy a vampire but a tool in a more elaborate exorcism. In the ritual of exorcism a long stake of wood or metal was driven through the body (chest, stomach, wherever) of a resting vampire; not to end the vampire's life (or unlife) but to pin it down to prevent it from rising while the other vampire slayers do their work. Only the Kozlak of Dalmatia will perish from a staking.

Fictional accounts of vampires shape-shifting into animals are a bit closer to the mark than most information found in books and movies, though there are very few legends that say anything about bats. Only about a third of the world's vampires possess shape-shifting powers at all, and out of the hundreds of vampire species around the world, only a handful (the South African Azeman, the Jaracacas of Brazil, the Croatian Kudlak, the Dalmatian Kozlak, and the Bhuta of India) can transform into bats. So, despite the fact that the root word for vampire can be translated as "bat," bats are in fact not that commonly connected to vampires. The most common creature for a vampire to morph into is a bird. Owls, crows, ravens, hens, and turkeys are common shapes. Cats are another popular beast-shape for vampires, as recounted in the Japanese legend of Õ Toyo and Prince Hizen, the Chordewa of Bengal, and the Jaracacas of Brazil. Other shapes seen in vampire folklore include such diverse creatures as the moth, snake, wolf (again, not as common as the movies suggest), fly, dog, tick, flea, mouse, rat, or bee.

Several vampires also take the form of fireballs or something resembling a Will-o'-the-Wisp. These include the Soucouyan of

Dominica, the Hungarian Lidérc Nadaly, the Zmeu of Moldavia, the Obayifo of Africa's Gold Coast, the Loogaroo of Haiti, the Asema of Surinam, and the Vjestitiza of Montenegro.

On the subject of vampiric strength, all of the sources—from folklore to the most current direct-to-video fang flick—seem to agree: they are very, very strong. The Draugr of Scandinavia, for example, is a vampiric ghost that inhabits and reanimates the bodies of dead Viking warriors, creating a monster so strong that no weapon can harm it. The Chiang-Shih of China actually entertain themselves by ripping their victims limb from limb with their bare hands, as do the Callicantzaros of Greece and the Czechoslovakian Nelapsi. Since the vampire is so powerful, getting close enough to one to fight it is generally a fatal gambit.

Some vampires do not require physical strength to kill their victims; some can do it merely by the intensity of their gaze. The Jigarkhwar of India and the Russian Eretica both possess lethal stares. Strangely, the Asuang vampire of the Philippines is best defeated by engaging it in a staring contest and waiting until it backs down and slinks away. Kind of makes him the schoolyard punk of the vampire world.

Sharpening the Genre

"To a certain extent, all of my work is influenced by folklore, particularly the postmodern sort exemplified by television shows like *In Search Of* and the *X-Files*, using the symbols and props of our modern life to evoke the same existential terrors that kept us crouching in our caves. Folklore is all about the things that lurk on the periphery of what we understand. What's wonderful about living in our scientific and rationalistic age is that the things on *our* periphery are all the more weird and compelling. The more we learn, the more refined our monsters become."
—Will Ludwigsen's short fiction has appeared in *Alfred Hitchcock's Mystery Magazine*, *Weird Tales*, *Cemetery Dance*, and many other magazines.

Villains, Killers, and Horror Movies

"The villains always have the best parts in movies. Darth Vader had the best part, the Wicked Witch had the best part in *The Wizard of Oz*—everybody loves villains. And these guys are just actors in makeup, but we all love them. They have a power to them. They're strong. Everybody knows about them. So they become incredibly familiar. It's hard to get people riled up and scared by them anymore because they're so familiar to us. For Halloween we dress up as scary characters, but we love them, enjoy them, and celebrate them. That's what it's all about.

John Carpenter,
photo by Sandy King

"Folklore is translated into a twentieth-century medium, the movies, as opposed to being told around a campfire. Now, there it is right in front of you on the screen. The horror film is always reinvented by the new generation. Then you keep seeing it again and again until it wears out. Then somebody else comes along and reinvents it. That's the good thing about it. Westerns didn't last, musicals didn't last—but horror films lasted. Odd, isn't it?" —John Carpenter directed many of our most iconic horror and sci-fi films, including *Halloween, Escape from New York, Big Trouble in Little China, Prince of Darkness, The Fog,* and *Starman.*

Decapitation is also a handy tool against vampires, whether in the movies or in real life. Sadly, popular fiction doesn't use this method enough, perhaps because it is too quick and simple a solution. A skilled swordsman, a woodsman with an axe, or a reaper with a scythe would each be ideal as a vampire slayer or slayer's assistant. The downside of this method of disposal is that one has to identify and locate the vampire, then get close enough to swing the weapon. Vampires are secretive by nature, and, being unnaturally fast and powerful, they generally offer a strong resistance.

One thing on which pop culture and fiction agree is that fire destroys vampires, just as it destroys everything else. It is often called "the great purifier," and in the battle against undead evil it certainly lives up to that claim.

A major rift between fiction and folklore is how a person becomes a vampire. In pop culture a person is bitten by a vampire, then has to drink some of the vampire's blood, and this exchange brings a person from life to unlife. Following death, the new vam-

---

Things That Scare

"Vampires, werewolves, and other monsters are a universal ethos, found in modern mythology, folklore, and legend in all corners of the world, and the dual nature of these creatures, both human and monster, offer glimpses of the best and worst of the human condition. The werewolf represents the idea that a terrifying beast lurks inside us, while vampires give form to our fear of darkness and death, and zombies and ghosts explore our mortality. The things we fear are the things we try to explain in rational terms, and these archetypes give us a means to try to explain the irrational. Humanity's mortality is the one thing that unites everyone, no matter what race or creed, and transient tales woven around the great unknown will continue to thrive as we try to give purpose to our existence. They explore the dark side of human nature; but in a lot of cases, many of the monsters possess near immortality, conquering the fear of death that haunts us all." —Shaun Jeffrey is the author of *Evilution* and the short story collection *Voyeurs of Death*.

pire rises from the grave after three days. But that process is another of Stoker's inventions. It's also another link to his personal beliefs. The process of exchanging blood and then resurrection after three days was his way of showing the vampire's mockery of the process of Jesus shedding—and symbolically sharing—His blood, then rising from the tomb after three days.

THE ALLURE OF THE VAMPIRE

Bela Lugosi by Bill Chancellor

The vampires of folklore are monsters. And even though some use sorcery to take the form of a beautiful woman or handsome man, beneath the glamour is a creature that is ugly inside as well as out. Most of them are unsympathetic, unattractive, and unwanted but through the sorcery of storytelling we've transformed them into romantic figures imbued with supernatural sexual appeal. We've made them tragic and sympathetic even when they are being outright predatory. From the perspective of the folklore purist, this is a rather puzzling distortion of the "truth;"[8] but when you consider the needs of the storyteller and an audience hungry for exciting new tales, it makes much more sense. A story of pure evil gets boring after a while. Even a story of natural predation gets tedious, which is why organizations as scientifically grounded as National Geographic have begun using personification in their wild animal specials. It's no longer "See the hungry lioness stalk her prey" but has become "In this episode, Daisy, our heroic young lioness, risks everything to provide for her cubs." We like to empathize with everything in nature. We give names to hurricanes; we turn the life stories of meerkats into complex soap operas; and a lot of us believe our house pets actually like being dressed in human clothes and treated like people instead of animals. It's no surprise we want to humanize the vampire.

Also, the complete bad guy, without dimension or redeeming elements, is a one-note character. That's why zombie films either concentrate on the dynamics of the human survivors, or, as in the case of some of the more recent zombie films, notably George A. Romero's *Land of the Dead*, some traces of personality are returned to the living dead in order to make them a more interesting participant in the tale.

Romanticizing the vampire isn't that much of a stretch, if you take the elements and look at them from a different perspective. Vampires are immortal, which means if they die young and pretty they stay young and pretty. Faces remain unlined and gravity doesn't make anything sag—vampirism is the ultimate Botox. Vampires don't get sick, which is a pretty attractive draw. No cancer, no hemorrhoids, no AIDS, not even a dose of the flu. Vampires are strong, which means there is an implied empowerment for everyone who feels weak or disempowered—which covers a large portion of humanity. Vampires are above—or perhaps apart from—ordinary laws and behavioral restraints. And then there's the act of the bite, which is often portrayed as a kind of kiss. Lips,

8. Okay, call it what you will.

The Romantic Vampire

"The vampire that came to us out of the 1800s in Europe changed the notion of what a vampire was up to that time, both in Europe and in other lands. Vampires were all malevolent spirits, sometimes in corrupted physical form, and terrifying. They were not the sophisticated upper-class gentleman or lady, if you will, that appeared in the first English-language novel *Varney the Vampire*, in the short story "Carmilla," and later *Dracula*, all from the UK, or in some of the stories out of France. These refined creatures could walk among us and were educated. They fit in and could go unnoticed but for their killer ways. This was not the filthy resuscitated corpse that dug its way out of the grave and rampaged, preying on its relatives. That change is with us still and in the last couple of decades has moved into what has come to be known as the romantic vampire, much of what we see now in fiction. The dark side has been brought into the light, the vampire absorbed, even loved. The terror has been sucked out of the undead and consequently we've had to replace him/her with zombies, which fill the space left by the horrifying, unstoppable nosferatu. Zombies are mindless, driven by their needs, killers, not really living, dirty, insane, and they go back to what folklore portrayed as the vampire before he cleaned up good." —Nancy Kilpatrick is the award-winning author of eighteen novels, including *The Power of the Blood* series and the nonfiction book *The Goth Bible* (St. Martins Press, 2004).

---

hot blood, and a little pain. The focus is shifted away from a rending of flesh and the severing of arteries so that the curse of vampirism becomes "the dark gift," as Anne Rice and so many others have called it.

This vampire personality makeover was kick-started in 1819 by John Polidori's short story, "The Vampyre," which featured Lord Ruthven, an elegant and refined nobleman. Ruthven was suave, his predatory nature more sexual than vicious, and his manners (except when he's actually killing someone) are impeccable. When Polidori's story was adapted into a play in 1820, *The Vampire or*

Urban Fantasy

"My main series is urban fantasy, which is often heavily rooted in folklore—populated by werewolves, witches, demons, ghosts. This genre (and the 'sister genre' of paranormal romance) have become enormously popular in the last few years, introducing a new generation and a new audience to these old stories."
—Kelley Armstrong is the author of the *New York Times* best-selling Otherworld urban fantasy series, which started with the werewolf novel *Bitten* in 2001.

Kelley Armstrong,
photo by J. Fricke

the *Bride of the Isles*, by J. R. Planche, it reached the cultured society of London and became a subject of polite discussion. Alexandre Dumas of *Three Musketeers* fame published *Les Mille et un Fantomes* (published in English as *The Pale Lady*), which sets the adventure in the Carpathian Mountains and deals with a Polish noblewoman involved with two brothers, one of whom is an unsavory vampire. And in 1860 *The Mysterious Stranger* was published by an anonymous author, in which the villain is a vampire Count from the same region of the world. It's pretty clear that these last two stories, which introduced us to the Carpathians as a center for vampire activity and vampires who were noblemen—significantly a Count in the 1860 story—that Bram Stoker mined these early tales for the creation of Count Dracula.

This is one of the clearest examples of how the vampire image in the popular view is drawn from layer upon layer of fiction far more than from folklore. Jules Verne even added to this new archetype with his *The Castle of the Carpathians* (1892) five years before *Dracula* was published. Stoker, by the way, had originally planned to set his novel in Styria (part of Austria), but was influenced into a location change, largely because of his readings of earlier vampire fiction and some delving into folklore.

Not all of these new literary vampires were noble born. In 1836, French author Théophile Gautier published the short story, "La Morte Amoreuse," later translated into English as "Clarimonde."[9] It told the story of a Catholic priest who fell in love with a female vampire. In the story the vampire is presented as beautiful and compelling—in essence faithful to the concept of many of the world's seductress vampires—but the story had a lovely and ethereal air, far removed from the violent and bloody resolution of affairs with folkloric French seductress vampires like the Green Ogresses or the White Ladies of Fau. Literary license compelled Gautier to focus on the romance and skip all that rending and feasting.

Likewise, not all nineteenth-century vampires were charming, as evidenced by Johann Ludwig Tieck's 1823 novelette *Wake Not the Dead*, in which the vampire shapeshifts into a man-eating serpent. And the titular monster in 1845's *Varney the Vampire or the Feast of Blood* was a real rotter. Although this is closer to the nature of the beast according to folklore, the story itself was not based on folklore. *Varney*, written by James Malcolm Rymer,[10] was published in serial form in 109 weekly installments as penny dreadfuls: eight-page booklets that sold for a penny (and which were also called penny bloods and blood and thunders).

The romantic transformation of the vampire continued, however, and as audiences clamored for more, the writers of the era realized just how flexible the vampire was in terms of storytelling potential. As a result the authors strayed further from folklore and deeper into the land of pure invention. Sometimes they did so with poor results (as with *Varney*, which though a landmark is a dreadful read), and sometimes with innovation and literary distinction. The vampires of fiction began to take on more than sexual allure and romantic charm—they began to be three-dimensional; they

9. Among other titles.
10. Some sources claim that Thomas Preskett Prest may have written the story, though this claim is not widely accepted.

Heroes and Monsters

"Most often a monster story is really a hero's journey: the antagonist is the monster and the hero wins in the end. Like any other genre it's all about new stories and twists with the same basic human struggle to overcome an obstacle, be it getting the girl, killing the monster, or overcoming evil. Great new stories with intriguing locations and new horrific things to deal with seem to be the basis of some of the new "monsters" and horror films. Even when the "monster" is a human or evil residing in our technology, it's about coming up with that

Ashlie Rhey as a vampire

scary character and executing the film shoot and edit in the manner that puts the audience in the state of fear, suspense, and horror." —Actress Ashlie Rhey starred in *Witchcraft 7* (1995) and *Playboy's Rising Stars and Starlets* (1998)

---

became people who were caught up in unnatural circumstances rather than monster archetypes. Perhaps the first truly three-dimensional vampire character was that of Carmilla, the female monster in the 1871 novella of that name by Joseph Sheridan Le Fanu. Though seduction is still the major theme, the story is given

Varney the Vampire

a new slant by having a female vampire seduce a female victim. This created an entirely new subgenre: homoerotic vampirism. Without Carmilla we would not have had Anne Rice's Vampire Chronicles and all its many imitators.

Perversely, when Bram Stoker created *Dracula* he did not make the count a romantic lead in the truest sense of the word. Drac was noble born and charismatic, but his charm was more a product of manipulation and black magic, though clearly a sexual subtext lurks right beneath the surface of each page. It wasn't until Dracula was adapted for stage and later film that the sexual potential of the character was fully explored. Béla Lugosi, who was a romantic

Envisioning Horror

Deadland by Michael Calandra

"Since a lot of my work features a model, I may try and use some horror themes to describe and accent her character. In my painting *Deadland*, I chose a Queen of the Undead theme for my model Bianca Beauchamp. I wanted her to be very dark, sexy, and in total control of her legions of the dead. By placing the dead characters behind her, I attempt to show her dominance over death. I also used only cool colors to illustrate their cold, dead world. The subject, painted in very warm contrasting colors, shows that she is unaffected by death, perhaps even beyond it. I created the skeleton figure behind her to show their dependence on her leadership. The chains and sickles hanging down symbolize the figures bound by death."

—Michael Calandra's art has appeared in *Heavy Metal Magazine* and *Art Scene International*.

leading man at the time, was the first who gave him the charm and the sexual charisma. And the movie production company wanted to make it very clear that Dracula—though a murderous predator—was a heterosexual murderous predator. The screenwriter and director were told that Dracula only sucks the blood of women. A few decades later Christopher Lee amped up the heterosexual charge in the Hammer films that had him feasting on

Vampire Cinema by Allen Koszowski

many a soft feminine throat, usually while a barely contained bosom heaved dramatically.

Louis Jourdan, Frank Langella, and Gary Oldman each added their own spins over the years, keeping the sexual tension high; though by no means has *Dracula*—and the rest of vampire fiction—ever settled down into a boy-meets-girl, boy-drinks-the-blood-of-girl sort of thing. Vampire films and novels have explored all aspects of human (and inhuman) sexuality. Hetero-,-homo-, and bisexual vampires are so common nowadays that a sexually ambiguous, or perhaps "omnivorous," vampire has become almost de rigueur.

Sexuality, in fact, is a more common theme in the modern vampire tale than horror. The whole paranormal romance subgenre is built on the exploration of the vampire as a romantic, tragic, and often misunderstood creature. Anne Rice owned this genre for years, chunking out huge novels filled with an ornate—even rococo—style that indulged in a lushness of language that was as sensual as the subject matter. Her stories were always from the vampires' point of view, and through characters like the conflicted Louis and the impulsive Lestat we share the experience of leaving humanity and becoming immortal. Rice's genius was to make the vampires' experience one that we, as human readers, could share and understand. Her first (and leanest) novel, *Interview With the Vampire* (1976), was one of the first—and certainly the best to date—novel in which the process of transitioning from human to vampire was explored with such insight that it became intensely personal for the readers. It was a best-seller, and is still on bookshelves over thirty years later. Subsequent books strayed from Louis's perspective and into the wickedly warped mind of Lestat, a sensual, sexual, and audacious character who was at once hero and villain, victim and predator, voice of reason and architect of chaos.

Rice also created an elaborate vampire mythology that strayed almost completely from folklore but was so authoritatively written that many readers believe that she, like Stoker, based her work on actual myths and legends. This pervasive belief, which has been cited in dozens of articles, interviews, and news stories, isn't all that surprising, especially considering that the generation who

Giving Life to Old Paradigms

"For me it comes in dreams. I wake up with a new fantastic idea (or at least I like to think so). For my *Dark Order Saga* I eliminated the myth that vampyres can't see themselves in mirrors because they're soulless . . . if you put a mirror in front of a corpse, it still has a reflection. And who brought silver into the equation? To this day, merging werewolf myth with vampyres irks me." —Ellis Mechallen is the creator of the sci-fi fantasy comic book *Veni. Vidi. Vici.*

reads her books grew up with her as the voice of vampire lore for their generation, just as a whole generation a century ago grew up with Bram Stoker's *Dracula.* This is no different than the way in which all folklore has spread: we believe what we experience, and we know what we hear. For almost four decades vampires have equaled Anne Rice to millions of people.

However, Anne Rice was not the first to use the interview format to tell a story from the vampire's point of view. Fred Saberhagen (1930–2007) did that a year earlier with *The Dracula Tape* (Warner, 1975), a novel that explored the morality of both vampires and humans, and which launched a series of excellent novels: *The Holmes-Dracula File* (1978); *An Old Friend of the Family* (1979); *Thorn* (1980); *Dominion* (1982); *A Matter of Taste* (1990); *A Question of Time* (1992); *Séance for a Vampire* (1994); *A Sharpness on the Neck* (1996); and *A Coldness in the Blood* (2002). In Saberhagen's novels Van Helsing and company are a bunch of obsessive and violent killers and Dracula is merely misunderstood. His seduction of Mina is just that, a seduction, and the exchange of blood is an erotic ritual. One of the most intriguing entries in the series is *The Holmes-Dracula File*, in which the narrative shifts back and forth between Dracula's views and Watson's account of the case.

Another significant voice in vampire fiction, though one who is not as pervasively influential, is Stephen King. He is the king of horror fiction, no doubt and more well-known even than Anne

Rice; however, he's only written a couple of vampire stories, and those have been overshadowed by other nonvampire works of his own creation. His truly significant contribution to vampire fiction was *'Salem's Lot*,[11] (Doubleday, 1975), in which a very old and very nasty vampire comes to a small New England town and raises a lot of hell. Aside from being a major bestseller and a contributing factor to King's rise to mega-stardom,[12] *'Salem's Lot* reintroduced the folkloric monster in true form: ugly, evil, and corrupt. Well, mostly true form . . . the vampire—Barlow—was in many ways modeled after Dracula, though he was far more destructive. Dracula kills only a handful of people in Stoker's novel; Barlow wipes out an entire town. But even though we have the return of the unrepentantly evil vampire, it still isn't quite a folkloric story. It has elements of it, but they're a grab bag of actual folklore and post-Dracula pop-culture fiction.

Hell of a story, though. It is also one of the very few major vampire novels of the last thirty years in which sexuality is not a key factor. Sure, there's sex among the supporting cast, but the monster in this story cares more about pain, misery, and issues of faith than he does about his libido. Barlow is no one's idea of a sexy nobleman out for a night of sinful fun.

Robert McCammon traveled through similar dark regions with his 1981 novel, *They Thirst*, in which a vampire overlord and his vampire biker minions invade Los Angeles. This book somehow got lost during the explosion of interest in Anne Rice and deserves a second look, particularly for the way in which the author explores emotional development (for good or ill) in vampires. Though not folkloric in substance, it nonetheless has an epic scope and all the twists and turns of one of the old folk ballads.

Other writers, however, wanted the sex. They knew that their readers had needs and they catered to those needs in increasingly explicit ways. Some managed to include the sex but retain the sen-

11. The original title was *Second Coming*, but King later changed it to *Jerusalem's Lot*. The publishers shortened it to *'Salem's Lot* because they felt it sounded too religious.

12. His books have sold more than 350 million copies.

Flipping the Vampire Paradigm

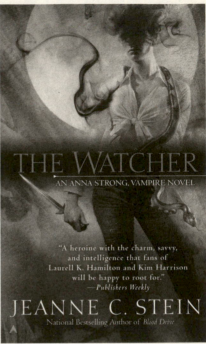

Jeanne C. Stein

"Since I write vampire novels, I have definitely been influenced by folklore; however, I have tweaked the mythos to suit my own paranormal universe. My vampires are not relegated to the dark of night but live among us. They have integrated themselves into society, although it is a society that is not aware of the special nature of some of its members. Authors can revitalize the existing monster paradigms by reversing the roles of monster and man—who is to say the vampire fighting evil is the bad guy when we humans commit terrible atrocities against each other? It's the question I ask in my books: who are the real monsters?"
—Jeanne C. Stein is the bestselling author of the *Anna Strong Chronicles* (Ace Books).

sual. Few managed this more deftly than Whitley Strieber with *The Hunger*, which tells the tale of immortal vampire Miriam Blaylock, whose bite transforms her lovers into human/vampire hybrids that, alas, do not share her immortality. As a result she tragically loses her lovers one after the other and is constantly searching—hungering, if you will—for a true immortal beloved. Catherine Deneuve played her in the 1980 film version and that film captured the languid sensuality of Strieber's story. Strieber returned to his vampire world with *The Last Vampyre* (Atria, 2001) in which the author explores the whole vampire society, most of which is fictional but with a few nods to folklore thrown in to keep informed readers on their toes. Then in the third installment, *Lilith's Dream* (Atria, 2002), he replaces Blaylock with a new and more ferocious lead: Lilith, the first wife of Adam and the mother of all vampires.

In recent years the paranormal romance genre has grown from a tiny subgenre—either of horror or, more often, of the romance market—into a monster of a market share. By 2004 close to two hundred new titles were being published per year, and that has grown steadily every year since, and sales of half a million copies per book have become fairly common.

One of the genre's key players, Sherrilyn Kenyon, has been writing books almost as fast as readers gobble them up. She writes several different series, including *The Dark-Hunters*, a group of immortal warriors pledged to the Greek goddess Artemis and dedicated to defending mankind against Daimons (vampires) and other supernatural threats. Though Kenyon does not delve deeply into vampire folklore, she draws heavily on Greek mythology for her storytelling framework, and that adds great richness to her tales.

Other key players in the paranormal romance genre include Kresley Cole, J. R. Ward, Patricia Briggs, Jacquelyn Frank, Charlaine Harris, Carrie Vaughn, Marjorie M. Liu, Charlaine Harris, Christine Feehan, Kim Harrison, Tanya Huff, and several dozen others. Like Kenyon, they seldom build on folkloric vampires, but they often bring in elements of other legends and myths, and in doing so keep their plots fresh and their readers hooked.

A second subgenre of the vampire genre is that of Dark Fantasy,

Horror Erotica

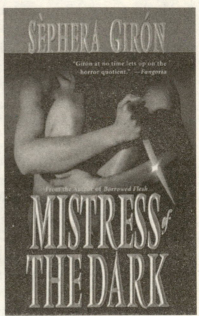

Sèphera Girón,
photo by Derek Sullivan

"Both horror and erotica elicit the same kind of physical response. Sexual energy is built on suspense, tension, adrenaline rush, and release and when you think about it, you have the same elements in a good horror story. It has always seemed like a natural pairing for me to blend sex with horror. Gothic novels have rich lush descriptions that are almost as sensual as a sex scene. Think about a monster stalking the prey; hearts pounding in the darkness, rapid breathing, eyes dilating, nerves tingling, the adrenaline rush of the hunt, the thrill of capture, the urge to do it again when it's over." —Sèphera Girón is the author of *Mistress of the Dark* and *Hungarian Rhapsody* (Neon, 2008).

which uses a similar romantic framework but which gets pretty weird and often very nasty. Dominating this genre is Laurell K. Hamilton, whose Anita Blake, Vampire Hunter series established a complex mythology—largely invented rather than borrowed from folklore—and then shapes the stories with extreme violence, very graphic sex, wicked humor, and lots of passionate intensity. Hamilton also writes the Merry Gentry series, about a faerie princess turned private investigator.

In film, vampire erotica has become its own subgenre, and some notable entries include several takes on the "Carmilla" storyline, including Roger Vadim's *Blood and Roses* (1961), Roy Ward Baker's *The Vampire Lovers* (1970), Jesus Franco's *Vampyros Lesbos* (1970), Vincente Aranda's *The Blood-Splattered Bride* (1972), and José Ramón Larraz's *Vampyres* (1974). In some cases filmmakers decided to go a step farther in the exploration of undead sexuality, occasionally crossing the line into soft- and hard-core pornography, which in turn spawned several spinoff subgenres: gay and lesbian vampire porn and S&M vampire films, in which romance takes a backseat in favor of the shock of explicit sex and (way too often) explicit violence. In these aspects of the genre, folklore is not even a fragment of the storytelling equation.

On television, shows like *Dark Shadows*, *Buffy the Vampire Slayer*, *Angel*, *Forever Knight*, and others continued the process of romanticizing the undead, but the inspiration for much of it was equal parts Anne Rice, Dracula, and Shakespeare. The tone was often Goth and the humans and vampires became ciphers for the Montagues and Capulets in supernatural takes on Romeo and Juliet.

Overall, the allure of the fictional vampire remains firm, just as the memory of the less appealing folkloric vampire continues to fade. It will be interesting to see what happens when authors, in need of something fresh, begin digging up the bones of the older vampires. It will happen . . . it's just a matter of when.

Vlad the Impaler

DIGGING UP THE TRUTH

There has been tremendous and long-running debate among vampire experts in different fields about the connection between the vampire of folklore and the vampire as depicted in pop culture. One hot-button issue is whether Bram Stoker based his fictional Dracula on the historical figure, or just borrowed the name and some locations to spark up a novel.

At the spearpoint of this debate were Raymond T. McNally (1931–2002), a former Boston College professor, and Radu Florescu (1925–), a Romanian scholar who holds the position of Emeritus Professor of History at Boston College. McNally and Florescu coauthored *In Search of Dracula: The History of Dracula and Vampires*, which was a bestseller in 1972. Prior to this no one had really linked Stoker's fictional count with Vlad Dracula, also known as Vlad the Impaler. McNally and Florescu insisted that Stoker had deliberately used Vlad as the basis for Dracula; while others (some of them Stoker scholars) say that the author had merely borrowed a name and location but never directly (or indirectly) claimed that his fictional character was the undead vampire-ghost of the Wallachian prince who died in 1476.

Funny thing is many in the pop-culture world take it as a given that Dracula and Vlad are one and the same. When we conducted

The Role of Folklore

"My most recent novel, *Mr. Twilight* (a Del Rey original cowritten by Michael Reaves) draws heavily on folklore. It has angels, demons, Dracula, epic pulp monsters, Native American shamanism—all woven together around the central theme of the power of human imagination. But the most engaging idea to me in *Mr. Twilight* was something that happened almost by accident when we introduced Vlad Tepes (a.k.a. Dracula). Michael had him arrive on the scene via an ancient and arcane television set and that set me to wondering about the power of the human imagination as it pertains to 'real' monsters. Vlad Tepes was a real person and a genuinely scary piece of work. In *Mr. Twilight*, it's the historical Vlad Tepes who enters the scene, but he's overlaid with the Bram Stoker/B-movie Dracula persona and, in some ways, imprisoned within it or circumscribed by it. It's an idea that I'd love to explore further." —Maya Kaathryn Bohnhoff is the author of six fantasy novels. Her short fiction has appeared in *Analog, Interzone, Amazing Stories, Jim Baen's Universe*, and *Paradox*.

a poll of a few hundred folks in the horror genre (ranging from filmmakers and novelists to fans) every single one of them thought that the connection was obvious and well known. Most were surprised that there was even a debate on the subject.

Filmmaker Lawson Welles,[13] who worked as a researcher for Dr. McNally and once slept overnight in Castle Dracula, told us: "In recent years, certain authors looking for a reputation of their own have taken the opposing viewpoint and claimed that there exists no concrete evidence to support Florescu and McNally's stance that Stoker based his vampire tale on the historical Vlad the Impaler. Doc McNally and I had an in joke about these people, saying they were staking a dead vampire instead of beating a dead horse. I am not saying Stoker was well-versed in the history of

13. Lawson Welles is the writer, director, producer, and star of the motion picture *Cricket Snapper*, released in 2005 by Phoenix Rising Films.

Vlad the Impaler or of Romania, but if you found an historical figure suitable for literary enhancement, would you be more interested in anally and carefully documenting your inspiration for future generations to be able to say: 'Oh, yes, he based Billy the Bat on so-and-so?' Or would you sit down, write the freaking story, and get the job done? Writers write, it's what we do. Stoker met Arminius Vámbéry, the Hungarian adventurer and folklore expert, who was well-versed in Vlad Dracula and vampires. Stoker even has Van Helsing mention his 'friend Arminius of Buda-Pesth' in the book. Stoker's description of Vlad in the novel is certainly jumbled and historically inaccurate, and just the thing I might have written had I returned home from dinner with Vámbéry after one too many brandies, the drink and the echoes of the legends of Vlad flying like satanic specters in my head."

The debate was given new life, and at the same time very likely put to rest, in 2005 with the publication of historian and literary novelist Elizabeth Kostova's first novel, *The Historian* (Little, Brown), which very neatly and completely draws a connection between Stoker's Dracula and the historical Vlad the Impaler.

Stoker is far from the only author to mine folklore for storytelling gems. Among the most compelling series of vampire novels of the late twentieth century are the tales of Le Comte de Saint-Germain by Chelsea Quinn Yarbro. The principal character is based on The Count of St. Germain (1710–1784), a rather remarkable historical figure who was—if all of the stories about him are to be believed—an alchemist, musician (piano and violin), courtier, adventurer, inventor, composer, and occultist. It's largely believed that he is something of a self-invented person, taking various names and titles over the course of his life, including Master Rakoczi and the variations on Sanctus Germanus (Latin for "Holy Brother").

So, who was he?

There's been debate over that point for centuries. Various claims—some made by him and others about him—suggest that he is an immortal, a god, a demon, an angel, or an alchemist who discovered the secret of eternal life. Different scholars have asserted that he is (or was) Francis Bacon, true heir to the British Throne, born to Queen Elizabeth and Lord Dudley, or the son of

Francis II Rákóczi, the Prince of Transylvania, or the illegitimate son of Maria Anna of Pfalz-Neuburg, the widow of Charles II of Spain; or the bastard son of the king of Portugal. The Venetian adventurer and author Giacomo Casanova wrote of him in his diary, referring to him as a "celebrated and learned imposter." Two authoritative biographies have been written so far: Isabel Cooper-Oakley's *The Count of St. Germain* (Ars Regia, 1912) and Jean Overton-Fuller's *The Comte de Saint-Germain: Last Scion of the House of Rakoczy* (East-West Publications, 1988). Though they agree on some points, they differ wildly on others.

Theosophists claim that St. Germain is one of the ascended masters[14]—a select group of spiritual figures that includes Jesus, Confucius, Gautama Buddha, Mary the Mother of Jesus, Lady Master Nada, Enoch, Pope John Paul II, Kwan Yin, Sanat Kumara, Kuthumiand. In her book *The Externalisation of the Hierarchy*,[15] Theosophist Alice A. Bailey claimed that Saint Germain was "the Lord of Civilization," and that it was his task to establish the new civilization of the Age of Aquarius.

According to Theosophy and the Ascended Master Teachings, Saint Germain has been incarnated many times. They maintain that he was the ruler of a prehistoric civilization that began as a colony from Atlantis and which flourished in the Sahara seventy thousand years ago; then later ruled Atlantis thirteen thousand years ago. They also claim that he was the Samuel, the last of the Hebrew judges from the eleventh century B.C.E.; that he was the Greek poet Hesiod; and that he was also Plato, St. Joseph (as in husband of Mary and guardian of Jesus), Saint Alban, Merlin, and many others.

Many writers have tapped this rather fantastic character to add substance to their fiction. Alexandre Dumas very likely based his Count of Monte Cristo on Saint Germain, particularly on one of the leading theories about the man that he was self-invented. Literary novelist Umberto Eco used St. Germain as the antagonist in his novel *Foucault's Pendulum* (Harcourt Brace, 1989). In her

14. Originally presented by H. P. Blavatsky in the 1870s in her essay: "Masters of Wisdom."

15. A compilation of earlier revelations published posthumously in 1957.

novel, *Dragonfly in Amber* (Delacorte, 1992), Diana Gabaldon uses the Count, but as a mere mortal.

The author who has truly made Le Comte de Saint-Germain her own is Chelsea Quinn Yarbro, who has written over two dozen richly textured romantic historical novels about the Count. Her stories take places in various periods of history, from ancient Rome to modern day. The first published book in the series was *Hotel Transylvania*, released in 1978 by St. Martin's Press. Yarbro's take on Saint-Germain casts him as a heroic figure who seems fated to be in the path of major events in history, such as the kingdom of Charlemagne, Europe during the Nazi invasion, Florence in the time of Lorenzo de Medici, and others. Unlike Stoker, who skated on the edges of historical research, Yarbro digs deep and fills her books with exquisite details. However, her vampires are in some ways conventional, built more along the lines of post-Dracula pop-culture versions than as creatures from folklore.

Yarbro, though never a household name like contemporary Anne Rice, nonetheless has a legion of devoted followers, and unlike Rice, whose novels play strongly to the Goth crowd, Yarbro's fan base is a mix of devotees of historical romance and the New Age crowd, and she certainly has deep New Age cred from having been the spiritual "channel" for a spiritual being named Michael, which she has shaped into the bestselling and highly influential *Messages from Michael*[16] series.

More than a century has passed since *Dracula* was published, which means that no one alive remembers the pre-*Dracula* attitudes toward vampires. No one alive remembers a time when vampire information came strictly from folktales. With each new generation there are new layers of fiction between our perception and the mind-set when a belief in vampires was commonplace. Our folklore has truly become a reflection of what we've seen on the big screen, read in novels, experienced on TV, or found on the Internet.

New variations on vampires constantly appear. In 1954 Richard Matheson gave us the first great science-based vampire story, *I Am Legend*, in which a plague sweeps the world and turns everybody

16. First published by Playboy Press in 1979.

into vampires except one man. The book, written more than half a century ago, stands as a remarkably keen cautionary tale about the spread of disease. Literary and social critics often cite it as an example of what can happen if disease is allowed to run rampant. The book has been adapted to film three times, though sadly with very mixed results. The first attempt was in 1964 with Vincent Price starring in a dreadfully slow and tedious Italian production titled *The Last Man on Earth (L'Ultimo uomo della Terra)*. Though this movie stayed moderately close to the novel, and even offered some logical thematic updates such as the source of the disease (an unknown plague rather than the result of mutations from a nuclear war) and the protagonist's profession (medical researcher rather than plant worker), it missed the real point of the story, particularly in the fact that the central character never grasps the significance of the story. In the book, protagonist Robert Neville clearly understands who he is and what he represents to the new and emerging vampire culture, and that revelation allows him a strange measure of peace. In the movie, Price goes down ranting, a man thoroughly confused and defeated.

When Charlton Heston took a swing at the story in 1971's *The Omega Man*, there are again some interesting additions such as the plague being the result of biological warfare between China and the USSR. The protagonist is now a military man and scientist who survives by injecting himself with an experimental drug. He struggles to recreate the drug while fending off attacks—not from vampires but from albino mutants in monks' robes and sunglasses. For some reason a lot of folks seem to dig this flick, though few of them that we polled had ever read the novel.

In 2007 Will Smith starred in a big-budget remake that was a huge commercial success. Though titled *I Am Legend*, it again veered sharply from the book and instead mined the two previous films for source material. Robert Neville was once again a military scientist and the disease this time was a retrovirus[17] that had been genetically altered to attack cancer cells. Instead it kills off most of the population and what survives are thousands of weird

17. The film's science is pretty faulty. The measles virus depicted in the film is not a retrovirus, but a part of the Paramyxovirus family.

Zombie Research

Dead Country

"Before we even started production on *Dead Country*, I tried to track down every obscure zombie movie I could find. I didn't just want to draw my inspiration solely from the mainstream stuff. I found Lucio Fulci's work to be very helpful indeed. I think that most of us like to believe in the fantastical, no matter how absurd it might be. We yearn for more than our conformist reality gives us. The idea of a monster hiding under the bed or lurking outside in the bushes is as exciting as it is terrifying. If anything, it's a great form of escapism for a lot of people." —Andrew Merkelbach directed and starred in the Australian zombie movie *Dead Country*. He has previously appeared in the 2005 science fiction film *Traveller: Red*.

I Am Legend Spoiler

If you haven't yet read Richard Matheson's *I Am Legend*, skip this sidebar and go buy the damn thing. It's short, it's brilliant, and you should leave right now to get a copy. If you have read it and don't know what we're ranting about when we say that the three film adaptations missed the point of the book, then here it is in a nutshell: Protagonist Robert Neville wages a daily war against the undead, believing that it is his moral imperative to rid the earth of them, regarding them as parasites and himself as the defender of mankind, even if he is all of mankind that's left. Then a new society emerges: vampires who have retained their conscious minds and who have worked to establish a new society in which infection is normal. Neville has killed many of them, just as he'd killed the less evolved evil vampires. When these new vampires hunt him down, arrest him, and condemn him to death as a mass murderer, Neville finally grasps the truth: They are the new humanity and he is the murderous parasite. Where once they were the creatures of myth and legend, they are now the "human" race and he, the thing that comes to kill while they sleep, is the new creature of folklore. He has become their boogeyman. He has become the cornerstone of their new folklore. Seen in this light, the title is beautiful and insightful, and the three film versions—even if you like them—are not what they could have been because they snubbed Matheson's intention.

CGI zombies that look unnervingly like a nude, bald Ted Danson. This film totally misses the point of the book, and the misfire is more keenly felt because this movie starts out with a bang and shows lots of promise, particularly in the sensitive, layered performance by Will Smith. But right around the time the first zombies show up, the film begins to crumble, and the ending is total sappy junk that not only ignores the point of the book but misuses the meaning of the title in a very lame way. Moviegoers didn't seem to care, though . . . the film grossed more than 580 million dollars worldwide.

Despite the fact that the novel *I Am Legend* is about vampires, it had little actual effect on the vampire genre. Instead it became the principal inspiration for George A. Romero and John Russo when they wrote the script for *Night of the Living Dead*, which means that it's the great grandfather of all zombie films. Go figure. A lot of folks have wondered—and your authors here are among them—what a George Romero film version of *I Am Legend* would have been like. Considering the biting social commentary sewn into the fabric of Romero's Living Dead films, it's a good bet he'd have both understood and retained Matheson's message.

Beginning with *I Am Legend* and really gaining steam with Anne Rice and Stephen King, vampire fiction took off in all directions, warping the paradigm and eventually just knocking the hell out of it, and generally relying on stronger storytelling elements than is typically found in the films. Colin Wilson, for example, blasted them into space in his 1976 novel *The Space Vampires*,[18] in which vampirism is seen as the result of an alien invasion. Dan Simmons's *Carrion Comfort* (Grand Central Publishing, 1990) gave us a bunch of truly vicious psychic vampires, including a former Nazi concentration camp guard. Michael Talbot (1953–1992) turned in another quirky book with *The Delicate Dependency*, in which vampires were a race of protectors (known as the Illuminali) fighting a losing battle to try and keep humanity from destroying itself. Suzy McKee's *The Vampire Tapestry* (Simon and Schuster, 1980), uses multiple points of view to explore the process of becoming a vampire and the nature of the vampire as a nonhuman predator. The approach gives the book an almost cryptozoological aspect, and makes for a compelling read.

Ray Garton gave vampire fiction a real twist with *Live Girls* (Pinnacle, 1987), in which the peep show and porn industry is infiltrated by vampires. The book was a real hit when it came out and has gathered a very strong cult following since. A number of other books and movies have since used the vampire stripper theme, though (sadly) none of them credit Garton as the pioneer for this delicious bit of perversity. He followed it up with the chilling *Night Life* (Leisure, 2007). Ray observes, "In *Live Girls*, I threw out

18. Published by Random House and filmed by Tobe Hooper in 1985 as *Lifeforce*.

Twisting the Vampire Myth

"There's a double appeal when you use 'classic' monsters such as vampires and werewolves in your stories. First, you have the shorthand—everyone knows what they are, and you don't really need to explain them too much. Vampires suck blood, avoid daylight, and so forth. Creating your own monsters is much harder—though, of course, it can be very fulfilling. Second, you have the opportunity to do something new with something old. Can you put a new spin on a vampire? That can be a great deal of fun! In my novel *Night Wings*, for example, I came up with the idea that vampires creating vampires is a bit like making photocopies—the further removed you are from the original, the blurrier the copy gets. So the first vampires are the classic Dracula type—intelligent, lively, and active. But as they get 'copied', they become more bestial. Then the originals have to have the copies killed off, to avoid them breeding even worse copies. So they employ a vampire hunter to slaughter their own progeny. But the hunter has his own agenda, and turns out to be worse than the creatures he's hunting." —John Peel writes young adult fantasy (the Diadem series, Llewellyn Publications), as well as media tie-in books, (*Doctor Who, Star Trek, The Avengers*).

---

the power that the image of the crucifix has always held over the vampire. That just didn't seem to fit into today's world. For one thing, that crucifix represents only one religion. For another, religion does not have the power over all of us that it once did. There was a time long ago when life in every town and village centered around the church. These days, it's more likely to center around the mall. So I dumped that bit of myth. Garlic, on the other hand, seemed more likely to work. In *Live Girls* and *Night Life*, the vampires have a terrible allergic reaction to it."

Fevre Dream by George R. R. Martin (Simon and Schuster, 1982) also explores the concept of a vampire subculture, which was a concept that had started to really take hold by the early 1980s and has since become almost the standard for vampire stories. In this historical novel, Martin gives us a heroic vampire in the form of

Joshua York, who partners with Mississippi captain Abner Marsh to build a strange riverboat called *Fevre Dream*, on which York searches for other vampires. York, you see, has created a kind of artificial blood and he hopes that by sharing this with his fellow vampires it will stop them from preying on humans. Of course an evil vampire opposes him and things go to hell in a paddle-wheeled handbasket. The novel is beautiful and riveting, and the story endlessly fascinating, rife with possibilities for further tales that, so far, Martin has chosen not to pursue.

Author Lee Killough penned a trilogy of vampire tales collectively known as the *Bloodwalk* series, in which a cop, Garreth Mikaelian, investigates a series of brutal murders and encounters a vampire. The first book in the series, *Blood Hunt* (Tor, 1987) deals with the search for the killer and the resulting confrontation. In the sequel, *Bloodlinks* (1988), Garreth has become infected by the vampire and we share his pain and torment as he undergoes the process of transformation from human to vampire. In the final book, *Blood Games* (Meisha Merlin Publishing, 2001), Garreth begins to experience the burden of immortality. Though only a

Folklore in Fiction

"I write horror, fantasy, urban fantasy, and erotic and sweet paranormal and fantasy romance, so I take a lot of my stuff from legends and myths, folklore, things like that. I try to add twists to them, so they won't be the same as those already published. For example, in the erotic paranormal romance novella, *Beast Magic* (published under the pen name of Sapphire Phelan; Phaze, 2007), the villainess is a werelioness. In fact, my hero is a werelion and a lot of shape-shifters, mainly lions, are in this. Since I had read of other shape-shifters besides werewolves in a book long ago, when I did this book (first one of a trilogy) I wanted to do more than werewolves. The next one will be wereleopards and the last one is werewolves (to make my publisher happy as werewolves do well in paranormal romance)." —Lee Killough/Sapphire Phelan's latest novel is *Crimson Promise* (Phaze, 2008).

vampire for fifteen years, he sees his friends begin to age and get sick while he remains young and eternally healthy.

Aside from being fun reads, the Killough books also anticipate the "vampire detective" later famous on TV in shows like *Forever Knight*, *Angel*, *Moonlight*, and *Blood Ties*. However this concept was first presented in Marvel Comics' *Tomb of Dracula* (issue #25, 1974) with the introduction of Hannibal King, a private detective turned into a vampire by the evil Deacon Frost. The character, in a radically different form, appears in *Blade: Trinity*, the third movie based on the comic series.

Other landmark vampire books include Kim Newman's *Anno-Dracula* (Pocket Books, 1993), which invites us into an alternate universe where Van Helsing and his crew failed to kill Dracula and the Count has married Queen Victoria and become the official Prince Consort. *Vampire Winter* (Pinnacle, 1990) by Lois Tilton

The Modern Film Audience

"Audiences are much smarter than they used to be. What they accepted as fact or explanation in films long ago wouldn't necessarily fly today. So, I think one of the best "new" makeovers to these classic figures is the scientific approach many filmmakers are taking to explaining their existence. For instance, in the eighties we had *The Lost Boys*; and our heroes used classic clichés everybody knew to defeat the vampires: holy water, garlic, stake through the heart, etcetera. The filmmakers didn't bother with any explanations as to why these methods work. They simply took the 'everybody knows that' approach. That was fine for the eighties, but would that work today? I don't think so. In *Blade*, the filmmakers not only explained why some of these methods work, but also invented science to back it up. Audiences just won't accept something to be true simply because the filmmakers say it is anymore. Those days are over. By adding science to the equation, filmmakers are taking these old icons to new places, while also sparking their audience's interest even further." —Robert Harari cowrote and directed the 2007 independent horror/slasher, *The Murder Game*

took us into the depths of nuclear winter, where night lasts way too long, which allows toothy night-hunters more time for their brand of fun and games. Both of these books expanded the boundaries of vampire storytelling in ways that have been widely imitated since.

Creating a new mythology for a vampire tale and exploring the psychodynamics of being an immortal predator have become cornerstones of our new vampire "folklore." We've seen this develop in the novels of Anne Rice, Fred Saberhagen, and Chelsea Quinn Yarbro, and we've watched it unfold on TV in several significant series. *Forever Knight*, a vampire adventure mystery series began as a 1989 CBS television movie with singer Rick Springfield playing detective Nick Knight; then in 1992 it debuted as a regular series that lasted three years during which it established a very detailed mythos and plunged deep into the heart and soul of the central characters. The protagonist is an eight-hundred-year-old vampire (Nicholas de Brabant) who repents of his evil ways and fights to redeem himself while at the same time struggling with a decidedly predatory nature. The series came to a dramatic and somewhat tragic (though perhaps ambiguous) ending after three years.

Angel, a spin-off of the enormously popular cult hit *Buffy the Vampire Slayer*, saw the supporting character of Angel, a vampire whose soul had been returned to him by Gypsies—not as a gift but as a curse so that remorse would forever torment him. Angel's path to redemption is a rocky one because while he was a predatory vampire he was one of the worst of all time, delighting in torture and mayhem. As a soulful vampire he fights the good fight to bring down the forces of evil and save as many people as possible. Unlike in many adventure shows, *Angel*'s supporting cast suffered a lot of damage. Main characters were frequently killed off and the series itself ended with a hopeless battle in which the heroic vamp and his remaining companions fight an endless army of monsters in a vain attempt to push back the hold evil has over the earth.

As he did with *Buffy*, creator Joss Whedon decided to continue the story of Angel in comic book form, and the "sixth season" begins after Angel and his crew have lost that fight. So things have gone from bad to worse and the path to redemption is even rockier. And by looking at one of the rarest aspects of the vampire legend, the redeemed vampire, these shows gave a nod to folklore. In folklore there is a kind of vampire called the Stregoni Benefici, a creature that had been evil and was eventually tamed and converted back to faith by a priest, after which the vampire became a kind of toothy hit man for the church, targeting other vampires. Angel and his sometimes enemy/sometimes friend Spike are presented as different takes on the reformed vampire concept.

Vampire TV shows and films often have a core group of loyal followers, which keeps them alive on DVD and on message boards, and gets the cast members invited to genre conventions. Few vampire-themed shows make it past three seasons (and most don't make it to the end of one), even when they have a cult following. The problem is that too often the cult following, though devoted, isn't very large.

For vampire films, cult buzz rarely translates to box-office success. In fact some of the most intriguing vampire films have been commercial disappointments, earning far less than expected, or even total financial duds. Consider these box office numbers: *30 Days of Night* ($39,568,996—based on Steve Niles's amazingly compelling comic and starring Josh Harnett, Melissa George, and a powerful Danny Huston); *From Dusk Till Dawn* ($25,836,616—despite a cast that included George Clooney, Salma Hayek, Quentin Tarantino, Harvey Keitel, and Juliette Lewis); *Shadow of the Vampire* ($8,293,784—a brilliant film starring an amazingly creepy Willem Dafoe in a part that was written expressly for him[19]; and a compelling John Malkovich); *The Hunger* ($5,979,292—with Susan Sarandon, Catherine Deneuve, and David Bowie), and *Near Dark*[20] (a perfect vampire film with Adrian Pasdar, Jenny Wright, Bill Paxton, and Lance Henriksen that scraped in a meager $3,369,307).

And yet vampire films are still being cranked out, with medium and big budgets being forked over for *Castlevania* (based on the popular video game), John Carpenter's *L.A. Gothic*; the return of lantern-jawed hero Bruce Campbell in *Bubba Nosferatu and the*

---

19. Dafoe was hired to play The Green Goblin in *Spider-Man* (2002) after the producers saw this performance.

20. Horror Geek Trivia: The word "vampire" is never mentioned in the film.

The Devil's Footprints

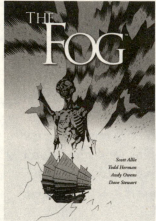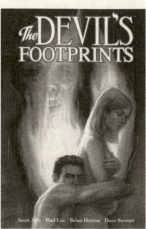

Scott Allie of Dark Horse Comics,
photo by Todd Herman

"*The Devil's Footprints* gets its title from a bit of folklore from my home town. It has to do with the history of my little New England community, but it also sort of becomes a metaphor for the life of the character. I was fishing for a title for the book, going to the obvious things, like *The Demonologist*, but not wanting to make it sound like a superhero book. And I thought of this story from my town, and how it would affect the character, and what it sort of had to say about him. Other aspects of the story come from other places' folklore, including an alternative sort of magical explanation of the vampire, which comes to define the protagonist's father in the book. There's a sense of mystery in folklore that's lacking in a lot of modern genre fiction, and I try to pay attention to how it works in folklore and pre-twentieth-century literature and tap into that. The sense of mystery in folklore is something horror fiction needs to really work. You lose the mystery, and there's nothing to fear."
—Scott Allie writes and edits for Dark Horse Comics and Glimmer Train Press. His work includes tributes to H. P. Lovecraft, *Buffy the Vampire Slayer*, and *Star Wars*.

Curse of the She-Vampires; adaptations of Ray Garton's *Live Girl* and Elizabeth Kostova's *The Historian*, a live-action remake of the 2000 anime *Blood: The Last Vampire*; *Cirque du Freak* (based on the successful series of young adult novels); *Underworld: Rise of the Lycans* (without Kate Beckinsale), and a few dozen others, including a Tim Burton reimagining of *Dark Shadows*[21] and the wonderfully titled *Rosencrantz and Guildenstern Are Undead*.

Vampires frequently try to invade our homes via television, sometimes with great success (*Dark Shadows*, *Buffy*) sometimes with no success (*Blade: The Series*), and a lot floating somewhere in the middle, as with *Blood Ties* and *True Blood*[22]—one of the stronger recent entires, with Anna Paquin as Sookie Stackhouse, a young woman who can read minds who encounters a vampire shortly after vamps outed themselves on national TV. Often vampire-themed shows have to fight for life with the aid of either critical praise or a devoted fan base—though neither of these is enough to keep the bloodsuckers on the boob tube if the ratings aren't high.

With all of the burgeoning vampire pop culture, and the need to spin something so original that it would stand out and get noticed, you'd think it would be easy to find a fair amount of shows and books based on the many and varied vampires and vampire-like creatures of folklore. And yet we don't see as much of that as we'd like to.

Maybe the next crop of writers will explore the many monsters of folklore—such as the ones presented in the next section—to give vampire tales a brand-new bite.

THE FAMILY OF THE FANG: VAMPIRES AROUND THE WORLD

Abchanchu: A theriomorphic blood-drinker from Bolivia in South America who assumes the form of an old man who pretends to be

---

21. At this writing it's "rumored" that Johnny Depp will step into the role of Barnabas Collins. Jonathan Frid created the character for TV and Ben Cross took his bite out of the part in the attempted TV reboot of the show.
22. Based on Charlaine Harris's excellent series of novels.

On Vampires

Acheri by Katerina Koukiotis

"I think the fact that vampires have been given a second chance at life by another bloodsucking creature can be seen as powerful but also sad at the same time. They are trapped and there is nothing they can do about it. Most people end up falling for them, wanting to help, even though they may end up victims." —Katerina Koukiotis is a traditional fantasy and portrait artist from Queens, N.Y.

lost and helpless. When some kindly stranger comes along to help the old duffer home, out come the fangs and the bloodlust.

Acheri: This nosferatu takes the form of a little girl who plays with human children and through apparently innocent contact spreads a terrible wasting disease. In the other (and more common) legends, she comes down from the mountains during festival times and blends in with the town children, but as her shadow passes over healthy children they instantly become ill and often die.

Adze: In Togo (formerly the Slave Coast of Africa) certain human sorcerers of the Ewe Tribe voluntarily open themselves to possession by vampiric spirits called Adzes. Once possessed this unholy human monster hybrid can shape-shift into mosquitoes or other flying insects and in those forms enter the houses of unsuspecting folk. The Adze is both a blood-drinker and a disease-carrying nosferatu. It rarely kills, however, preferring to keep its victim alive as a steady source of nourishment. Mosquito netting might keep it out, and a flyswatter can kill it, but because the Adze is cleverer than your average flying bug, it is adept at escaping harm while targeting its prey.

Akhkharu: a species of seductress vampire from ancient Assyria that fed on the life essence of its victims by seducing and, quite literally, screwing its victims to death. And before you think that there are worse ways to go, bear in mind that at the outset of this unnatural seduction the Akhkharu is quite a wrinkled old hag; she's only young and beautiful at the point where her victim is drained of all sexual and vital energy. Not exactly a "cougar."[23]

Algul (also **Alghul** and **Bloodsucking Djinn**): An Arabic vampire whose name translates as "horse leech," the Algul is a female blood-drinker who preys on the newly buried corpses of dead children. The Algul can be heard howling in the nighttime darkness, often mimicking the calls of night birds and desert scavengers such as the jackal.

---

23. Modern slang for an older woman who seduces younger men.

Old Hag

Alp and **Mara:** The Alp[24] is the male form of a species of vampiric elf from German folklore; the Mara (or Mart) is the female. These monsters are night predators and often invade the sleep of their victims, transforming dreams into nightmares and then feeding on the discharge of terror. Like the Old Hag, the Alp or Mara crouch down on the chest of their victim, increasing the pressure until the victim can no longer breathe. Sometimes death ensues; sometimes the monster leaves the gasping victim only to return again and again until the poor bugger is drained of all vitality. These attacks are called alpdrücken, which means "elf pressure."

24. Not to be confused with the Alp-luachra, an evil fairy from Irish mythology.

In all of its many aberrant manifestations, the Alp wears a tarnkappe, or "cap of concealment," which gives it a variety of magical powers, including invisibility and theriomorphy. If the hat is stolen, the Alp loses this power of concealment and its powers are reduced. In such cases the Alp can be driven out by prayers or spells, though actually destroying the creature appears to be impossible.

Though they primarily feed on breath and life force, they have been known to drink blood from the nipples of children or young men. When they are not being overtly murderous, these elf-vampires love to play annoying pranks, such as tangling the hair of their victims into "elf-knots," pulling out nose hairs, causing breast milk to turn sour, and other equally unpleasant things. Like many creatures of world myth, the Alp is often created when a child is born with a caul[25] over its face. A child born with such a "mark" is frequently believed to be doomed to a life of evil—or a rebirth into a supernatural life of evil after natural death.

Alp-Luachra: This is a very nasty little monster from Irish legend that takes the form of a newt and crawls into the mouth of a sleeping person. Historical sources differ on what the critter does next. Some say that it crawls down into the stomach and feeds on the undigested food in its victim's stomach. Other tales say that it feeds on the sleeper itself, munching on flesh and connective tissue. The first tale is the most common, however, and there are folk stories and songs about a clever potential victim who ate lots of salted beef and when the Alp-luachra went belly-diving and gobbled up all that salt it threw itself into the creek to assuage its thirst and drowned. Few mourned its passing.

Aluka (also **Aluga**): One of the most ancient blood-drinkers is the demonic "king of the vampires" known as the Aluka. The name itself has the same root origin as the Algul of Arabia, and means "horse leech."[26] The Latin translation of Aluka is "sanguisuga,"

---

25. A caul is an amniotic sac that, in rare cases, adheres to the face after birth. Cultures vary as to whether this is a sign of evil or of great positive psychic power.

26. The term "horse leech" first appears in Proverbs 30:15.

which means "bloodsucker." The reference is not to some mere parasitic insect but rather a demon of great power with an unquenchable thirst for blood.

Aptrgangr (also **Haugbui**): This is a fierce monster from Norse legend created when a demonic spirit inhabits a recently deceased corpse. The name means "after goer," a reference to something that walks even though it is dead. The other name, Haubui, means "howe" or "barrow," a reference to a grave. The Aptrgangr is similar to the Draugr (see p. 69) except that it seldom strayed from its grave, whereas the Draugr frequently raided local villages. When enraged, the Aptrgangr could swell to enormous size and was possessed of tremendous strength.

Asema: Trinidad's Asema shares many unsavory qualities with other vampires throughout the region, most notably the Haitian Loogaroo and the Azeman of Suriname. The Asema spends her days in the guise of an old woman (in very rare cases, as an old man). When the sun sets it sheds its skin and its evil supernatural

---

Urban Legends

"In the past man invented monsters to explain his fears or why things were done in a certain way. Folkloric beings were essentially a survival tool. Urban legend is a modern way to say the word folklore. All urban legends play on people's fear and give you a lesson on things you ought not do. Long ago we would say to our children that meeting your paramour for a midnight embrace was dangerous because that is when monsters roamed about most freely. Now we tell kids that if you go parking, the man with the hook for a hand will gut you both. Then, as now, parents don't want their babies having babies. Monsters, be they vampires, lake monsters, or gods who live atop cloud-covered mountains, are all catalysts for some other aspect of human life."
—Theresa Bane has been featured on the Discovery Channel for her knowledge and expertise on the mythology of the vampire. She is the author of *Actual Factual: Dracula, a Compendium of Vampires* (NeDeo, 2007).

self emerges as a blue ball of light. In this form it will ride the night winds in search of prey, alighting on sleeping humans and drinking their blood. Sunlight neither harms nor weakens the Asema, but it does make it harder for her to take anyone unawares. The Asema hunts at night strictly because of the advantage offered by darkness. Popular forms of protection work against Asema. These include eating herbs that will make one's blood bitter, or by eating a lot of garlic. Like many vampires, the Asema can also be foiled by scattering rice or sesame seeds outside one's door, forcing it to linger and count them one at a time.

Astral Vampires:[27] These are vampires who exist in spirit form and it is only the spirit that is supernatural. Normally these are humans with all of the normal strengths and weaknesses of ordinary folks; but these people can enter into trance states during which they can astrally project[28] their spirit so that it can roam free and prey on human victims. These free-roaming spirits feed on life force or spiritual energy rather than blood. This form of vampirism is often confused with "Psychic Vampires," discussed elsewhere in this section.

Asuang (also **Aswang**): Easily the most fearsome and feared creature of Filipino folklore is the shape-shifting Asuang. The Asuang often takes the form of a black-skinned man, but to hunt it rips its own head and intestines free from its torso, and this viscera flies through the night sky to hunt for prey.[29] The Asuang utters a compelling cry as it flies, "Kikik," which draws its victims to it through some supernatural compulsion. The word "Asuang" means "sorcerer," though most often the victim was not a magic user in life but is instead the victim of a magical sickness of unknown origin. Instead it gains supernatural powers only after this unnatural disease has completely subsumed its human parts;

27. A term coined by Theosophist Franz Hartmann.
28. Astral projection is the practice of deliberately separating one's consciousness from the physical body in order to move unhindered by any limitations.
29. Other monsters that do this include Like the Phi Song Nang of Thailand, the Malaysian Penanggalan, the Krasue of Cambodia, and the Vietnamese Ma Cà Rông (see individual listings).

afterward the doomed person has no control at all over what he does. However, by day the Asuang looks as human as anyone else in the village, works at a job, even has a family and friends. The demonic spirit within is clever and deceptive, and it maintains an excellent disguise that can fool people for decades. The Asuang is also smart enough to never hunt in its own village, and travels many miles at night to neighboring villages to hunt. However, the day after it has fed, the Asuang looks almost pregnant, its belly bloated and distended with consumed blood. When the Asuang attacks it will stand upside down and then belch forth an odor so powerful and overwhelming that the victim will be rendered as helpless as if subjected to nerve gas. Then, while the victim is paralyzed—though not necessarily unconscious—the Asuang will begin to feed, starting with the heart and working down to the intestines.

Aswid: In Book Two of the Eyrbyggia Saga,[30] there is a story of two great Icelandic warriors, Aswid and Asmund, who were heroes and generals as well as being the best of friends. They struck a blood oath that if one of them died, the other would go to the grave with his friend. After Aswid grew ill and died, his friend buried him in a great tomb along with many items of tribute, including Aswid's horses, weapons and his favorite dog. True to his word, Asmund had himself sealed into the tomb and then sat down to decide how best to end his own life. Before he could come to a decision Aswid awoke from death—not as a ghost but as a bloodthirsty vampire. Aswid attacked and killed the dog and horses and consumed their flesh and then attacked his old friend, forcing Asmund to draw his sword and fight back. Three centuries later, a small group of men decided to excavate the tomb, ignoring the local legends that the grave was haunted. When they broke the seals and entered the tomb, they lowered a rope with the intention of climbing down, but instead an old man climbed up. It was Asmund, who claimed that he had struggled with Aswid for three hundred years and only the arrival of the excavating party provided enough of a distraction

30. The saga of the inhabitants of Eyrr, a farm on Snæfellsnes in Iceland.

to break the deadlock and allow the general to finally end the unnatural existence of Aswid. And, as soon as the old man told his tale, he died. Asmund was buried with full military honors, while the beheaded corpse of the vampire was removed from the tomb, burned, and the ashes scattered.

Azeman: This vampire from Suriname (formerly Dutch Guyana) takes the form of a wizened old woman by day but at night she shape-shifts into a bat or some other creature of the night. Despite the frequency with which book and movie vampires transform into bats, it's very uncommon in folklore. The Azeman is a rare exception. The Azeman steals in and seeks out a sleeping person whose foot is exposed. With great and subtle care, she uses her needle-sharp fangs to scrape away a piece of flesh from the big toe. When the blood begins to flow, the Azeman drinks hungrily until she is bloated, then crawls out of the house and flies off. Since she is only bat-sized, her feeding is rarely fatal, but the victim is left drained and weakened, and often suffers from the onset of disease.

Bajang: A Malaysian vampire that takes the shape of a hungry polecat and goes hunting for children. Sometimes the Bajang is an independent monster, working according to its own wicked agenda. It can sometimes be more or less tamed by a witch or warlock into being their familiar. Bajang familiars will then be handed down from one generation to the next as a protector of the family and a weapon to be used against rivals. The enslaved Bajang is kept in a bamboo vessel called a tabong, which is protected by various spells and charms, and closed by a stopper made from special leaves. While the Bajang is imprisoned it is fed with eggs, and even though it is a slave, the Bajang will turn on its owner if it is not given enough food. When used as a weapon against its master's enemies, the Bajang does not rend and tear; rather it infects the master's enemies with a terrible wasting illness that, if not diagnosed and treated correctly, is fatal. Many folktales have it that the Bajang is another of those tragic creatures that inhabit the corpse of a still-born child. Unlike child vampires of Mexico and Croatia, the Bajang is brought into being through incantations. Other legends suggest that the Bajang is the male version of the female Langsuir.

Bas: The Chewong people of Malaysia believe in a vampiric being called the Bas, a vampire-like creature that feeds on the *ruwai* (loosely translated as soul, vitality, or life) of livestock, particularly swine. The Bas will not venture into any town or village. It can even be frightened off by a simple campfire if the Bas takes it as a sign of civilization. Some scholars and medical professionals believe that the Bas legend grew out of an attempt to explain plagues or the spread of other communicable diseases.

Bebarlangs: In the rural jungles of the Philippines, there is a tribe of essential vampires called the Bebarlangs who are humans who have developed astral projection to such a high degree that they can send their astral bodies to neighboring villages to feed on the life essence of sleeping victims. These invisible predators some-times attack in packs and can wipe out a family or a whole village in a single night. More advanced Bebarlangs can also intrude into a sleeping person's mind and steal his secrets as well as his life force. A charm is made from drops of blood, bits of hair, and fin-gernail parings mixed with wax and mud taken from just outside the person's front door. These materials are fashioned into a small icon of a holy person or angel, then hung over one person's bed or worn around the neck on a cord. Only then will the person be safe from this psychic attack.

Blautsauger: This vampire, whose name literally means "blood sucker," is found throughout Austria, Germany, and Bosnia-Herzegovina, referring to one or more vampire species. The Aus-trian Blautsauger appears to have more in common with its German cousins than with the Bosnian variety. The Austrian Blautsauger is a living dead revenant who has the typical pale skin, rotting flesh, and gaunt features of a zombie. The most common way to become a Blautsauger is to eat the flesh of any animal that has been killed by a wolf. Like the zombies of popular films, the Blautsauger is a flesh-eater as well as a blood-drinker. The Bosnian version of the Blautsauger has no skeleton at all but holds its shape through supernatural will. Its body is covered in stiff hair, but oth-erwise looks more or less human. It has the power of transforma-tion and can become a rat or a gray wolf. It tricks people into eating a small clot of dirt from its own tomb. It holds the dirt behind its back and works its wiles on the unsuspecting, enticing them into believing it has a food treat or other goodie. But once the unfortunate person tastes the bit of dirt he will instantly begin to fade, his bones will begin to melt, and rough hair will begin growing all over him. He will become a Blautsauger himself.

Like many vampires of eastern Europe, the Blautsauger sleeps in its grave during the day and rises at night to feed on the living. It doesn't fear the sun, but prefers to hunt at night like other nocturnal predators, using darkness to help it sneak up on its prey. It is rarely merciful. A Blautsauger can only be prevented from entering a house by smearing all doorways and windows with a paste made from mashed garlic and an attar of hawthorn flowers. The Blautsauger can most easily be killed while it sleeps using the standard ritual of exorcism.

Blood-Drinker: These are the "classic" vampires, largely because of the source of their sustenance, but in folklore, blood-drinkers are varied and often wildly dissimilar, both to each other and to popular impressions of them.

Bockshexe: This is a subspecies of the German Alp that can transform into a great, dark-haired goat and walk about on two legs. This variation almost certainly has roots in the horned-devil hysteria of the Inquisition Era (1478 C.E.[31]), and overlaps with theriocephaly—the worldwide mythological phenomenon of humans with animal heads, such as the various depictions of goat-headed devils like Baphomet.

Bouda: In Morocco, Tanzania, and Ethiopia there is a kind of living vampire that uses sorcery to transform into a were-hyena. Like most theriomorphs, the Bouda is alive, However, it drinks human blood as well as feasts on flesh. Strong and cunning, most Bouda are blacksmiths, a trade that allows them to fashion powerful magical charms to enhance their shape-shifting ability. When it is in animal form, the Bouda looks every bit like a normal hyena except that it wears an amulet that maintains a link to its humanity.

---

31. C.E. (Common Era) is used here in place of AD (*anno domini*), as it has become more common in international usage. Along the same lines B.C.E. (Before Common Era) is used in place of BC.

Without the amulet it will become a true hyena (and as a result, less dangerous). The Bouda possesses no supernatural invulnerability and can be killed by ordinar weapons in either form; it is an unnatural devious creature, which makes it difficult to hunt and trap.

Breath-Taker: Are usually invisible, though not always. They come in various forms, are often small, and generally prey on the weak and sick; however the legend of the Old Hag[32] falls partly into this category and partly into the next.

Brukulaco (also **Bruculaco**): The regions of Thessaly and Epirus in Greece have long been haunted by the spirits of the undead, including the formidable Brukulaco. This vampire is created when a person is excommunicated from the church, effectively severing the person from the grace and protection of God. In some cases the curse can be passed on to the son of an excommunicant. After death, the corpse transforms into a swollen, monstrous shape with skin as hard as tree bark. It smashes its way out of its grave and lopes off into the night, body hunched and head held low, teeth bared, very similar to the interpretations of werewolves seen in films like *The Howling* and *Dog Soldiers*. The beast has a barrel chest that, when struck, booms like a drum. Its arms are packed with muscles and each long finger tapers into a razor-sharp claw as long as a steak knife. Despite this appearance, it is considered to be a species of vampire rather than a werewolf.

Once the Brukulaco has set out to feed, it will utter a strange plaintive cry. If someone comes to investigate the sound, the Brukulaco will slaughter him and feast on his blood and flesh. Like the vampires of Germany, the Brukulaco also spreads the plague. This kills more people than its nightly attacks.

In the region of Thessaloniki there is a somewhat different version of the Brukulaco legend. There it is believed that when a person suffering from catalepsy lapses into a fit, his soul leaves the body and enters that of an nearby wolf. At once the wolf becomes a killer and will hunt down livestock and human alike.

---

32. See Old Hag entry in Chapter 3 for more on this monster.

Folklore in Science Fiction

"Science fiction has certainly taken many of the traditional myths and 'futurized' them. In thrillers, serial killers are basically a type of werewolf, men who are monsters inside. In fact, that might be the origin of the first werewolf stories, normal-seeming people who can turn into monsters. *Frankenstein* was originally called 'the modern Prometheus,' a retelling of that old Greek myth. *Dracula* suddenly brought a bunch of obscure vampire legends into public consciousness. These myths will continue to evolve and influence each other."—Kevin J. Anderson has published over ninety-five novels, forty-four of which have been national or international best-sellers. He is best known for his science fiction epic *The Saga of Seven Suns*, as well as his *Dune* novels written with Brian Herbert, many *Star Wars* novels, and *The Last Days of Krypton*.

Bruxsa: One of the most dangerous vampires on earth is Portugal's Bruxsa. This is a vampire who becomes so by choice, having been a witch who cast an evil enchantment on herself. More modern tales of the Bruxsa have whitewashed it, describing it either as a witch, a common pop-culture version of a vampire, or even a misunderstood immortal. But as you go further back into Brazilian folklore, the Bruxsa's nature becomes far less savory and not at all sympathetic. By the light of day the Bruxsa leads a normal life, appearing as a human—though extremely beautiful—woman. She can marry, bear children, attend church, and essentially pass unnoticed among her prey; but by night she transforms into a bird and flies into the darkness to seek her unnatural amusements. The Bruxsa loves to torment lost travelers, leading them astray, confusing them to the point of despair, then attacking them. Her means of choice, like that of many vampires, is the blood of children. Some legends hint that she even bears her own children for the sole purpose of having food at hand.

The Bruxsa has vast magical powers. Immortal and invulnerable, the Bruxsa can also cast spells that cause drought and sickness, and bring rains that drown fields at just the wrong time in the growing cycle. Though there are no known methods of slaying the Bruxsa at this time, there are ways to protect a child against her attack. Various magical amulets can be obtained from priests or mystics (and sometimes from Gypsies, who have no love for the undead). These charms are made of soil from a shrine of the Virgin Mary, mixed with hairs from the child's head and seven drops of the mother's tears. The items are mixed together, put into a small ceramic or carved wood amulet, and worn on a silver chain.

Buo: A rare vampire species from Borneo, the Buo has huge penetrating eyes, great fangs, and an unquenchable thirst for blood. They are the reanimated corpses of great warriors. When they rise they retain their old fighting skill but add to that the unnatural strength of the undead. The only sure way to destroy one is to completely dismember it and burn the parts separately.

Callicantzari (also **Kallikantzaros**): According to the folklore of Christian Greeks, any child born between Christmas and New Year's Day (or, in some tales, between Christmas and the Epiphany, January 6th) is at risk for becoming the vampire called a Callicantzari. This is an extremely fearsome beast whose nature encompasses many of the worst qualities of vampire and werewolf. The Callicantzari exhibits insanely violent behavior, but only during the span of days between Christmas and New Year. It has powerful talonlike fingernails with which it rips its victims to shreds. Some scientists have postulated that the legend of the Callicantzari is a way of explaining the rare and extreme aberrant psychological condition of necrophagism, where a person eats the body parts of someone who was recently murdered.

This monster has been known to abduct women and mate with them, and any offspring of that unhappy union are born as Callicantzari who quickly grow to adult size. Luckily the hunting season for the creature is brief and during the rest of the year it descends to the underworld to raise its young and plot its next campaign of murder and bloodshed.

Canchu (also **Pumapmicuc**): Pre-Columbian Peru suffered from an infestation of Canchus, a kind of bloodsucker whose favorite meal was the hot blood of powerful warriors in the full flush of youthful vigor. Not daring to attack these stalwarts while they were awake, the Canchus would sneak in to feed while a warrior was fast asleep. Sometimes they would kill the warriors by draining them dry of blood; other times they would leave the man alive and allow him to regain his strength, then return again and again in order to feed on the powerful blood. Rural stories in more recent times[33] hold that the Canchus—lacking a warrior class to prey upon—will now attack any healthy person. Mountain passes are their favorite hunting grounds, especially during moonless nights or snowstorms. Songs will drive this monster away, and the folk song "Canchu, Canchu" is popular with Peruvian folk bands. In the song, a wise traveler protects his two lame-brained sons from the vampire's clutches by making then sing heroic songs all night, thus tricking the Canchus into believing they are all stalwart warriors who are clearly still wide awake.

Charismatic Shape-Shifter: These vampires take the form of a compellingly beautiful woman or man in order to lure a victim into a tryst. Once alone, the creature then reverts back to its true form and attacks with great violence, feeding on blood or flesh.

Chedipe: In Indian folklore there are a number of different types of vampire prostitutes, including the vicious Chedipe. In folk art the Chedipe is depicted as a vulgar woman riding a huge male tiger under a moonlit sky. This powerful female vampire will cast a spell over an entire household and then enter while all are in a trance. There it will select a strong male to be the victim and suck his blood through his toes. Sometimes the Chedipe will sexually attack the man while he sleeps, polluting the sanctity of the household. It delights her to destroy a family's love, trust, and marital purity, because the Chedipe also feeds on sorrow and misery. The vampire's bite is rarely fatal, but the Chedipe may return again and again, taking more blood before the body can replenish what has previously been stolen. The victim soon weakens and begins to waste away, and if he does not seek treatment he will die.

---

33. There have been reports as recently as 2004. Local police who investigated these sightings have found no actionable evidence.

Chiang-Shih: In China a person who dies as a result of suicide, murder, hanging, drowning, or during the commission of a crime will rise as a Chiang-Shih, a very violent vampire, driven by pure bloodlust and heedless of any consequences. They act insanely because they are the manifestations of the irrational aspects of the soul. Chiang-Shih have great difficulty walking due to the pain and stiffness of being a decaying corpse, so they hop instead. In fact, a series of horror-comedy-martial arts movies have been made about the hopping vampires of China. Whereas hopping scenes in the movies are largely shot for laughs, the creatures of legend are no laughing matter. They are vicious and sadistic and always hungry for blood. They are vastly strong and enjoy tearing their victims limb from limb. Some Chiang-Shih have been known to sexually assault female victims. Taoist monks are often called into villages to defeat Chiang-Shih. The priests prepare charms which they write with chicken blood on small pieces of yellow paper. The trick is then to affix these small paper charms to the Chiang-Shih's forehead, which is easier said than done with a monster that can kill with its breath or tear a man limb from limb. But once accomplished, the Chiang-Shih is instantly helpless. Of course, many Chiang-Shih movies contain at least one scene of the small pieces of paper accidentally falling off a Chiang-Shih's forehead.

Children of Judas: A cult of red-haired vampires that cause havoc throughout Serbia, Romania, and Bulgaria. They are known for their killing style: they can drain their victims entirely of blood with one bite. Their bite mark is unique in that it resembles the Latin symbol for the number thirty, XXX, which stands for the number of silver pieces Judas received for betraying Jesus. Judas is seen as a vampiric character because of his actions during Jesus last few days. Having participated in the Last Supper (a Passover dinner), he drank from Jesus' cup, which was symbolically held out to the Apostles as the blood of Christ. That very night Judas went and betrayed Jesus to the authorities, resulting in His arrest and crucifixion. Judas apparently repented of his crime and hanged himself in remorse. He is considered by most Christians as the embodiment of evil and is forever damned.

The crucifixion of Jesus as a result of His betrayal by Judas is

Folklore and the Blues

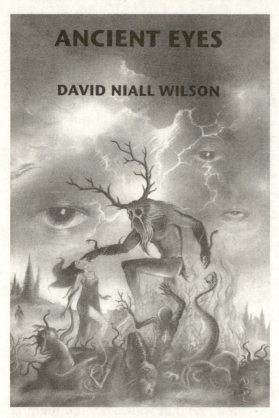

"In my novel *Deep Blue*, I covered some of the folklore associated with the blues, and also archaic, old-world spiritual practices like snake handling and the Sin Eater. In *Ancient Eyes*, I touch on the 'Great Horned God' and the old 'Earth Mother,' from Europe. . . . These are recurring themes for me. I'd say that almost every time I sit down to write, some aspect of historic folklore plays a part in the result. History, for me, is the best mental playground and the surest source of inspiration. I have an extensive library of history, folklore, occult, spiritual, and religious works that I draw on for stories."

—David Niall Wilson has been writing horror, fantasy, and science fiction since the mid 1980s. He is a multiple Bram Stoker Award winner with sixteen novels and over 150 published short stories. His latest novel is *Vintage Soul*.

---

probably the basis for the belief that crucifixes are anathema to vampires. However, this concept holds far more weight in fiction than it does in folklore. Though there have not been any reports in recent years of attacks by this vampire society, the Children of Judas concept pops up every now and then in popular fiction. In the vampire film *Dracula 2000*, Judas was named as the first vampire, a fact at odds with the more ancient histories of vampirism around the world. They were also used as supporting characters in Marvel Comic's *Dracula Lives* #3, October 1975.

Chordewa: This creature from among the Oraons caste of western Bengal is both witch and essential vampire, and is a theriomorph capable of transforming her very soul into the shape of a large black cat. This cat then ingratiates itself with potential victims, acting very friendly, eating the victims' food, and even showing "affection" by licking people on their lips. This lick, however, is a kiss of death: it is both an infection and a kind of transmission port from which the cat will gradually drain the victim's life force. In other legends all the cat creature has to do is lick a person's shadow to inflict the wasting disease.

Churel: Pregnant Indian women who die during the festival of Divali (the Hindu Festival of Light) are in danger of returning as bloodsucking revenants called Churel. These Churel are hideous vampires with lolling black tongues thick coarse lips caked with rouge, wild and tangled hair, heavy sagging breasts, and feet that are twisted around backward. Because they have died so unfairly—carrying new life—they are bitter and vengeful and return to take out their resentment on the living. The Churel attack young families, handsome men, and anything else that would remind them of what they have lost. But their greatest enmity is directed toward their relatives, whom they blame for allowing them to die when their need for care was greatest. The best way to defeat a Churel is to preven its creation, either by attending a pregnant woman and providing the best possible care or by burying her with absolute attention to every detail of the sacred burial rites and celebrating her life in song and prayer. If a Churel comes into existence, only a Hindu Pundit (priest) can drive it out using prayer and incense and offerings. But this is difficult, and often the Churel is driven away for a time, only to return again months or years later.

Cihuateteo (also **Civatateo**): This Aztec vampire is a revenant of a woman who died in childbirth. Unique among these similar vampires, however, the Cihuateteo's child is also a vampire. The undead mother and child haunt the night and attack children, crippling them with a dreadful paralysis or infecting them with a wasting sickness. Sometimes the Cihuateteo and her child drink their victims' blood, but most often they feed on the essence of fear, and on the life force discharged as a person wastes away and dies of a lingering disease. The Cihuateteo have pale faces and pasty skin. They dress in costumes like those worn by Tlazolteotl, the goddess of sorcery, lust, and evil. Fending off a Cihuateteo is very difficult and usually requires holy charms that were sacred to the ancient Aztecs. Modern crosses will not work, even if the Cihuateteo was a Christian in life. Only the adult Cihuateteo is vulnerable to Aztec charms; her child, who never knew the rites and rituals of any religion, is immune to them. The only weapon known to work against both creatures is fire, and even then it will merely drive them off. No known method of totally destroying this vampiric pair is yet known.

Craqueuhhe: This is one of Europe's most savage monsters, a true anthropophagous vampire—which means that it is not just a blood-drinker but a flesh-eater as well. The Craqueuhhe is a revenant, a corpse animated from dead flesh that rises from the grave of a person who has died in sin or who was never baptized. This creature is more zombie in appearance than vampire, like a decaying corpse with sunken eyes, greasy hair clotted with dirt, fingernails broken from having clawed its way out of its coffin, and the stench of decay about it. Maggots and other insects crawl through tears in its flesh and infest its clothing. The Craqueuhhe can hunt no matter how badly its body is impaired or injured at the time of its natural death. Accounts of Craqueuhhe shambling along on shattered legs, with arms torn out, or with other massively disfiguring injuries are very common. By the same token, the creature's complete disregard for concepts like pain or crippling injury make it difficult to fight and even more difficult to kill. Gunshots pass right through it and knives are useless. And despite its decaying and wretched appearance, the Craqueuhhe is extremely fast and very powerful. Only fire and beheading will stop the creature. The zombies of films like *Night of the Living Dead* depict creatures more in keeping with the Craqueuhhe than with any version of the traditional Haitian zombie. The character of Kenneth Boyd in Jonathan Maberry's Pine Deep Trilogy (*Ghost Road Blues*, *Dead Man's Song*, and *Bad Moon Rising*) is a Craqueuhhe.

Dearg-Dul: Ireland, home of many ghost tales and legends of faerie folk, is also home to the deadly Dearg-Dul. This is an ancient vampire whose name means "red bloodsucker" and whose bloody crimes date back to druidic times. Unlike other revenants, the Dearg-Dul do not appear as moldering corpses. In fact, stories tell of male and female Dearg-Dul appearing as beautiful and sexually appealing specters that lure their victims to trysting places and then kill them. The druids—wise in the ways of the supernatural world—have fought these creatures for a thousand years and have devised ways of stopping them. Once the grave of a suspected Dearg-Dul is identified, the druids erect a heavy cairn of stones over it. Even with their unnatural strength, the Dearg-Dul cannot dislodge thousands of pounds of rock. Trapped in their graves, the vampires will eventually degenerate into dust.

Dockele (also **Dockeli**, **Dockje**): This is another Alps subspecies, albeit an extremely rare one, with sightings limited to the more remote mountain regions of Germany. Like the Bockshexe, the Dockele is also a theriomorph[34] that often takes the shape of a cat while hunting.

Doppelsauger: Breast-feeding vampires are common in Europe, especially in Germany, but the Doppelsauger of Hanoverian legend goes a very nasty step further and actually consumes the breasts as well. A Doppelsauger is created when a mother has allowed a child who has been weaned to begin breastfeeding again. Hence the name Doppelsauger, or "double-sucker." Why this is such a mortal sin is open to debate. However, if that child were to die it would be condemned to return to haunt the living as a Doppelsauger. First, while still in its grave—and once its unnatural hunger awakens— it will eat its own breast. Once it has consumed that, it rises from

---

34. Theriomorph (from the Greek *therion*, meaning "wild animal" or "beast," and *anthrōpos*, meaning "man") is a shape-shifter, or a being that can deliberately change its physical appearance through magical transformation. Not to be confused with a "glamour," which is an illusion caused by magic.

the grave as a fearsome revenant to feed on the breasts of its family members. The Doppelsauger typically attacks only its own relatives, but it will attack others out of need.

Various preventative strategies are open to the family of the dead child to reduce the risk of its becoming a Doppelsauger. The key is to make sure it cannot begin eating itself while in the grave. Denied this initial and unwholesome meal, the Doppelsauger will lack the strength necessary to break free of its coffin and rise from the grave. Blocks are put in place to prevent the jaws from working, such as a metal coin wedged between its teeth or semicircular wooden board placed under its chin to make it impossible for the corpse to bite at itself. Wrappings are often wound around the body to deny it the use of its hands, and care is taken to make sure cloth from the shroud or burial garments does not come into close contact with the mouth.

Draugr: Ancient Norse legends tell of powerful ghost-vampires who inhabit the graves of dead Vikings and reanimate the corpses. The creature that rises from these graves is a virtually indestructible killing machine able to withstand any weapon. The Draugr raids local villages to steal treasure, which it then takes back to its new lair. Once it amasses a hoard it guards it jealously and savagely rips apart anyone who attempts to take so much as a single copper penny. The only person who can defeat a Draugr is a hero, but the hero must do so in unarmed combat. If the Draugr lives long enough, it develops vast supernatural power, including control over the weather, and can call up storms and thick fogs which it uses to shroud its lair so that no one can easily find it. When it goes out to hunt it often takes the form of a hunting bird or a fierce gray wolf. Draugr are mentioned in various Norse epics, including the Grettis Saga (in which a Draugr is shown to be able to live among humans without being detected) and the Eyrbyggja Saga (in which the story is varied to include a shepherd who returns as a Draugr). This monster is also the theme of *The Saga of Draugr* by Heulend Horn, a Viking heavy metal band from Argentina (and, no, that's not a typo).

Ekimmu: The eerie Ekimmu is a ghostly creature that, if not properly buried, can rise from its unquiet grave to prey on the living.

Those who have died sudden and violent deaths become Ekimmu, especially murder victims, women who died during childbirth or their stillborn children, those who have been poisoned or who ate spoiled food, those who were interred without proper burial rites, victims of drowning, victims of starvation, and the unburied on battlefields. Even the recent dead who have perished without ever having been fulfilled in love—or who have been scorned and died lonely and bitter—can rise from the grave as an Ekimmu.

The Ekimmu is a tormented soul, caught in the twilight between this world and the next, unable to move on because of unresolved matters on earth, unable to sever the ties that bind it to this world. Bitter and angry, the Ekimmu takes out its wrath on the living, killing wantonly and wreaking havoc with anyone who lives near its burial place. The Ekimmu is most often seen in the form of a rotting corpse staggering stiffly through the night. In other accounts it appears as a foul night wind, as a deadly shadow, or in the form of a shadowy phantom. But in whatever form it assumes, the Ekimmu is a vile and malicious monster.

Empusa (also **Mormolykiai**; plural **Empusae**): These blood-drinking demons were in the service of Hecate, the Greek Goddess of the Crossroads. The Empusae often went about disguised as humans, but their true forms were reportedly very hideous, and they were believed to have one leg of brass and one like that of a donkey. These vile vampires have been written about in stories, histories, folktales, and plays for thousand of years, but the most famous and important account was that by Philostratus in his *Life of Apollonius of Tyana*. Philostratus wrote of the handsome youth Menippus, who was enticed by an Empusa disguised as a Phoenician woman. Apollonius confronted the Empusa, and the Empusa revealed itself and admitted to fattening up Menippus so that she might devour him.

Eng-Banka: Another Malaysian Essential Vampire that takes the appearance of a fierce dog creature that steals a person's soul, resulting in death within a few days. Though the Eng-Banka is quick and clever, it is no more powerful than an ordinary dog and can be killed by any conventional method. However, the corpse of a slain Eng-Banka should be burned and the ashes scattered to prevent the spirit from returning to the region. Because the Eng-Banka appears as a dog, or a doglike creature, many rural Malaysians fear dogs that they do not know. They often carry charms to protect them against being approached by strange dogs.

Erestun (also called **Xloptuny**): Russia has quite a variety of vampire species troubling its long, dark nights. One of the worst is the Erestun, a vampire created when a sorcerer takes over a person's body while the victim is on the brink of death. At such times the link between body and soul is tenuous and the sorcerer can, essentially, force the rightful spiritual inhabitant out of the body and occupy it himself. At this point the dying person makes a miraculous recovery. Unfortunately, the Erestun needs to feed on blood in order to maintain the health of its new vehicle and the likeliest targets for the Erestun are the relatives of the body's former owner.

Eretiku (also **Eretnik**, **Eretitsa**, **Erestun**, **Eretnitsa**): These vampire-sorcerers from Russia and neighboring countries take their name from the root word eretic (heretic) and these vampires rise from the graves of blasphemers[35] who practiced dark sorcery. In Northern Russian tales, the Eretiku is a woman who sold her soul to the devil during her lifetime and returned from the grave to trouble the world of the living. Adopting the form of an old hag by day, the Eretiku would seek out others of her kind and form a coven to meet in the dark shadows of a deep forest ravine. In the East-Central Russian version, the Elatomsk is a woman who had sold her soul to the devil for great magical powers, and after dying a human death returns as a kind of poltergeist called a doorknocker. Most versions of this monster sleep in graves and make disgusting and disruptive noises in alehouses, public bathhouses, and other places.

Essential Vampire: Also known as Energy Vampires, this forms the largest overall category of vampires in the supernatural world. These monster do not feed on blood but instead (like the Astral Vampire) take nourishment from life energy, breath, emotion, sexual energy, and other vital forces.

---

35. The belief that heretics return from the dead to harass the living is viewed as an explanation—or, perhaps an excuse—for the brutality surrounding the medieval Russian campaign against blasphemers.

Estrie: One of the most fearsome (and feared) vampires in Hebrew folklore is the Estrie. These are a kind of female witch-vampire that has the sole purpose of attacking humans for blood. An Estrie will attack any person at will, but favors the blood of children above all. The Estrie are shape-shifters, capable of adopting various forms to deceive their prey. When an Estrie takes to the night air to fly above villages and farms it will revert back to its horrific demonic shape. Killing an Estrie does not require magical weapons; ordinary swords and spears will work, and fire is always useful. Should a human injure an Estrie, the creature will die unless it somehow contrives to steal some salt and bread from the house of its enemy. Consuming these things will restore the Estrie to health, and by the next evening it will be able to hunt again.

Farkaskoldus: This Hungarian predator is another interesting blend of vampire and werewolf, resisting classification as either and embracing characteristics of both. The Farkaskoldus is an resurrected spirit that returns to seek revenge, rising from the grave of a person (usually a shepherd) who has been abused or unfairly treated in life. Though essentially a werewolf in action, it drinks blood rather than hunting, for meat. The majority of legends hold that once the Farkaskoldus has gotten whatever justice is desired, its spirit will be able to rest and it will return to the grave, never to rise again. In some folktales the Farkaskoldus, once freed of its compulsion to seek redress, will begin attacking anyone until it is hunted down and killed.

Flesh-Eater: This is a much larger class of monsters and includes many species of vampire as well as all species of werewolves, various kinds of living dead, ghouls, and even some faerie folk, gnomes, and imps.

Ghost Witches of Nigeria: The Yakö people of Nigeria believe that some witches can turn into invisible vampires while astral projecting. Though incorporeal, these witches feast on blood. The presence of an ulcer is, according to local legend, a sure sign that a person has become the prey of one of these ghost witches. Anthropologist Daryll Forde wrote a chilling account of this phenomenon in his book *Yakö Studies* (Oxford University Press, 1964).

Gierach: Much like the Upier of Poland, the Gierach of Prussia kills with the power of pronouncement: it climbs to the top of a house, steeple, or bell tower and speaks the name of its victim, and that person dies within hours or days. Most people in the village hear the call of the Gierach as the cry of a nightbird but the victim hears his or her own name being called. Because of this, many rural Prussians consider owls to be evil, vampires in disguise, or at very least omens of ill fortune. The Gierach is a

---

Food for Thought by Brom

"I'm an artist; I paint what I see and I see monsters everywhere."

---

revenant essential vampire that feeds on the despair of its doomed victim. However it can be thwarted easily by using one of the tried-and-true methods for distracting Eastern European vampires: Scatter poppy seeds on its grave and it will be compelled to stop and count them all night. Another trick is to leave a stocking, woven mat, or fishing net atop the grave. The vampire will not be able to go hunting until it has unraveled every thread.

Gjakpirë: An Albanian vampire about which little is known today. It is generally considered to be a revenant and a blood-drinker, much like the Lugat, though it is not as difficult to kill. Folktales suggest that the Gjakpirës were cowardly vampires because they could easily be killed. Therefore, they used deception and trickery to gain access to a sleeping person, then would take just a little blood but not enough to cause alarm. The Gjakpirës traveled by night, often in the form of dark nightbirds, and would change back into their natural shapes (that of reanimated corpses) prior to attacking their victims. Often a Gjakpirë would lie by the side of a road, appearing to be simply an injured traveler, and wait for a good Samaritan to come along and offer aid. Once the well-intentioned person was within reach, the Gjakpirë would stab him in the groin or throat with a sharpened stick, then wait for the victim to become weak with blood loss before attacking and lapping up the blood.

Glaistig: This monster from the Scottish Highlands has the upper torso of a beautiful woman and the legs of a goat, a fact she hides under a flowing green skirt. The Glaistig will dance seductively in order to lure a man to a secluded place, then enchant the man to dance with her until he collapses from sheer exhaustion. In many tales the Glaistigs are blood-drinkers, and in the final stages of the dance they tear at their victims' throats and shoulders and feast on the spurting blood. Folktales suggest that Glaistig is a twisted variation of a water sprite, and indeed her name means "water imp." Travelers around the more remote lochs and rivers in the Highlands are often tricked into thinking they're in for a bit of elfish canoodling when they meet the Glaistig, but it never quite ends as the lustful gent expects.

Green Ogresses: France has a reputation for some very nasty vampires, many of whom take the form of beautiful women in order to lure unsuspecting (but horny) men into secluded areas, typically near ponds or swamps, and then chow down with their own version of a picnic lunch. Only a man with the purest soul can resist them and escape . . . and those are fairly few and far between.

His-Hsue-Keui: A general Chinese term for vampire and translates as "suck-blood demon." See also Chiang-Shih.

Human Vampire: These are not supernatural beings at all[36] but are otherwise ordinary humans who either live as vampires by choice or because they believe it is their nature. Some social anthropologists argue that this phenomenon is an outgrowth of the Goth subculture that developed in Great Britain in the early 1980s as part of the Goth (or Gothic) rock scene; however, there's some evidence that it was in wide (though not open) practice for many years prior to the advent of the Goths. Aspects of the Human Vampire you'll encounter elsewhere in this chapter are Sanguinarians, Lifestylers, Psychic Vampires, and Role Players.

Impundulu: Among the Pondo, the Zulu, and the Xhosa peoples of Southern Africa there is a common legend of a vampire species called the Impundulu, whose name means "lightning bird." The creature, which often takes the form of a black-and-white bird of immense size, is the servant of a witch who uses it to gather information and attack her enemies. The creature has vast powers that include summoning and hurling lightning with its talons. When not in bird form, the Impundulu transforms into a man or woman of great beauty and unnatural charisma who seduces humans and feasts on their blood. Its appetite for hot blood is unquenchable, and if the witch did not exert control over the monster it would go on a rampage of slaughter. When used against the witch's enemies the Impundulu preys upon livestock, weakening them and spreading disease. It is thought by some field biologists that the Impundulu myth was created as a way of explaining wasting diseases

36. Some practicing members of the vampire community will likely disagree with us on this, and we won't argue the point.

such as the prion disease spongiform encephalopathy (mad cow disease) or diseases carried by insects or bacteria in polluted water. An Impundulu who is no longer under the control of a witch is called an Ishologu, and is one of the most feared monsters in African folklore.

Incubi/Succubi: These are (almost always) invisible spirits who visit sleeping humans at night and engage in sex for the sole purpose of feeding on sexual energy, potency, or, in some rare cases, sexual fidelity. Incubi are male sexual vampires and Succubi are female.

Jenglot: Even among vampires this one is odd—a doll-sized bloodsucker with a skeleton face and conjoined feet that was once a full-grown human being. Some anthropologists contend that the Jenglot is not an actual vampire but a fetish doll used to symbolize some other vampires such as the Pontianak or Langsuir. Local Malays argue that it is a separate species of vampire that grows in size as it feeds. Some even claim to have kept them as pets, feeding them animal blood (or in some cases human blood purchased from the Red Cross). The Jenglot is never seen to actually drink the blood but somehow absorbs the essence of it through some mystical means.

Kathakano: Never trust a smiling vampire. Though not a true aphorism, it is certainly good advice when in Crete. The native blood drinker of that island is the Kathakano, a revenant who constantly grins. From a few yards away on a darkened country road or badly lit city street, the Kathakano might appear to be nothing more than a friendly stranger, or at worst a happy drunk. But then it draws closer and spits tainted blood at its victims, burning them with some foul acid produced by its unnatural body. Blinded and in agony, the victims are helpless as the Kathakano rushes forward and bites them with its smiling mouth full of sharp, white teeth. Like most vampires of Eastern Europe, the Kathakano can be tracked to its grave and it is helpless while sleeping. Once the grave has been opened, the corpse should be beheaded and the head boiled in a large pot filled with a mixture of one part vinegar and two parts water from melted snow. As soon as the mixture boils, the head should be unwrapped and lowered by tongs into the liquid. The head is left to boil for one hour, the time kept according to a church clock tower or a priest's pocket watch. After this process is complete, the head is carried back to the grave and the body is reburied. In some cases the head and corpse are cremated and the ashes poured back into the grave.

Keres (also **Ker**): In ancient Greek mythology, there is a race of demonic creatures who served as the very personification of violent death, whether through battle, murder, or accident: the Keres. These creatures appeared as women clothed in bloody garments, but behind their painted lips they have long fangs and their bone-white hands are tipped with wickedly sharp talons. The Keres served the Fates, who measured the length of a man's life on the day of his birth and who represented the inevitability of death; so when a person was near death as a result of violence, the Keres would ensure that they did not linger (or recover) and would descend to battlefields or the scenes of accidents and would rip the souls out of the dying. Once a soul was freed to begin its journey to Hades, the body was theirs to consume with great hunger and relish. When there was a great battle, scores of these she-creatures would flock like carrion birds over the battle and would often squabble and fight among themselves for the choicest spoils of war. The Greek poet Hesiod wrote of the origins of the Keres in his classic *Theogony*. They've appeared in Homer's *Iliad* and *The Odyssey* as well as numerous other classic writings.

Kozlak: Spread along the edge of the Adriatic, between Croatia and Albania, is the nation of Dalmatia, home of the vampire-poltergeist called the Kozlak. If a child dies because it has not been properly breast-fed, there is a great risk that it will become a Kozlak, returning to haunt its neglectful mother and the whole community. The angry infant spirit smashes crockery and throws things around the house, and can even muster the strength to pull hay carts around the yard, sometimes overturning them. Occasionally the creature manifests itself as a bat or other small predator and attacks the family's cattle, drinking blood and spreading disease. If the creature's rage spills out of the house and into the village, the resulting destruction generally creates an outcry resulting in some quick and

Making It New

Queen of Bones by Linda Peltola

"It is a challenge for any artist to bring something new to a paradigm that has already been very strongly developed throughout time and that's expected to be presented in a certain way to honor the tradition, but I believe that when an artist takes a bold leap and places a mythological character in the present day, the contrast becomes obvious—it's no longer just folklore, it's something that's right here and now, it's more believable when presented in the surroundings of our age of 'sense' and science, and

that makes it even more frightening to most people. That's when the question rises in your mind: 'What if that really happened now?' At that point, you can no longer rely so strongly on your idea of what's true and what's ancient folklore."
—Linda Peltola was born in Finland and does bohemian design work for progressive companies. She is preparing the first collection of her art to be published in the United States.

---

decisive action. Traditionally the villagers appeal to the Franciscan Brothers for help, and a monk trained in fighting supernatural evil is dispatched to save the village.

The monk creates a special amulet to protect himself against the Kozlak by incanting prayers over the amulet. He must also obtain a thorn from a hawthorn bush that was grown high in the mountains and at a point where there is no view of the sea. With the amulet and the thorn, the monk goes to the graveyard where the Kozlak's mortal remains are buried. There he sits and prays until his chants summon the Kozlak spirit from its grave. Once the Kozlak has risen, the monk leaps up and transfixes it with a sharpened stick of hawthorn wood. This destroys the evil spirit, leaving the resting remains sanctified and harmless, and the village in peace.

There is an interesting historical oddity about the Kozlak: it is the only known vampire species that can be destroyed merely by a stake through the heart. Unlike the vampires in popular fiction, vampires of folklore are not generally destroyed by a stake, but simply held immobile so other methods of exorcism can be performed.

Krasue (or **Phi-krasue**, **Pi-Kasu**): A monster found throughout Southeast Asia, particularly Cambodia, Indonesia, Laos, Malaysia, and Thailand. It manifests as the floating head of a woman with its intestines dangling beneath. In various folktales the monster is reported to feed on blood, human waste, cow dung, or life essence. It has been the focus of a number of films including *Nieng Arp* (1977), *Mystics in Bali* (1981), *Krasue* (2002), and *Krasue Valentine* (2006). It was even used for laughs in a Thai commercial for Sylvania light bulbs.

Krvoijac: Throughout the Balkans, vampirism is heavily linked with the spread and practice of Christianity. This is never more so than in the case of the Krvoijac of Bulgaria. All that is required of a person to become a Krvoijac is to smoke tobacco or drink alcohol during Lent, and the transformation is upon them. Fairly harsh punishment for breaking the vows of abstinence. When a person is so cursed they die and are buried normally, but over the next forty days their skeleton melts to a gelatinous state and then is reformed as part of their unnatural immortal body. This new vampiric anatomy helps give the creature the strength necessary to tear apart its shroud, smash through the lid of its coffin, and claw its way up through the earth to escape the grave. When the Krvoijac rises it is a blood drinker and appears very much like a reanimated corpse, with pale rotting flesh, sunken eyes, and horrible breath.

The forty-day transformation of a blasphemer from human to Krvoijac represents the forty days Jesus wandered in the desert without food or drink. In Lent this was a purification process that helped the mortal Jesus prepare to accept the Holy Spirit and thereafter take up the mission for which He had been born. In the case of the Krvoijac the forty-day period is an unholy mockery of the forty days of Lent.

To destroy a Krvoijac, a vampire-hunting priest called a Djadadjii must use his holy powers to invoke the creature's spirit, drawing it out of the ground through prayer, and then directing the spirit to enter a bottle that he has specifically prepared. The bottle is then taken to a great bonfire and hurled into the flames. Only in this manner can the evil soul be destroyed. Once this has been accomplished, the body, still in the grave, becomes nothing more than a lifeless corpse and troubles the village no longer.

Kudlak and **Kresnik** (also **Krsnik**): The Kudlak, a vampire subspecies found on the Croatian peninsula of Istria as well as Serbia, Bosnia, and Slovenia, is a creature that truly exemplifies the nature of good and evil. In those lands, when a person is born with a caul (a veil covering the face), it is a sign that the child will either grow up to be evil (a Kudlak) or good (a Kresnik). The color of the amniotic membrane indicates which: pale, white, or clear indicate a pure nature; blood red or dark reveals an evil soul. The child is doomed from birth to be either a hero or villain, and there's not much that can be done to turn aside the arrow of destiny.

The Kudlak will grow up with evil alive in his heart and will do all manner of harm while still a living being. But at night the soul of this tainted being will leave the body and roam the dark in the shape of a locust, night bird, or bat, or perhaps stalk the byways as a wolf; attacking the innocent, sometimes killing outright, sometimes amusing itself by merely maiming or tormenting. The Kudlak can also cast spells over the community, resulting in crop failures, bad weather, stillbirths, and other calamities. When the living Kudlak finally dies (whether naturally or through violence), it will rise again as an undead revenant, a true vampire. And then the real reign of terror will begin. If fate chooses to let a person born with a caul become a Kresnik, his destiny will be to become a champion and protector of his people. He, too, can leave his body and adopt the form of an animal or bird, but his sole purpose is to seek out the Kudlak and destroy it in any of its evil guises. The Kresnik[37] is fierce and strong and can confront the Kudlak in either its living or undead form.

Langsuir (also **Lansuyar**): Malaysia and Java share a number of cultural similarities, not the least of which are their troubles with vampires created from stillbirths and deaths of women during childbirth. The Malaysian Langsuir is a female vampire[38] of overwhelming beauty who died from grief when her child was stillborn. Forty days after her burial she will rise from her grave as a vampire and fly away into the trees, forever haunting the region and hunting humans for their blood. Though she has changed into a spirit of heart-rending beauty, the Langsuir can be identified as something other than human by her unnaturally long nails, green robes, and long silky black hair that hangs so low it swirls about her ankles. The long hair hides a second mouth that has formed at the back of her neck, and it is through this second mouth that she drinks the blood of children. The Langsuir is also a flesh-eater and

---

37. Some modern versions of this legend get the names backward and list the Kresnik as the evil one.

38. The male of the species is the Bajang (see listing).

she will hunt, alone or in packs, eating raw fish caught in streams or attacking livestock.

Like the Javanese vampires, the Languir can be crippled by burying it with its mouth filled with glass beads (in order to prevent it from making its hunting call or using its seductive voice to lure prey). Similarly, hens' eggs are placed in the vampire's armpits and long needles are driven through the hands to disable its ability to fly.

A Langsuir can even be cured and restored to normal humanity (a very rare turn of events in the world of vampires). To accomplish this, the Langsuir has to be captured and restrained. Her long hair must be shorn off and stuffed into the unnatural mouth at the back of her neck, and her fingernails should be cut all the way down to the skin. If these things are done correctly, the Langsuir will be restored to normalcy. She can even marry, have children, and live a normal life except in one regard: if she were to make merry and feel intense emotions, she would revert back to her vampiric self. Therefore the Langsuir must be sure to live a dour, somber life. The stillborn child of a Langsuir is reborn as a Pontianak (see entry).

Leanan Sídhe: One of the stranger and more enchanting vampires of Celtic folklore is the Leanan Sídhe,[39] known also as the "Dark Muse," and tales vary as to whether she is an essential vampire or a blood-drinker. Or neither. The more modern tales have revised and romanticized the creature so that she's more often a benign fairy babe rather than the supernatural predator she was for centuries, as recounted in the older folktales and songs. In either case she is one of the Aos Sí, or fairy folk (pronounced "ess shee") who takes a human lover but whose needs are so powerful that they literally burn the life force out of the human. Mind you, her lovers are always willing, because the Leanan Sídhe earns her reputation as a muse by inspiring that human's greatest work and deepest thought; but the price is a shortened life. There's a metaphor for addiction that has not been lost on writers, including Arthur Conan Doyle, who wrote of Holmes's need for cocaine in order to be at the height of his powers.

The root of the name comes from two Gaelic words: *leannan*

---

39. Leanan Sídhe is the spelling in Irish Gaelic; in Scottish Gaelic it is liannan shìth; on the Isle of Man it's Leanhaun Shee.

("sweetheart" or "concubine") and *Sídhe* ("of the fairy mounds"). John Keats's poem "La Belle Dame Sans Merci" suggests that the Leanan Sídhe only pretends to be a flirty lover but that once she has her victim in thrall she reveals her true self and the unfortunate victim winds up trapped in a half-life, providing ongoing sus-

Altering Folklore for Use in Fiction

  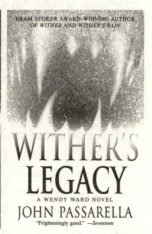

John Passarella,
photo by Andrea Passarella

"In my novel *Wither's Legacy*, the creature terrorizing the town is based on the Canadian Wendigo. I tell an origin story informed by my research of the Wendigo in folklore and the fur trapping/trading industry as it existed almost 250 years ago in what is now Canada. I use those elements as a starting point, then proceed to disregard some aspects of the legend (e.g., gargantuan size), while inventing my own 'unknown' qualities, such as mastery and control over winter weather and how to end the curse. In my novelette, *Breathless*, my Wiccan character, Wendy Ward, faces the Yuki-Onna demon from Japanese folklore and, again, I abide by some of the conventions while adding some inventions of my own." —John Passarella is the Bram Stoker Award–winning author of the Wither series of novels.

tenance for the essential vampire. This is probably drawn from the Leanhaun Shee, a variation from the Isle of Man.

Lifestyle Vampires: People who live the vampire life constantly and identify with vampires as kindred spirits but who do not believe themselves to be supernatural beings. This aspect of the subculture is most closely tied to both Goth and the post–Anne Rice audience.

Lilitu: This race of Sumerian vampires (the male is called Lilu; the female is the Lil) are perhaps the very first recorded[40] blood-drinkers, dating back to legends six thousand years old. They were evil beings that entered houses by night and drank the lifeblood of babies and young children. These demons inhabited the desert wastes and were seen as negative spiritual influences on sexuality and fertility, used primarily to curse someone else with barrenness Either separately or together they were regarded as extremely dangerous to pregnant women and newborns. The offspring of Lilitu parents is called an Ardat-Lili ("Maiden Lilitu"), and became a spirit of sexual dysfunction and frustration, causing spouses to stray, husbands to become abusive, wives to turn cold and vicious, and both partners to lapse into degenerate ways.

Living Vampires: Supernatural creatures that have vampiric qualities but who are not dead; and because they are alive, they are hard to detect and can more easily infiltrate a community.

Lobishomen: The sinister creature from Brazil preys mainly on women, though it seldom kills its victims. Instead it draws only enough blood to nourish itself. However, its bite creates a kind of infection that turns the woman into an insatiable nymphomaniac. As a result she often becomes a sexual vampire, preying on men other than her husband and destroying the sanctity of her marriage vows. In this way the Lobishomen accomplishes its evil purpose.

Portugal has a legend of a Lobishomen that is often overlapped with the legend of the Bruxa: vampire witches who attack children

---

40. The Lilitu were one of several demons spoken of in the Epic of Gilgamesh.

to suck their blood. In some areas where the Portuguese settled in Brazil, the Lobishomen is regarded more as a werewolf than a vampire. In werewolf fiction, the herb wolfsbane is commonly cited as a protection against lycanthropes, much as garlic is used against vampires. The same holds true in the folklore of the Lobishomen. Wolfsbane is planted on graves to keep the dead from rising as werewolves. In cases where a witch is suspected of being a werewolf, the herb is crushed into a paste with sweet onion and smeared around doors and windows.

Most sightings of the Lobishomen describe a small creature, hunchbacked and scampering on stumpy legs. Its face is horrifying, with pale and bloodless lips, jagged black teeth, jaundiced skin, and stiff bristling hair like that of a jungle ape. Disposing of a Lobishomen is fairly tough because it is clever and elusive, but it has one often fatal weakness in that it has no head for alcoholic beverages. Leaving cups of strong wine will lure it to get drunk, at which point it can be overcome by several strong men, crucified to a tree, and then stabbed to death. The corpse is then burned. In centuries past it was believed that a knife or sword that had been used to kill a Lobishomen was tainted and had to be melted down or otherwise destroyed. But in the ninth century the belief sprang up that such weapons had become imbued with special powers and were kept as talismans, often hung over thresholds to send a clear message to other evil creatures: Keep out!

Ma Cà Rông: Often seen only as a floating head and entrails (like the Asuang of the Philippines, the Phi Song Nan of Thailand, and the Malaysian Penanggalan), the Ma Cà Rông of Vietnamese legend is a grotesque and deadly creature of darkness. This foul beast does not hunt humans for blood like other vampires but feeds on cow dung (which, even for vampires, is pretty disgusting). The Ma Cà Rông is brought into being when a person dies at a "sacred hour," called "than trùng." Than means "spirit" and trùng means "coincidence." So this is not a situation where someone died with a tainted soul; they were just unfortunate enough to die at an unlucky hour.

Mananangal (also **Wakwak**): The Filipino version of the Malaysian Penanggalan (see listing).

Mandurugo: One of the more "traditional" of the many Filipino vampires is the Mandurugo, whose name literally means "bloodsucker." The creature is most active in the province of Capiz, in the northern region of Panay Island. Legends of it have spread throughout the Philippines. These creatures appear in the form of beautiful and seductive women during daylight hours, but at night they transform into flying monsters. Mandurugo can live ordinary lives and use their beauty to land a healthy young husband, but it is not out of love that they marry. A Mandurugo will enchant her husband into a deep sleep and feed from him by drinking a little blood each night. When a Mandurugo is hungry for fresh blood or blood in greater quantities, she takes to the night winds and hunts down a fresh quarry. Fire is one of the few things that can destroy the Mandurugo. Knives and swords will only cause injury. Bullets have little effect beyond causing momentary pain: they may slow the Mandurugo down, but they will not stop this monster.

Masan: One of the more tragic (yet horrifying) Hindu vampires of India is the Masan. This blood-drinker is the ghost of a child who, usually due to improper burial rituals, has not passed on to the afterlife or a new incarnation. The ghost becomes trapped on earth as an immortal monster, naturally filled with rage at being damned. It seeks to inflict as much vengeful harm as it can on the living. Wicked and spiteful in its unholy afterlife, the Masan delights in torture and murder. Because it died as a child, it vents its fury on the world by preying on living children. The Masan takes human form, often that of a child, though not always the child it was before it died. It befriends other children and lures them into secluded spots where it then attacks and kills them, feeding on their blood.

The Masan has vast magical powers and is known for casting hypnotic spells or laying curses. It is so vile and peevish that it will even curse a child that chances to walk in its shadow. One way the Masan selects its prey is to loiter on a public street and follow any woman whose gown happens to drag across its shadow. Once it reaches her home, the creature will prey upon any children therein, either attacking them as soon as the mother is not watching, or luring them outside to "play" and murdering them in quiet. The predatory habits of the female Masan are somewhat different. She sleeps by day in the cold ashes of a funeral pyre and rises at night to attack unwary travelers passing by the burial grounds. Completely covered in black ashes from the funeral pyre, the Masani blends in with the night. She will attack anyone—man, woman, child, even livestock.

Mjertovjec: Sometimes the shadowy line between what is a vampire and what is a werewolf becomes all but impossible to distinguish, and in many cultures they are inextricably linked. The Mjertovjec is a prime example: when a werewolf (or, in some cases a witch) dies, it can be reincarnated as a strange kind of vampire called a Mjertovjec. There are other ways in which a person can be cursed into becoming a Mjertovjec. If a person becomes an apostate (someone who has abandoned his faith or defied the church), or openly curses the Church or God, then doom is on them. Also, if a person merely acts like a werewolf—attacking people and biting them—then he suffers the same fate. The Mjertovjec appears as a disembodied head and thorax, with a dark red or purple face and many sharp teeth. From the hour of midnight until the rooster has cried three times it holds sway over the hour of darkness, and will attack the unwary with great strength and a terrible thirst for blood.

To prevent a Mjertovjec from haunting the countryside, villagers spread poppy seeds on the road between the cemetery and the house where the creature dwelled while it was alive. Like many Slavic vampires, the Mjertovjec is compelled to stop and count the seeds, thus wasting the entire night. A wise vampire slayer would secretly follow the Mjertovjec back along the trail of seeds to its resting place. In order to destroy the Mjertovjec, the vampire slayer has to wait until the disembodied head and thorax have left the grave again (or were busy counting seeds in the road). Only then can an iron shaft be driven through the creature's chest. Once transfixed, the spirit is cast loose from the body and destroyed. But even so the corpse itself has to be burned quickly or the Mjertovjec might somehow return.

Mormo: Unlike most creatures from ancient Greek myth, this night-wasting essential vampire lingers into the modern world,

On Werewolves

Among Werewolves by Eldred Tjie

"There is something about the metamorphosis that comes with werewolves that has an escapist flavor about it. To change into something else, to get into a different body and able to do things that you couldn't originally do . . . to let out the anger and frustrations built up over time . . . *that* is a very attractive element that I'm sure many people would agree with me on."
—Eldred Tjie is currently working professionally in the field of computer animation and does illustrations as a hobby.

though today it's more often a name given to a local version of the Boogeyman. In ancient times the Mormos were female demons that attacked sleeping children for their blood, leaving them cold and dead for their parents to find. Some scholars speculate that this was the way the ancient Greeks tried to rationalize the otherwise inexplicable tragedy of SIDS (Sudden Infant Death Syndrome). Oddly, among the many world cultures that tell of a child-killing demon, that creature is almost always female. It is like an anti-mother, a demon who demonstrates the exact opposite of the nurturing and protective actions of a true mother: it kills instead of nurtures, feeds upon rather than nurses.

Moroi: Romania is known more for ghost stories than vampires (despite what you read in fiction). However, the ghosts of that country often possess some vampire qualities. The Moroi, whose name comes from the Slavic word for "nightmare," is either an essential vampire that rises as an invisible spirit from the grave or a living person who draws life and energy from other people. In this latter case the Moroi is not always aware of the evil it does (unlike its more vicious cousin the Strigoi).

Motetzdam: A generic Hebrew word for "bloodsucker," used to describe any species of vampire.

Mullo: For long centuries, there has been a strong link between Gypsies and vampires. Despite some fictional references to the contrary, the Gypsies are not friends to the vampire; like every other culture, the Romany hate and fear these creatures of evil, particularly the Mullo (literally "one who is dead"). These creatures are revenants that rise from the graves of those who have died from sudden death, violence, or other unnatural causes or suffered improperly performed burial rites. A death at the hands of one's relatives can create a Mullo, especially where a relative keeps the deceased person's possessions instead of passing them on as is the typical Romany custom. Many Gypsies are wise enough to take measures to prevent a dead person from becoming a Mullo. At the time of burial they will place small pieces of steel in the newly deceased person's mouth, over the eyes and ears, and between the fingers. Then a stake made from newly cut hawthorn will be

The Folklore Behind the Fiction

"My novel *Cursed Be The Child* makes extensive use of Romany folklore and customs—although, like the Gypsies, I occasionally decided to create an age-old Romany tradition on the spot. It worked for Maria Ouspenskaya when she was filming *The Wolf-Man*. In the novella *Buckeye Jim in Egypt*, I used the traditional folk song 'Buckeye Jim' as part of the basis for the character. BJ is a banjo player who wanders through Little Egypt (Southern Illinois, which is, as one wag put it, 'just to the south of prosperity'), healing the sick, restoring sight to the blind, and other nice stuff.

"Turns out he's the 'Widow's Son,' like Lazarus, raised from the dead by Jesus, though the incident didn't get as much press. The Southern Illinois folklore is all based on the legit stuff—including the stories of Egypt's Robin Hood, Charlie Birger, the last man legally hanged in the state who stood on the gallows and said, 'It's a beautiful world . . . Goodbye.' "
—Mort Castle is the author of *The Strangers* (Overlook Connection, 2005) and editor of *On Writing Horror: A Handbook by the Horror Writers Association* (Writers Digest Books, 2006).

driven through the legs or hawthorn splinters will be placed in the socks. Even if the Mullo comes to life it would be unable to stand or walk, and would soon perish again from lack of nourishment.

Throughout history the Mullo has taken many forms, including a ghost, a rotting corpse, an animal-human cross, or a pale stranger wearing dark clothes. It's likely the Mullo is a shape-shifter, which increases its level of threat. It's also a sexual predator known for both seduction and rape. Some tales suggest that a Mullo can lead a fairly normal life as a human being, even to the point of marrying; but their sexual hungers will soon fatally exhaust their mates. Animals such as dogs, cats, or farm animals can become Mullo; and in some rare cases, plants as well. Pumpkins and other kinds of gourds or melons kept in the house too long might actually start to move about, make strange noises, and leak blood.

Destroying a Mullo usually requires contracting the services of a professional vampire slayer called a dhampyr (also dhampire, dhampir, etcetera). The dhampyr is the male offspring of a human and a vampire and possesses special powers that enable him to sense the presence of evil. If a Mullo has not yet risen from its grave, or is resting in a coffin or tomb, the dhampyr will open the grave and quickly drive long iron needles into the corpse's heart to immobilize it. A variety of rituals are used to rid the body of the supernatural taint and purify the physical remains. These include pouring boiling water over the corpse, beheading, the use of garlic and hawthorn, dismemberment, and sometimes incineration.

Nachzehrer: This Germanic vampire shares much in common with the Doppelsauger in that it begins feeding on it own clothing and flesh while still in the grave and then rises to attack its living relatives. Nachzehrers are created when a child born with a caul dies, or when someone has drowned. Upon first awakening, the Nachzehrer lies in its grave with its left eye open and slowly gnaws upon its shroud or its flesh. Family members can often tell that a recently buried relative has become a Nachzehrer because they will begin to sicken and die as soon as the vampire awakens in its grave. When the creature has fed enough to have the strength to rise, it directs its appetites on the living; if any of its family still live, they'll be the first victims. The Nachzehrer is also a nosferatu known for spreading various plagues. Throughout German history it has reappeared in times of famine and disease, a dark pestilential presence. The best protection against this dreaded vampire is placing scissors beneath one's pillow with the points facing toward the head of the bed. This charm also works well against the Alp and the Blautsauger.

Nelapsi: The most dreaded vampire in the Czech Republic and Slovakia[41] is the deadly Nelapsi, a creature that delights in destroying entire villages. This vampire will invade a town, glut itself on the blood of humans and livestock, and leave the region a lifeless wasteland. The Nelapsi uses strong teeth to tear at its victims and

41. These two nations were formerly known as Czechoslovakia until 1993.

often smothers them with a fierce strength. It is believed that the Nelapsi has two hearts and two separate souls, which makes killing the vampire far more difficult. When confronted, the Nelapsi has the power to kill with a single fierce glance of its flaming red eyes. It generally brings with it a virulent plague that slays the few people that survive the vampire's blood thirst. The villagers know that the best defense against the Nelapsi is to prevent its creation, and luckily have methods for ensuring this. One way is to make sure to bump a coffin on the dead person's threshold while carrying the burden out to be buried. This "shakes loose" any bad luck clinging to the coffin so it will not attract any evil spirits.

Poppy seeds should be strewn along the road between the deceased's home and the graveyard, all around the grave, and inside the open grave itself. More seeds, perhaps some millet, should be used to fill the corpse's nose and mouth. Vampires like the Nelapsi are enthralled by seeds and will always stop to count them. With thousands of seeds scattered within and around the grave, the creature will feel compelled to count each one and won't have time to rise. Some folktales suggest that it is not the seeds but the poppy flower that should be placed inside the grave. The belief is that the narcotic effect of the opium will keep the revenant in a dreamlike state and therefore make it unwilling or unable to rise.

Neuntoter: Another German nosferatu is the Neuntoter ("killer of nine"), a revenant whose body is covered with open sores and suppurating wounds. He spreads disease wherever he goes. Its unusual name refers to the popular belief that it took nine days for a buried corpse to fully transform into this type of monster. Many believe that a child born with teeth is destined to become a Neuntoter after its own natural death. These children will be carefully watched, and when they eventually die—even as older adults—their birth "defect" will be remembered and the appropriate actions will be taken.

Nobusuma: According to Japanese folklore, a bat that lives to be a thousand years old will evolve into a form somewhere between animal and human, called a Nobusuma (Japanese for "most ancient"). The Nobusuma has a body like that of a flying squirrel, with wings that attach to the ankles of each of its four limbs. The Nobusuma is not a blood-drinker. Instead it comes out at night and sucks the breath out of sleeping victims while tapping on the chests. Oddly, if another person witnesses a Nobusuma's attack, the victim will survive and live a long and healthy life. But if there are no human witnesses, the victim will die within three days.

Nodeppo: An even older Japanese batlike creature is the Nodeppo. There are no accurate accounts of Nodeppo sightings because anyone who has seen it has died. There are tales, however, of people who saw the creature's horrific face reflected in mirrors or pools of water. Though these people survived the immediate encounter, many became ill and died within a few months. The Nodeppo swoops down and wraps its victims in its great dark wings, then sucks all of the breath out of them, instantly killing them. Travelers most often fall prey to this beast, but a wise traveler can protect himself by carrying a few nanomani leaves close to his skin.

Nora: Part evil imp and part vampire, the Hungarian Nora is a small hairless creature that is otherwise human in appearance. It runs on all fours like an animal. Often making itself invisible, the Nora generally attacks women who are immoral or who speak and act irreverently, biting them on the breasts and drinking their supposedly "tainted" blood. The creature's bite causes an allergic reaction that makes the victim's breasts swell to startling size, thus revealing both her shame and the fact that the woman has been the victim of this sprite. The cure for the Nora's bite is an ointment or poultice made from crushed garlic, applied liberally to the breasts. This helps reduce the swelling and prevents further attacks.

Nosferatu: A Romanian word that is widely used in folklore to describe any of the many vampires around the world who spread disease. The word nosferatu translates as "plague carrier." In his novel, *Dracula*, Bram Stoker incorrectly translates it as "undead."

Obayifo (also called **Asiman**): The Obayifo of Ghana is the supernatural spirit of a living witch or sorcerer who is able to leave his/her body and flit through the air as a malicious spirit in the form of a ball of light. The Obayifo preys primarily on infants and young children, drinking blood and sometimes leaving the victim alive but horribly diseased. When it is unable to get human blood, the Obayifo will feed on the juices of fruits and vegetables. In places where it feeds on crops, it often causes blight, and if the Obayifo is fraught with great hunger it may wind up destroying an entire field, leaving the fruits withered to dry husks and the plants diseased and inedible.

Bloodlust by Vinessa J. Olp

Obur (also **Ubour**): This Bulgarian vampire is a strange blend of vampire and poltergeist. The Obur is created when a person has died a sudden and violent death. Upon burial the spirit refuses to leave the body and either ascend to heaven or descend to hell. It is trapped and lingers on the mortal plane, creating havoc. The Obur spirit is manifested inside a corpse during the forty days following burial. When that time has passed, it claws its way out of the grave and begins its mischief. The Obur possesses a strange static charge: when it is in the vicnity, sparks crackle in the air and it is surrounded by the smell of ozone (often mistaken for brimstone). The Obur acts primarily like a poltergeist, creating destruction, hurling things about, destroying furniture, and focusing most of its destructive attentions on its own family. The creature is fond of making loud, sudden noises, like firecrackers, and disturbing any peace its former family members might enjoy.

The Obur is a blood drinker but not primarily so. It prefers normal human food and will be satisfied with that until there is no more to be had. Only then will it turn on humans and attack them for their blood. When that happens, the Obur will glut itself on blood. The name Obur is actually an old Turkish word meaning "glutton," and considering the creature's insatiable hunger for food (and blood) is an apt choice. But its unnatural hungers were also often its downfall, because the Obur could be lured into a trap using rich food as bait. Some folktales say that excrement could also attract it. Only the Vampirdzhija—a blend of witch-finder and vampire slayer—have the ability to sense an Obur while it is still in its grave and forming its vampiric skeleton; but must wait until the creature has actually risen before undertaking its destruction. Like the Djadadjii who face the Krvoijac (see listing) the Vampirdzhija will summon the spirit of the Obur and consign it to a bottle, which is then burned.

Ogoljen: A particularly bloodthirsty revenant from Bohemia, the Ogoljen is very savage and terribly strong. It can be stopped by fire or beheading, and once brought down has to be properly buried to keep it from rising again. Dirt from its burial site is both a charm against it and a potent inhibiting magic which, when placed in the navel of the resting Ogoljen, will prevent it from rising.

Ohyn: Fear of the unknown is common throughout the world, and is an obvious root cause of many monster beliefs. Sadly, this extends to rare genetic anomalies, which many cultures view as "alien." In Western Asia and most of Europe red hair[42] and left-handedness were rare enough to be viewed as unnatural; but world-wide birth defects of various kinds have been held as proof of the Devil's attempt to corrupt human flesh. In pre-twentieth-century Poland, a baby being born with teeth was seen as unnatural, and if the child also had a caul, then it was proof that the child was cursed and though it may live a normal (and even devout) life after natural death it was doomed to rise from the grave as an Ohyn, a blood-drinking revenant vampire. Some families, seeing these "defects" hurriedly removed the caul and pulled the infant's teeth before anyone else in the village could see them. The concept is incredibly horrible. Stillborn babies were also seen as evil—proof that the Devil has taken the child's soul before it could take its first breath. The villagers would go in fear that the infant's spirit would rise as an invisible version of the Ohyn—one that fed on breath rather than blood. If a stillborn child had milk teeth, the people believed that the revenant would use those tiny teeth to chew at its own flesh and bones until it is strong enough to rise from the grave. In some stories it rises as a floating child (though in art it's often anachronistically depicted as a toddler rather than a newborn); in other tales it rose in adult human form; and in others it was an invisible ghost. When in human form—small or large—it was a blood-drinker; otherwise it was an essential vampire and spreader of disease.

Otgiruru: The Herero people of Namibia are plagued by a species of vampire called an Otgiruru, which is the demonic reincarnation of a dead sorcerer. Unable, or perhaps, unwilling to depart into the afterlife, the ghost looks for some way to create a new body. Unlike revenant vampires, the Otgiruru uses its supernatural will to construct a new body composed of dirt and offal from the earth. The most common form is a hulking doglike creature, but the mind and will within is that of the cunning sorcerer. In its monster-dog form, the Otgiruru lures victims with its plaintive

42. In Christian folklore the prejudice against red hair is based on the belief that Judas Iscariot was redheaded and that anyone with red hair is descended from him. Another view was that red hair is the "Mark of Cain" spoken of in Genesis.

and compelling howl, then attacks the inquisitive tribesmen for their blood. It often pretends to be a family pet or familiar village dog that has been injured, playing off the sympathies of kind hearts who can't stand to see or hear an animal suffer. Though the Otgiruru is a vicious monster, it will only confront one person at a time and flees from groups of two or more. A spear can pierce it but will not kill the creature. Tribesmen use a spear to pin it to the ground so that it can be hacked to pieces and then burned.

Oupire: The Oupire of Moravia is a typical Slavonic revenant and plague-spreading nosferatu in that it is a human who returned from the dead to prey on its family and village by both bite and disease. Oupires attack livestock as well as humans, depending on their hunger.

Owenga: In the North African nation of Guinea the ghosts of dead sorcerers or people who lived evil and corrupt lives often return to earth in physical form as vampires called Owengas. These monsters prey upon the people from their own villages and cannot be killed by any means, but can be appeased by blood offerings. Animal blood is most often used, especially the blood of female animals that have never mated. The blood is usually placed in wooden bowls and left outside huts at night. Sometimes an Owenga will accept the blood offerings and leave the village in peace. But if it is angered by the quality or quantity of the offering, it will return and spread deadly disease throughout the village. If blood is spilled by accident and not cleaned up, the Owenga will return even stronger. This has instilled in the natives of Guinea a custom of immediately cleaning up all spilled blood and burning any object that is stained with blood. A village that adheres strictly to this will often be free from an Owenga for generations.

Pelesit and the **Polong:** Vampires take many forms around the world, and quite a few are found in Malaysia, from animal vampires to the troubled ghosts of children to one of the strangest of all: symbiotic vampires. The Pelesit and the Polong are two blood-drinkers that team up to overwhelm and destroy a victim from within. The Pelesit arrives first, usually in the form of a house cricket. It burrows into a victim's head and begins to feed on the blood of the host. At the same time, it causes erratic behavior and madness in the victim, causing the person to rant and rave (often for some inexplicable reason, about cats). Once thus entrenched, the Pelesit invites a second creature, a bottle-imp called a Polong. This second creature is even stranger, appearing as a one-inch-tall woman. These two creatures are fashioned by a witch when the witch murders a man and fills a bottle with his blood. The witch then casts various spells over the bottle, and when the enchantment is done the creatures are manifested in the physical world. Often these creatures are sent to a specific victim at the witch's direction. The terms of the witch's bargain are simple: the Polong, with the aid of the Pelesit, attacks the victim in exchange for being allowed to feed on the victim's living blood. When they are not feeding on an enemy, the imps must be fed by the witch with his or her own blood. If the Pelesit and Polong are not properly fed they will turn on their creator.

Penanggalan: This bizarre Malaysian creature is one of the most gruesome vampires in the world and is created when women are startled during deep prayer. The shock causes their heads to leap off their bodies, dragging along their entrails and a twisted spine. These women become vampires and remain in this disgusting form throughout their immortal lives. The Penanggalan generally dwell in trees and possess the ability to fly. The creature's flapping entrails drip a noxious fluid that spreads pestilence and disease. Should a Penanggalan linger too long in one place, the pooling fluids from its entrails will transform into a thorny, bioluminescent plant. The Penanggalan preys on the blood of newborn babies or pregnant women. Sometimes it will force a pregnant woman to give birth so it can devour the newborn child. Penanggalan are also thought to drain a mother's breasts of milk, or pollute the milk so that the nursing child will grow sick. To combat this, mothers should be given milk thistle. Milk thistle is a plant that has a variety of curative powers, including stimulating the production of breast milk. All pregnant women and young children are kept inside at night to keep them safe from a Penanggalan's attack. A hunting Penanggalan will flit from house to house, looking for children or pregnant women in homes that are not properly protected. Malaysian women who fear the coming of a Penanggalan will strew dried thistle along their windowsills. The vampire will not come near these sharp thorns, fearing to get them caught in her entrails. There are also rare cases where a witch will become a Penanggalan by choice. When a witch-Penanggalan returns to her secret lair she can immerse herself in a vat of vinegar and shrink her distorted self into a size that can be squeezed back into her body. Thereafter, during daylight hours, she will look and act normal; but come sunset the monster will emerge once more.

Pijavica (also **Pijauica**): This Slavonic blood-drinker rises from the graves of sinners who died unrepentant, who died during the commission of a sin, or who died after having been excommunicated from the church. A Pijavica can also be created from someone who had committed incest at any time during his life, an act viewed by Christians of that region as being a deliberate blasphemy against the relationship of Mary and Jesus. Often the Pijavica is resurrected by another evil person through a ceremony that involves animal sacrifices, a mixture of ashes from incense and candle wax, a child's urine, and the hairs of the deceased. This ceremony takes several hours and it can take several days before the flesh is reanimated and the creature rises. Once it has risen, the human who has invoked the creature must offer it a bowl of fresh blood (animal or human) within its first hour or the Pijavica will die again. After this point, no magic can restore it. In other tales of the Pijavica, it rises on its own sometime between the date of its death and the anniversary of its birthday. Once risen it is weak and must feed on animals for the first twelve nights until it gains enough strength to begin hunting humans. Like many vampires, the Pijavica's bite can spread disease, both to humans and livestock.

It's a glutton among vampires, consuming all of the blood of a grown human each night, and its sated face is so flushed with blood that it accounts for its name, which means "one who is red-faced with drink." In modern parlance the term is used as a harsh nickname for drunkards. The Pijavica often pretends to be a drunken person, singing loud songs or making jokes and beckoning others of the village to accompany it to the next tavern or inn. The Pijavica's favorite prey is the surviving members of its family. If it dies in a distant town, or if it does not have any living relatives, it will stake out any random family and begin killing their members one by one.

In direct confrontation, the Pijavica is nearly unbeatable. It is extremely powerful and fast and has an animal's quick, ruthless, and efficient fighting instincts. When it is awake and hunting, ordinary weapons are of little use, partly because its body is supernaturally resistant to harm and partly because it is so formidable a fighter that it can defeat even an experienced swordsman. However if luck is on the side of a skilled marksman, a bullet to the creature's brain will render it temporarily immobile. The safest means of stopping this creature is to wait until it is resting (in its grave if it is a revenant Pijavica, or in its hiding place if it is a living vampire) and then, using a sword or axe, cut its head off with a single stroke. The head should be placed between the Pijavica's legs and the body sewn into a shroud and buried deep. Or it can be burned and its ashes buried with a mixture of garlic and poppy flowers.

Pontianak (also **Kuntilanak**, **Matianak**, **Boentianak**, **Kunti**): There are several versions of this Malaysian monster but the two most common are the vampiric ghost of a woman who died during childbirth or the ghost of a stillborn child of a Langsuir (see listing). In both cases the vampire it becomes is insane, vicious, and bloodthirsty and will plague the village in which it once lived. The Pontianak is a favorite subject for filmmakers, and some of the better movies about the monster include the Malay films *Anak Pontianak* (1958), *Pontianak Kembali* (1963), *Pontianak Gua Musang* (1964); and the Indonesian flicks *Kuntilanak merah Terowongan Casablanca* and *Lawang Sewu :Dendam Kuntilanak* (both from 2007).

Pryccolitch: This fierce Romanian creature is another combination of vampire and werewolf, possessing the cunning of the former and the sheer destructive power of the latter. The Pryccolitch is a living vampire, and while alive it transforms into a werewolf and feeds on flesh, but once killed it rises from its grave as a blood-drinking revenant vampire. A curse laid on someone's head, heart, or soul—by a witch or a scorned and spiteful person—can transform a normal human into a Pryccolitch. Cursing someone, even in jest, can have dire consequences, because there are folktales that tell of idle curses resulting in someone being transformed into this bloodthirsty killer. The transformation into a Pryccolitch begins by the person's soul either going cold or leaving the body entirely. This absence allows evil spirits to enter. These spirits teach the newly transformed monster about its nature and guide it in its campaign of terror and murder, helping it to choose the right victims and always reminding it to be cautious and sly. The Pryccolitch can only transform into its monstrous shape while hidden from human eyes. The metamorphosis is very quick but painful, similar to the agonizing transformation shown in the movie *An American Werewolf in London*. Once transformed into wolf shape, the Pryccolitch hunts freely and kills openly. Pryccolitch accounts from the eighteenth and nineteenth centuries described it as mostly preying on livestock, but earlier accounts were frightening tales of the creature attacking families and wiping out entire villages.

Psychic Vampires: There are two forms of psychic vampires. One is human and the other is decidedly not. Human psychic vampires are people who either deliberately or, more often, subconsciously use passive-aggressive or codependent behavior to drain others of emotional, mental, and psychological energy. You've met them in the office, or in the PTA, or maybe one of them is your mother-in-law. Supernatural psychic vampires are creatures whose physical bodies have been destroyed or have completely putrefied or turned to dust. What is left is a kind of ghost whose presence pollutes an entire region. Psychic vampires often manifest as nosferatu and spread disease and pestilence. Psychic vampires can create other vampires at will by causing the bodies of any sinful person to rise from the dead, and these newly created vampires are generally your typical blood-drinking revenant.

Ramanga: One of the strangest vampires in the world is the Ramanga of Madagascar. Ramangas (which means "blue blood") are living men who are employed by village elders and nobles to eat discarded nail parings or spilled blood. It is the pervading belief in Macedonia that items like nail clippings and blood possess vast magical powers and, should they fall into the wrong hands, can be used to work evil magic against the person from whom they came. Since some people believe that a person's soul resides in their blood, this extreme custom can somewhat be understood. Nobles maintain one or more Ramangas to collect and ingest these items

Why We Love Monsters

Herschell Gordon Lewis

"Monsters bridge a gap between blind religion and assumed fact. Throughout history, continuing through the Middle Ages and, to some believers, even today, existence of monsters explains some otherwise inexplicable feats of strength and cruelty. Filmmakers have the technical capability of instilling reality into the folklore. Beginning with the original *King Kong* and continuing through the realistic computer-generated imagery available today, a film brings a monster or a science-fiction creature to life. These films live in history but no longer have any dramatic impact. The industry, and public sophistication, have relegated them to curiosities. Certainly they were responsible for the origination of the true horror movie, as well as the subsequent splatter film."
—Herschell Gordon Lewis is called "The Godfather of Gore" because he directed the first splatter film—*Blood Feast*—and a number of others in that genre.

so that no one else can gain access to them. Nobles who can afford it utilize a traveling Ramanga to accompany them on every journey so this grisly task will always be handled quickly and efficiently, keeping them safe from sorcery.

Revenant: A true "living dead" being that has risen from the grave as a vampire, ghost, zombie, or angel. In this book the term "revenant" is used to classify those vampires that are human corpses that have returned from the dead.

Role Player Vampires: People involved in online vampire role-playing games such as *Vampire: The Masquerade, Vampire: The Eternal Struggle, BloodLust*, and others.

Sampiro: Legend has it that any Albanian who is of Turkish ancestry will, upon his death, rise again as a vampire called a Sampiro. At this point, the creature will construct steel shoes and, still wrapped in its burial shroud, haunt the countryside, spreading death and disease. Vampire hunters look for a will-o-the-wisp and follow it back to the Sampiro's grave; and if the disinterred corpse looks like someone who has just died—or worse, like someone who is still alive—then it is proof that they have found the resting place of the evil Sampiro. The standard ritual of exorcism is then performed to destroy the monster.

Sanguinarians: Also known as "real vampires," this group takes its name from the Latin word sanguineus ("bloodthirsty", or "blood-red in color") and is distinct from other human vampires in that they actually crave human blood, and often believe that blood is necessary for their survival. Sanguinarians are not predators and only accept blood according to very specific rules involving non-vampire "Donors." There are three types of "colors" of Donor:

- Crimson, who donate their own blood.
- Crystal, who give up psychic energy.
- Amber, who give anything that is asked of them.

The abiding belief among Sanguinarians is that their blood hunger is a naturally occurring (though poorly reported and documented) medical condition. The pattern for its emergence is unknown and is generally not believed to be hereditary. To Sanguinarians,[43] vampirism is not a game but an actual way of life bordering on, and perhaps actually becoming, a religion. They even have a strict code of lifestyle rules called the Black Veil which spells out what can and cannot be done in terms of safety, control, and other elements.

Sanguinarian by Vinessa J. Olp

Sexual Vampire: Also called Seductress or Seducer Vampire, these predators use sexuality to deceive their victims and set them up for an attack. Many Sexual Vampires are also essential vampires, but often there are other distinct qualities that set them apart. Within this group there are two primary subgroups. Most vampires in this category are female, though there are certainly examples of male vampires using the tactic of seduction.

Shtriga: A vicious female witch-vampire who preys on infants. Many legends suggest that the Shtriga is a woman who was barren

43. Often called "True" Vampires.

or whose child died young and who now seeks revenge on the world for the injustices of Fate. Other tales cast her as a spinster who has never known love and has therefore grown bitter and old. She has turned to black magic to strike back at the people who shunned her and—by her perceptions—denied her the grace of love and family. The Shtriga is a theriomorph that transforms into a moth, bee, or other flying insect. It will steal in through an open window, settle on a sleeping child, and drain away its life essence. The Shtriga has been the hated villain in the bad dreams of many a parent, and has been blamed for many Sudden Infant Death Syndrome (SIDS) losses as late as the twentieth century. These crib

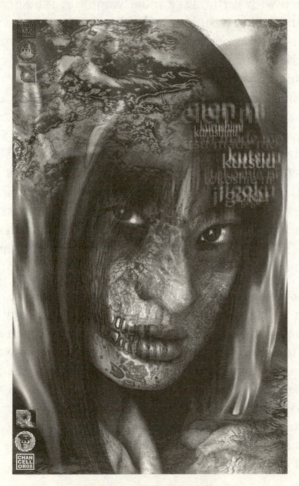

Shtriga by Bill Chancellor

deaths, though less inexplicable now, could have no other explanation to simple villagers, who felt there had to be some dark supernatural agent at work.

Children are not the Shtriga's only victims. These evil creatures also prey on adults by spreading diseases and bringing discord to the community. By day the Shtriga is able to live undiscovered among ordinary people, passing herself off as a member of the community and even attending church. But once a person is suspected of being a Shtriga there are two potential methods of detection. During a church service the suspect would be handed a piece of the Host (in this case it would be a piece of bread rather than a wafer) spiced with garlic. Like most vampires, the Shtriga cannot eat garlic and will be visibly repelled by it—alerting the rest of the parishioners to the demon in their midst. The second way of detecting the presence of a Shtriga is to place a small cross made from the bones of a pig on the doors of the church after the service has begun and everyone is inside. When the service is concluded, the Shtriga will not be able to cross the threshold to exit the church. Another charm works quite well against the Shtriga but is very dangerous to obtain. A person has to follow a Shtriga that has assumed mortal form back to its home. Legend has it that the Shtriga will vomit up some of the blood she's consumed. Once she leaves or goes to sleep, the intrepid vampire slayer has to scrape some of the blood onto a silver coin, wrap the coin in cloth, and wear it constantly. The Shtriga is unable to inflict harm on the wearer of a charm such as this.

Sluagh (also **Sluagh Sídhe**): These restless spirits of the dead appear throughout Irish and Scottish folktales and songs. They are essential vampires who feed on pain, misery, and the human soul itself. The belief is that they were once human sinners who were unwelcome either in heaven or hell and returned to Earth as pernicious ghosts They almost always come from the west, so it became common to keep west-facing windows shut. Some Sluagh hunt in packs and invade whole villages. The Sluagh can be detected most easily by their strong smell, a reek like that of decaying flesh. The odor grows more pungent with age.

On Irish Heritage

"The Irish, it is said, are a nation of storytellers, though I think that term can be applied to any country or region in which hard times force the people to look within rather than without for the genesis of their fear. I grew up around old men in smoky taverns telling tall tales that thrilled me and left a lasting impression, so as such I think all of my work is, in one way or another, inspired by folklore. Stories get passed on, and just as those stories change, so too do they change those who tell them. Without this background, I very much doubt I'd be doing what I do today.

"I have also revisited my homeland in a tale or two, most notably with *The Hides*, more recently with a short story entitled 'Tonight the Moon is Ours' which involved, among other things, impressionable youths, unrequited love, and fairy stones—those towering slabs that stand in the middle of Irish fields and are believed to be the portals to the Kingdom of the Faeries. Sure, it sounds ridiculous, but try asking a local farmer to move one and see how he responds."

—Kealan Patrick Burke is the Bram Stoker Award–winning author of *Kin*, *Currency of Souls*, and *The Turtle Boy*.

Soucouyan: The tiny island nation of Dominica[44] in the Lesser Antilles (between Martinique and Guadalupe), is the home of the Soucouyan, a skin-shedding vampire. As the sun goes down the Soucouyan shucks her disguise—that of a helpless old woman—and rises into the air as a ball of fire that swoops down on the unsuspecting, knocking them to the ground and feeding on their blood. The Soucouyan does not always kill, but when it does the drained corpse will as often as not become a vampire as well. The Soucouyan must reclaim her skin by first light of morning. Discarded skins are often collected and used as powerful ingredients in some of the charms and potions of Obeah magic. Possession of a discarded Soucouyan skin also gives a magician great power over the vampire.

44. Not to be confused with the Dominican Republic.

Sriz: Opinions differ as to whether the Sriz is a vampire, ghost, demon, or some other unidentified species of supernatural creature. The Sriz is a ritualistic killer who climbs to the top of a church steeple and calls out the names of his victims. The victims invariably die, some from heart failure, others in violent accidents, still others or various wasting diseases. The creature does not feed on flesh or blood, but is a kind of emotional vampire, gaining sustenance from the discharge of pure terror released by those who succumb to its call. The surest way to defend against the creature is to ring church bells, especially during times of prayer. The Sriz cannot abide "holy music" of any kind and will be driven off.[45] If a church has been desanctified, it is important for the villagers to cover the rooftop with bits of jagged metal or broken glass so the Sriz cannot perch atop it. In some mid-eighteenth-century folktales, the Sriz was attracted to the sound of bells rung in a desanctified church, so removal of the bells became an important part of officially abandoning a church.

Strigoi: The name Strigoi is based on a much older Roman term, strix, meaning "screech owl," which has also come to be identified with vampires and witches. The witches of Romania are known for a variety of black magic, but they also possess a vampiric quality, both alive and after death. The living Strigoi draws life essence from her victims while the dead Strigoi rises as a physical revenant to consume the blood of livestock and humans. If a person is a Strigoi while alive they will certainly rise from the grave and continue harassing the living. Strigoi can be identified at birth by the presence of a caul, a third nipple, or a tail. Being the seventh child in a family (which is lucky in other cultures) is a sure sign of evil in Romania, especially if all of her previous siblings were of the same sex.

The Strigoi are extremely popular in fiction, appearing in video games: *Warhammer, Ben Jordan: Case 3, The Witcher, Ace Combat 6*, etcetera; music "Ravenna Strigoi Mortii" by black metal

---

45. Whether intentional or not, the use of church bells to drive away an evil presence was a set-piece in *Spider-Man 3*. Granted it was established that the alien symbiot "black costume" could not abide loud noise, the scene played out like one of the Sriz folktales.

Strigoi by Bill Chancellor

band Dark Funeral; fiction: *The Hunt* (Ace, 1999) by Susan Size-more, *Children of the Night* (Grand Central, 1992) by Dan Sim-mons, *Descendant* (Severn House, 2006) by Graham Masterton; on TV in the "Darkness Visible" episode of *Hercules: The Legendary Journeys* and the "Something Wicked" episode of *Supernatural*;[46] and in the movies *Dracula* (2000) and *30 Days of Night* (2007).

Strix (also known as **Stryx**; plural **Striges**): In ancient Rome, the deadly Strix was a common danger for villagers and city dwellers

46. Called "shtriga" in the show.

alike. These were female living vampires, able to live normally among humans during the day and go undetected. At night the Strix would transform herself into a crow or owl and fly off looking for prey, invisible against the night sky. When she found a lonely traveler, saw a shepherd watching his flock by moonlight, or spied a sleeping person through an open window, the Strix would attack swiftly and glut herself on blood. Though she would attack anyone, she preferred the innocent blood of young children. The classical writer Ovid wrote in his book *Fasti* that Striges attacked children at night in a form of a screech owl. He wrote that they used their beaks and talons to wound an infant's chest, and then drank the blood from these lacerations. Thereafter the Striges would return night after night to trouble their prey until the child wasted away and died. If the parents discovered (or suspected) that a Strix was preying on their child, their only recourse was to appeal to a demigoddess named Carna. This powerful spirit then appeared and went through the home performing sacred rituals that would ban the Strix from returning. Her final act would be to place a branch of whitethorn[47] in the window of the infant's room.

Sukuyan: Like the Asema, the Sukuyan shed their skin at nightfall and fly off into the darkness as a ball of blue light. However, they are much faster and can actually travel at speeds approaching the speed of light itself, suggesting that they achieve a kind of energy state of being. Also like the Asema, the Sukuyan seek out humans, preferably asleep and unaware, and alight on them to drink their blood. The Sukuyan has far more power than the Asema and is a more dangerous and cunning predator. If cornered or trapped, the Sukuyan will shape-shift into an animal form and try to slip away or adopt the form of a predator such as a jungle cat, ape, hunting bird, large dog, or other creature and fight back using a fearsome armament of claws, talons, beaks, or fangs. In direct combat the Sukuyan can be driven off by steel or flame, but it cannot be killed while it is hunting. Special charms filled with garlic or pollen help keep the monster at bay. The key to destroying the Sukuyan is to find where it hides its skin and steal it. Denied the chance to

47. Whitethorn is a species of hawthorn, which is a common proof against vampires throughout Europe, even today.

return to its skin after feeding, the Sukuyan will eventually fade away and die.

Sundal Bolong: The Javanese Sundal Bolong is a seductress vampire that attacks only the bravest and most handsome men of a village. The Sundal Bolong assumes human form and dresses all in white (very much like the French White Ladies of Fau), luring men to secret places such as a hut in the woods, a cleared space in the forest, a grotto, or some other remote and secluded spot. After using them sexually (presumably to feed off their potent sexual energy), it transforms back into its hideous natural shape and attacks the depleted victims, tearing them apart and feasting on flesh and blood.

But the Sundal Bolong does not always kill quickly. It is one of the cruelest of the vampire species and enjoys the torment and suffering of its victims. It may curse a victim with a painful and wasting disease—something particularly dreaded by strong warriors—or inflict injuries while stranding the victim deep in the forest, harassing him as he struggles to make it back to his village. Should the victim actually make it all the way back to his village despite the injuries and indignities he has suffered, the Sundal Bolong will wait until help is actually moments away and then kill him with a flick of her claws across his throat. In some versions of the Sundal Bolong legend, it possesses similar qualities to the Polong of Malaysia in that it is a diminutive creature that sneaks into bedrooms at night and drinks blood from the thumbs of the sleepers. In this variation of the Sundal Bolong tale, the vampires can be captured and placed in bottles specially prepared by priests.

Talamaur: The Talamaur, from the Bank Islands off the coast of Australia, are not traditional vampires inasmuch as they do not drink blood, but they are equally evil creatures who feed on the pain and despair of the people of their own village. They are Living Vampires who possess the ability to speak with the dead. Some natives go in fear of these dead spirits and wisely want no contact; others crave to speak with departed loved ones and would risk the dangers of the Talamaur to make that connection. The Talamaur deceive these trusting folks by claiming to act simply as mediums, but the Talamaur have a darker purpose. They do far more than contact the dead—they can control them, enslave them, make them into familiars. Then they use these servant ghosts to do all manner of evil in their communities, even sending them as agents of destruction against their own families. Being a Talamaur is not a crime. It is even a profession that some advertise in order to make a living, and some Talamaurs may have good intentions (or hide their crimes behind occasional good deeds). But when a village begins to feel the presence of evil and see the evidence at hand, the villagers will launch an investigation. Those within the community who understand the nature of such magic devise a method of reversing the evil of the Talamaur and its familiar. The evil Talamaur is taken by force to a sacred space and forced to smell the smoke of burning leaves until it confesses its evil nature and reveals the names of the creatures under its control. It also has to list all of its crimes and name all of its victims past, present, and future. Once the crimes are confessed openly the spell is broken, the familiar is released back to the spirit world, and the reign of evil is ended. The Talamaur's life is often ended as well.

Tarunga: Some Talamaurs from the Bank Islands are very powerful sorcerer-vampires who can go into a trance and separate their spirits from their bodies. The spirit—known as a Tarunga—consumes the lingering life essence of a person who has recently died. Once this evil has begun to affect a village, the people begin looking for signs that a Tarunga is in their community. Some people begin having visions or vivid dreams which tell of the Tarunga. Watchers will be posted by newly dug graves listening for the telltale sounds of a Tarunga's approach: a whisper-soft scratching sound, like cat claws on a door.

Tase: In Burma the distinction between vampire and ghost is indistinct. In fact the vampire the Burmese fear most is, technically, a bloodsucking ghost. Unlike revenants (reanimated corpses), the Tase is the disembodied spirit that lingers on earth to prey on the living for their blood and also to spread plague and other diseases. There are three subspecies of Tase: Hminza Tase, Thabet Tase, and Thaye Tase, each one possessing their own evil and pernicious qualities:

1. Hminza Tase are the most rare of the three subspecies. They are evil demons who enter and possess the bodies of animals such as crocodiles, dogs, hunting birds, owls, and tigers. Once they have inhabited the animals they slaughter all others of the animals' species in a given area, staking out a hunting ground. Once it has been cleared of competitors, the Hminza Tase begin using a combination of animal cunning and demonic intelligence to lure humans into remote spots in order to attack them. The attack of a Hminza Tase is savage

Thabet Tase by Bill Chancellor

and leaves the victims torn to pieces, a state that disguises the nearly total loss of blood.

2. **Thabet Tase**, are the vengeful spirits of women who have died during childbirth and who return to the world of the living as essential vampires that feed on the sexual essence of men. They are skilled seducers and it is said that no man can resist their charms, especially while asleep and dreaming. It is the special delight of the Thabet Tase to disrupt a new marriage so severely that no child will be conceived between the newlyweds.

3. **Thaye Tase** are hideous giants that appear near twilight to spread diseases such as cholera, typhus, and smallpox. The Thaye Tase are the angry and confused spirits of people who died violently and are somehow caught between this world and the next. This feeling of being trapped apparently either drives them mad or brings out the worst qualities in them, because for amusement the Thaye Tase appear beside the beds of the dying and taunt the sufferers by mocking them for their helplessness and pain.

Proper burial rites help keep the Tase in their graves, but some folktales suggest that one of the older customs was to forgo the custom of using gravestones so that the risen spirit will not know who he is (or was) and will therefore be unable to locate his own village, family, and friends. Though not a prevention per se, this did keep familiar Tase ghosts from visiting. When a Tase is suspected, the only method of combating it is to drive it off by loud noises such as the beating of drums, clanging of pots, and firecrackers. The Tase, for all their other powers, cannot abide loud noise.

Tenatz: The legend of this monster might explain how some vampires are able to rise from and return to their graves without churning the soil: the Tenatz shape-shift into mice and then burrow down through the earth. The Tenatz are revenants, reanimated through postmortem demonic possession. Once freed of their graves, they transform back into their true corpselike forms and roam the countryside looking for victims. The Tenatz are thirsty blood-drinkers but not overly brave, preferring to attack sleeping victims rather than those who are wide awake and potentially difficult prey. A Tenatz can be destroyed by fire and decapitation, and staking it will render it helpless and unable to rise from its coffin. Severing the creature's hamstring is also a common custom for limiting its activities.

Tlacique: A race of vampire-witches among Mexico's Nahautl Indians. They possess a variety of supernatural powers that help them attack their prey and elude capture, including the ability to transform into blazing balls of flame. They can fly like fireballs across the sky, or dance through the woods like a Will-o'-the-Wisp, and often attack their prey in these fiery shapes. For some unknown reason their touch does not burn their victims, but mesmerizes them. The victims then slip into a stupor while the Tlacique drinks their blood. If pursued, Tlaciques sometimes turn into ordinary animals, most usually fowl like turkeys. In this innocuous form they can blend in with farm animals, going unnoticed while feeding a bit here and there from animals as well as farmers.

Tlahuelpuchi: An Aztec vampire that attacks infants and young children for their blood, this creature is a shape-shifter that can adopt any form: cat, dog, bird. Their preferred shape, however, is a turkey. While in animal guise, the Tlahuelpuchi glow with an unholy light. This allows the creature to easily be spotted and pursued (although pursuit should only be done in armed groups, never by a single person). To avoid pursuit, the Tlahuelpuchi will shape-shift into very fast animals such as cats, elusive animals such as birds, or, more often, nearly invisible creatures such as ticks or fleas. The Tlahuelpuchi is not a revenant but a person born under a curse, doomed to be a living vampire. Though the Tlahuelpuchi can be male or female, the females are far more common and much more powerful. The Tlahuelpuchi do not reside in trees or graves, but pass as ordinary humans during the daytime. These creatures cannot escape their doom, though some are unaware of it and live contented lives during the day, not knowing that they transform into monsters at night. Other Tlahuelpuchi know what they are, and dwell with their human families, hiding their true evil natures. A Tlahuelpuchi residing with its family will seldom be turned in for its crimes, no matter how extreme or heinous. This is not due to familial love, but because if a Tlahuelpuchi is caught and killed, its curse will instantly pass to the betrayer. It is also possible for the victim of a Tlahuelpuchi to rise from the grave as one of these foul creatures. To prevent victims from becoming Tlahuelpuchi, a village shaman must use precise burial rites to establish an air of sanctity around both the corpse and the grave.

Unlike most vampires, the Tlahuelpuchi only needs to feed once a month. It may feed more often if possible, but should it miss its monthly feeding it will die. At night, when everyone is asleep, a Tlahuelpuchi will shape-shift into one of its chosen forms and go hunting for innocent blood. Like other predators, the Tlahuelpuchi are fiercely territorial and will violently defend their hunting grounds. Though the Tlahuelpuchi may enter any house without invitation they are bound by strange rituals. Before entering they must assume bird shape and fly over the house from north to south then east to west, forming a cross pattern. This casts an enchantment that allow them entry. To save the victim's soul, a local shaman must disenchant the victim by "uncrossing" them.

Proper precautions include placing garlic and onions around doors, windows, and an infant's bed. The Tlahuelpuchi fears sharp metal, so an open pair of scissors left on a nightstand near a crib is often enough of a deterrent to keep the child safe. Protective spells and charms can deny the creature its food and starve it to death. Some villagers pin small religious medallions and icons to their children's clothing as further protection, and it is believed that mirrors can sometimes scare this monster off.

Uber: Actually the Turkish word for "witch," Uber is considered by many scholars to be one of the source words for "vampire." The domestic Turkish vampire is very similar to revenant vampires all through that region of the world. It is a corpse that has risen, usually that of someone who has died during an act of violence, or the corpse of a foreigner who was not a Muslim and died on Turkish soil.

Upier (also **Wampir**, **Viesczy**): This is a generic Eastern European vampire—very common in Poland and Russia, that has serpentine qualities, particularly in the fact that it has a vicious barbed stinger under its tongue that it uses instead of fangs. The Upierczi are not born as monsters but are revenants that rise from the graves of certain kinds of recently dead humans, typically those born with teeth or with a caul, much like the Ohyn. During its human life the Upier is often hyperactive and agitated[48] and shows a constantly flushed and intense face; after its death (by whatever natural means), the revenant rises to become one of the Upierczi. Like an animal, the Upier makes a nest for itself, usually in a stone crypt or some other enduring and moderately watertight vessel. Either it picks a suitable place and then constructs (or carries in) a nesting basin, or it finds a very remote spot where such an item already exists and then stakes out that spot as its own. Any creatures venturing into the area are doomed to a quick but painful death. The Upier is primarily a daylight vampire, actively hunting during the hours of noon to midnight When it finally returns to its resting place it fills its nesting basin with blood and sleeps immersed in the liquid.

The Upier will sometimes ring a church bell, and anyone who hears it—or heeds it—is doomed to die by its fell hand. The single best way to prevent a corpse from rising as one of the Upierczi is to bury it facedown. It will become confused and will consume its own flesh until it is too wasted to move. Another protection against the Upier is called "Blood Bread." This unsavory but potent item is made by locating the coffin of a vampire that has already been destroyed and gathering up some of its blood. This blood is mixed with water and flour and baked into a loaf, which is then shared among a family. Anyone eating the blood bread will be safe from the Upier's bite These precautions are adhered to with great care because tales of revenge by an Upier would freeze the blood of even the most stalwart slayer.

There is only one way to destroy an Upier: fire. The creature must be thoroughly incinerated. Even in the midst of its fiery death, however, the Upier has one last power: as it burns, its body

---

48. This sounds suspiciously like ADD or ADHD, and since so many monster legends are based on unnatural behavior (or physical deformities), it's likely that hyperactive kids in the centuries before videogames and iPods were getting a bad rap.

will burst open and out will pour thousands of vermin—rats, maggots, roaches, centipedes, and other equally base creatures. If any of these escape, then the spirit of the Upier will likewise escape to seek revenge. So the vampire slayers must build a huge bonfire, make sure that the Upier is in the center, and that all of the fuel is thoroughly doused with oil before torches are put to the wood.

Upyr: Yet another variation of the Eastern European vampire, the Upyr[49] sleeps by day in its grave or in a secluded hiding place, then rises at sunset to hunt for blood, often taking the form of a great hunting dog. The Upyr is a brutal killer that attacks children from one family and then turns its bloodlust onto the surviving adults. Because it a vicious family destroyer, the Upyr has earned a reputation as one of the most feared and loathed of the Slavic blood-drinkers. It can be immobilized by a long stake through the heart but only destroyed by the formal ritual of exorcism.

Ustrel: In Bulgaria, a child born on a Saturday but who died before he could be baptized the following Sunday was doomed to become a type of vampire called an Ustrel. This is a strange kind of vampire, even for the Balkans. It dies as an infant, and upon rising it is usually the size of a small child. But it can continue to grow in size and strength, and it possesses intelligence and cunning on a par with adult predatory animals like foxes or wolves. The Ustrel will return to its grave after a night of feasting (on animals like cows or sheep), but unlike many similar kinds of revenants it can eventually outgrow the need to rest in the earth. If an Ustrel is able to glut itself for ten successive nights it becomes so powerful that it no longer needs to rest in its grave. From then on it lives secretly among the herd, sleeping after feasting all night and returning to its grave before dawn. Sometimes it would sleep through the daylight hours between the horns of a ram or a young bull, or hidden between the hind legs of a cow.

The Ustrel stakes out a specific herd and works its way through the animals. Sometimes the Ustrel's appetites are not too ravenous

49. Upyr is sometimes used as a general term for all kinds of Russian vampires, including the Erestun and Eretiku. The name is also a variation of Upier, though many of the legends are significantly different.

and it goes undetected, the attacks on the animals being ascribed to wolves and other predators. But if the vampire becomes too greedy and attacks half a dozen sheep or cows in a single night, then the villagers know that an Ustrel is in their community. Immediately they call in a Vampirdzhija[50] to set about tracking down the blood-drinker because only a true Vampirdzhija can actually see an Ustrel and track it to its resting place.

The Vampirdzhija initiates a ritual called the "lighting of the need-fire" which begins the complicated procedure of defeating the Ustrel. On the first day (generally a Saturday, just after dawn), all of the livestock in town are gathered together into a central place and the villagers extinguish all fires in town. Then the villagers gather together and drive their herds toward the closest crossroads, where a pair of bonfires have been prepared. Once the herds approach, the bonfires are ignited by the old method of rubbing two sticks together. The shepherds, under the direction of the Vampirdzhija, drive the herds between the newly blazing bonfires. The passage between the flames makes the unseen Ustrel lose its grip on whatever animal it is resting upon, and the creature drops helpless to the road.

Though invisible, the Ustrel is still mortal in some ways, and its body can be felt and even touched. It can certainly be smelled, because the bonfires and the presence of the Ustrel attract the hungry forest wolves that come in once the herds and the villagers leave. They devour the Ustrel completely. As they leave the crossroads, some of the villagers take brands lit in the fires and carry them back to the village to relight all of the home-and cookfires. The bonfires are allowed to burn themselves out, and for several days afterward no one dares to approach the crossroads for fear that the Ustrel is still lingering and not yet devoured. If the Ustrel survives for a day or so before the wolves come, it may follow any person home and begin again its reign of terror.

U'tlûñ'tä (also known as **Nûñ'yunu'ï**): A Cherokee legend tells of a terrible bloodthirsty ogress who slaughters people and eats their livers. Known as the U'tlûñ'tä ("spear finger"), this she-creature

---

50. See listing for Ubor.

can adopt any shape or appearance to suit her purpose. In her normal form she looks very much like an old woman, except that her whole body is covered with skin as hard as rock that no weapon can penetrate.[51] On her right hand she has a long, stony forefinger made from hard bone, shaped like an awl or the head of a spear (hence the name). She uses this ghastly weapon to stab whomever she encounters.

U'tlûñ'tä by Bill Chancellor

51. Her other name, Nûñ'yunu'ï, means "stone-dress" because of her rock-hard skin.

Vampir (also **Viper**, **Vepir**, **Vapir**): This is a general term used to describe any of the various vampires of Bulgaria. Another common variation, Vampyr, is the Magyar spelling for vampire.

Vampire: The general name given by the English-speaking world to supernatural predatory monsters who feed on the blood, psychic energy, emotion, or life essence of others.

Vjestitiza: In Montenegro and nearby Serbia, there is a female witch-vampire who (along with so many of her kind) preys mainly on children. This beast, the Vjestitiza, is generally described as an old crone who undergoes a transformation when she settles down to sleep each night. Her vampiric soul, in the form of a glowing ball of light, leaves her physical body and hunts for young blood. The Vjestitiza can also transform into animals, such as a hen, a black moth, or a fly. The Vjestitiza's fireball state may merely be a transitional stage between woman and animal The transformed Vjestitiza enters the house of her prey and feeds on her victim's blood. Sometimes she will even cut out the heart and take it with her. On some nights, several Vjestitiza will hold coven meetings in beast shape. They discuss evil spells and ancient lore and occasionally share hearts they have stolen from sleeping children. An old woman wishing to join the coven and gain supernatural powers must first swear a blood oath to uphold the rule and defend the coven's secrecy. Breaking faith with her dark sisters will result in a horrible death.

A Vjestitiza is at the very peak of her powers during the first cold week of March. Knowing this, the wise folk of the village perform rituals of protection to deny a Vjestitiza access to their houses. The prescribed method is to stir the ashes in a home's hearth with two horns, then stick the horns into the pile of ashes. If a woman is suspected of being a Vjestitiza, she will be arrested by the villagers and put on trial. However, the "trial" is very much like those held in Eastern and Western Europe. It is popularly believed that no witch can drown, so they tie the suspect up and throw her into the river. If she floats, then she is clearly guilty. If she drowns, she is innocent. Such rough justice makes it dicey to be a suspected Vjestitiza, inasmuch as the result is the same for the innocent and the guilty.

Vlkodlak (also **Lampire**): The Serbian Vlkodlak is one of those rare creatures that begins its reign of terror as a werewolf but, once killed, returns to life as a vampire,[52] but then goes a step further and becomes human again! As a werewolf it is simply a living human who transforms into a wolf, and though this transformation is unnatural, neither the human nor the wolf possesses any additional supernatural abilities. Once it rises from the dead as a Vlkodlak, the creature becomes more complex and far more dangerous. Its vampiric appearance is that of a wretched and corrupt drunkard with florid skin the color of blood, and for seven years it exists as a blood-drinking revenant. However, if it makes it through those years, feeding continually, the Vlkodlak will undergo a second transformation and will become an ordinary human being once more. Of course, when this new human grows old and dies . . . it will rise again from the grave as a new Vlkodlak and the bloody cycle starts over again.

The Vlkodlak can also be created when someone has fallen under what is known as the Serbian Curse, which says that if a person sees a werewolf and escapes, then that person is doomed to become a vampire after death, no matter how that death occurs. Eating mutton from a sheep slaughtered by a werewolf will create the same cursed state. A person conceived through incest, who had committed incest with his own mother, or who died a violent death will also become a Vikodlak. To prevent a suspected corpse from rising as a Vlkodlak, the toes and thumbs of the body should be cut off and a nail driven into its neck to cripple the body. Garlic can also be thrown into the coffin to keep evil spirits from entering the corpse. These are only containment methods: to actually kill the Vlkodlak a hawthorn branch needs to be thrust through its navel and ignited by candles obtained from a deathbed vigil.

Vourdalak (also **Wurdalak**): The legend of the Vourdalak is an old one, told in various songs and stories through Russia, most notably in Leo Tolstoy's 1893 short story, "The Family of the Vourdalak," which was adapted for the screen as "The Wurdalack," a truly

---

52. The Mjertovjec of Belarus is another of these strange creatures.

unnerving segment in Mario Bava's 1963 movie *Black Sabbath*, featuring Boris Karloff. In most tales, the Vourdalak is depicted as a hauntingly beautiful woman who lures travelers to their deaths in secluded spots, though in other tales it could be a man or a child of either sex. Many legends of the Vourdalak seem to blend with that of the Eretiku by suggesting that the creature is a blasphemer who has made a deal with the dark forces in return for dreadful supernatural powers. As a rule the Vourdalak feeds on children, though some stories tell of it slaughtering whole families, and generally these victims are the monster's own family

Vrykolaka: Legends of the fierce Vrykolaka are well documented in the folklore of both Greece and Macedonia, with echoes of these superstitions lingering well into the late nineteenth century. The Vrykolaka is a vampire created when a person has either committed suicide (a mortal sin resulting in damnation), or dies a violent death (resulting in an unquiet spirit filled with rage and confusion). A grossly immoral—or amoral—person was also a likely candidate for becoming this species of vampire. Once such a person dies, his or her body becomes the host of a bloodthirsty vampiric demon.

The name Vrykolaka can be variously translated as "wolf-pelt" or "werewolf," which is odd since this species of vampire does not share any qualities with werewolves. The Vrykolaka gains vast powers as it grows older. It is very hard to identify, and few methods of destroying it are known. The idea that a vampire cannot enter a house unless invited is largely the result of authors such as Bram Stoker. However, that bit of fiction may actually have its roots in the legend of this Greek monster, because the Vrykolaka does indeed require an invite. The creature will stand outside and call the name of its desired victim, hoping either to be invited inside or for the person to come out. Mind you, the call of this monster is seductive and probably works on some psychic level that affects the subconscious will; it's not like the vampire stands outside and yells, "Yo! C'mon out and let me chomp on you."

Once it's within striking distance of its prey, the Vrykolaka will leap onto the victim, bear him to the ground, and smother him with its body. In some accounts the Vrykolaka is invisible and the

victim merely feels a crushing weight on his chest. People who
have escaped the vampire's attack describe symptoms very much
like those of a heart attack: a great weight on the chest, shortness
of breath, and pain. This appears to tie in to the legends of the Old
Hag and the medical phenomenon called sleep paralysis; however
the Vrykolaka attacks while the victim is awake and ambulatory.

The people of the island of Chios in the Aegean Sea (reported to
be the birthplace of the poet Homer) believe that placing a cross
made from wax or cotton (or both) on the lips of a corpse can help
prevent the corpse from becoming a Vrykolaka. Another preventative tactic involves a priest inscribing "Jesus Christ Conquers" on
a shard of pottery belonging either to the family of the deceased or
to the local church, and burying it with the corpse. Greek scholar
and theologian Leone Allacci,[53] wrote extensively about the Vryko-
lakas in his treatise, *De Graecorum Hodie Quorundam Opina-
tionibus*,[54] Cologne 1645:

> The Vrykolaka is the body of a man of wicked and debauched life,
> very often one who has been excommunicated by his bishop. Such
> bodies do not, like other corpses, suffer decomposition after bur-
> ial nor fall to dust, but having, so it seems, a skin of extreme tough-
> ness becomes swollen and distended all over, so that the joints can
> scarcely be bent; the skin becomes stretched like the parchment
> of a drum, and when struck gives out the same sound. This mon-
> ster is said to be so fearfully destructive to men that it actually
> makes its appearance in the daytime, even at high noon, nor does
> it then confine its visits to houses, but even in the fields and in
> hedged vineyards and upon the open highway it will suddenly ad-
> vance upon persons who are laboring, or travelers as they walk
> along, and by the horror of its hideous aspect it will slay them
> without laying hold on them or even speaking a word.

Waster: This is another name for essential vampires. As most of
the Wasters appear at night, they are frequently referred to, in folklore, as Night Wasters or Night Comers.

53. Also known as Leo Allatius (1586–1669).
54. The translation of this quote is from *The Vampire: His Kith and Kin* by
Montague Summers, published by Routledge, Kegan Paul, Trench, Trubner &
Co, 1928.

White Ladies of Fau: In the Jura region of France, there is a legend of faerie women who are so beautiful than no man can resist them. Known as *la dames blanche*, these "White Ladies" are not interested in luring men into a ferny grotto for an afternoon of supernatural nookie. Instead, once they get a man into their secluded den, they reveal their true faces—which no living man has seen but which legend insists is too hideous to behold—and they rip the guy apart, feasting on both flesh and blood. The legend has been whitewashed and romanticized by writers throughout the centuries, most notably in the story of Melusina, of whom much has been written. Most of them were collected by the scholar Jean d'Arras in the sixteenth century and presented in two volumes, *Chronique de Melusine* and *Le Liure de Melusine en Fracoys* (the latter of which was published posthumously). D'Arras's research had drawn heavily on earlier research by William de Portenach, but de Portenach's writings were sadly lost, though both of D'Arras's works still exist. These tales differ as to Melusina's exact nature. In various legends Melusina is a tragic heroine under a curse, a monster trying to pass as a human, or a demon living among humans in order to sow discord. In each legend there is one constant: Melusina always requests that her lover respect her wish that one day a month she could be sequestered away where no one could see her. Such promises never last and each doomed lover invariably spies on her (usually because he could not bear to be parted from her for even a single night). When Melusina is seen in her hiding place she is caught in some state of transformation: in the nicer stories Melusina would be bathing in a tub with her mermaid's tail flopped over the rim, but in other tales she would be in a hidden forest pool feasting on human flesh.

Wume: The Togolese have a strong moral sense, and much of their rich oral storytelling tradition is built around tales of right and wrong. The Wume is present in many of these stories as a worst-case scenario for a person's afterlife: Live an evil life and you are damned to spend eternity as a hated and feared creature of evil. The Wume was a human being who either died under a curse or who was a criminal in life and was doomed to damnation after death The Wume is a persistent vampire; evil, hungry, and very hard to kill. The beast is immensely powerful and very crafty, so no single slayer is likely to overcome it. The preferred method of destruction is to capture it (which takes the combined effort of many men), bind it securely, then find a secret place and bury it deep in an unmarked grave.

2 THEY HUNT
Hell Hounds and Monster Dogs

Hell Hound by Lincoln Renall

BAD DOG!

The dog isn't always man's best friend.

Wolves have been around for sixty million years. Except for tropical rain forests, wolves have inhabited every kind of habitat in the world, from the frozen Arctic to the dusty steppes to the deep forests. Currently there are thirty-two remaining species of wolf. Twenty-four of these species exist in North America and the remaining eight can be found in Eurasia. The smallest and rarest breed is the Mexican Wolf (*Canis lupus baileyi*) and the bigger varieties include the Russian Wolf (*Canis lupus communis*); a declining population found in Central Russia) and the MacKenzie Valley Wolf (*Canis lupus occidentalis*; found in the Northern Rockies and parts of Canada). Many other species, including the fearsome Dire Wolf (*Canus dirus*) have become extinct.

About one hundred thousand years ago the wolf genetic line split and the first protodogs emerged. Science is still trying to sort exactly how and why dogs emerged from wolves, and there is a huge knowledge gap between the original schism and the earliest records of domestication, which date back to 17,000 and 14,000 years ago, during the late Upper Paleolithic,[1] when humans began the process of domesticating dogs. The jump from wild wolf to domesticated dog is unusually fast in terms of the normal process of evolution. One theory is that juvenile wolves became separated from their pack and mated with other juvenile wolves, an event that resulted in the establishment of different behavior patterns than those of the mature pack. Such behavioral changes influenced the animals' interaction with their environment and that resulted in developmental differences. Within a few thousand generations, these new creatures no longer acted like wolves, and from there the dog emerged, with other changes caused by alterations in diet, interbreeding, and other conditions.

Dogs, from the start, have been transformative creatures. Dogs are virtually unique among animals in that new varieties or breeds of them can be created in sustainable form within a generation or two. Consider that in 1873 there were only forty known dog breeds while today there over eight hundred recognized breeds, ranging from the almost-not-even-there one-pound Chihuahua to Zorba, an English mastiff cited by the Guinness Book of World Records[2] as the heaviest and tallest dog ever, with a weight of 343 pounds and a length of more than eight feet from nose to tail

This transformative and malleable nature is reflected in much of the folklore surrounding both dogs and wolves, and that includes the ability to deliberately change shape so common in werewolf legends. Myth and legend is filled with dogs, ranging from the noble wolf of Jack London tales to the hyperintelligent Lassie and Rin Tin Tin to demonic hellhounds and wolf-men. Dog stories, like dogs themselves, seem to come in all shapes and sizes.

1. The third and last era of the Old Stone Age, variously dated between 10,000 and 40,000 years ago.
2. In the 1989 edition

What Makes the Ultimate Predator?

Thriller writer Janice Gable Bashman polled some experts:

▸ "It has intelligence, the ability to circle, corner, and out-strategize prey . . . then factor in ferocious killing adaptations—huge jaws and teeth, claws, sheer girth, sinew, superior hearing, smell, and the ability to see in the dark. Ultimate predators can smell your blood and sweat, hear your heart pounding inside your chest while you hide, as well as detect every shallow breath you take, then are able, via sheer force, to come through a normal human barrier (like a wall or door) to get to you."—L. A. Banks, bestselling author of *The Thirteenth* (St. Martins Press, 2009), Book 12 of the Vampire Huntress Series

▸ "Any predator faces two big challenges. The first is to be able to find prey—powers that can detect hidden prey from great distances. The second is to have enough weaponry to bring it down quickly and safely. Therefore, the ultimate predator needs an array of almost supersenses."—Ian McGree, producer, NHNZ Ltd. & Animal Planet's *The Most Extreme*

▸ "Intelligence. Cunning. Speed. Strength. Endurance. And, teeth, lots and lots of teeth. The ultimate predator is one that can hide among its prey, blend in with its environment, and then strike when it is least expected."—David Gallaher, writer and co-creator of the High Moon comic series, published by DC Comics/Warner Brothers

▸ "Most of all, the ultimate predator requires enormous amounts of patience and cunning."—Dave Wellington, bestselling author of *Monster Planet*

MONSTER DOGS

There have been monstrous dogs in folklore since the ancient Greeks. Cerberus, the three-headed guardian of the underworld, should probably be given the role of de facto pack leader, but other notable canine creatures abound. In both Egyptian and Eskimo cultures dogs were believed to be guides to the afterlife. The Greek

Goddess of the hunt, Diana, was thought to ride with spectral hounds who would locate lost souls. And generally the Greeks thought dogs could foresee evil.

Often dogs are believed to be omens of either good or bad luck. In Russia, if a dog howls by an open door, it's considered an omen of death. In central Europe, a dog howling during a child's birth is supposed to signal an unhappy life for the child. In several places around the world, there was a belief that dogs are witches who took animal form and that they howl when other witches are nearby. In England and France it was believed that if a dog howls three times in a row and then stops, it is supposed to signal the moment of a death. All through Europe and Colonial America it was thought that hearing a dog barking first thing in the morning is a sign of misfortune. In Ireland, a strange dog digging up your garden means illness or death is on the way. In Ireland, Scotland, and the deep American South folks still say that if a dog sleeps with its tail straight out and its paws turned up, bad news is on the way, and that the direction the tail is pointing indicates the direction from which the bad news will come. And you'll find these beliefs worldwide thanks to immigration and cultural blending: A dog running between two newlyweds is an indication of many fights between them to come; if a dog runs between a woman's legs, the husband should have reason to doubt her fidelity; if a dog runs and hides under a table, expect a strong thunderstorm to occur; a dog scratching or rolling on the ground for a long period also means rain will come; a dog howling for no reason is thought to be howling at ghosts. The same holds for dogs that suddenly stare at something in the room no one else can see.

Conversely, in England it is a sure sign of good luck to have a strange dog follow you. And in Western Europe, having a black-and-white dog cross your path while you are on the way to a meeting means good luck at the meeting. In Europe, a person bitten by a wild dog should eat a sandwich consisting of hairs from the dog and rosemary, leading to the cure for hangovers known as "the hair of the dog that bit you." In Scotland, a new friendship will follow a strange dog coming to your house.

The color of a dog is supposed to indicate the darkness of its soul, and some black dogs are thought to be embodiments of

The Power of the Monster

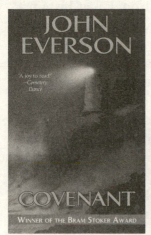

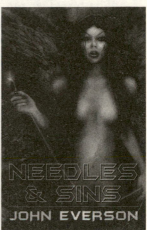

John Everson, photo by Geri Everson

"You only have to spend one night in the middle of the wilds to understand the power of the monster. And this monster is not some bizarre alien creation, but an exaggeration of what we know is out there. I've spent some time in the North Woods of Wisconsin alone—with only a handful of other humans in a five-mile radius. The nights are dark and eerie. And filled with sound. The sounds of wolves, or whistling air . . . or was that a bear? The fact is, the animals we know inhabit those dark woods only grow in stature (and tooth) in our minds as the nights go on and we shiver alone in bed. Imbuing the hunger of the wolf with the intellect of a man steps up the terror factor of those midnight howls." —John Everson is the Bram Stoker Award–winning author of *Covenant* (Leisure Books, 2008) and the short story collection *Needles & Sins* (Necro Books, 2007). He is also the cofounder of Dark Arts Books.

unquiet souls, whereas others are thought to be protective guides to travelers. Black poodles are placed on gravestones of German clergy who did not follow their religion too closely.

Seeing three white dogs together is considered good luck. A greyhound with a white spot on its forehead is considered good luck.

And white dogs have been used to sniff out evil of all kinds, from witches to vampires.

The broadest range of hellhound tales come from Great Britain, and frequently over the last thousand years there have been tales of packs of ghost hounds roaming the countryside. These hounds foretell death or disaster. To avoid spotting them, a person should drop facedown onto the ground when they hear the dogs coming. The most feared of these is a black spectral dog called the Barghest, and is considered to be a harbinger of death.

In Scotland and Northern England there is a very old legend of massive hounds that haunt the sites of battle and lap up the blood of the fallen. These Blood Dogs coalesce out of morning mist on the day after a battle and then slink around the field, digging in the dirt to get at bloody seepage, and often feasting on the bodies of the unburied dead. Blood Dogs have gray bodies, dark red eyes, and hot breath that can scorch the earth. Despite their hulking size the Blood Dogs leave no mark on the ground and their baying sounds like the wind.

The Scottish version of the story differs slightly from the English version in that the Blood Dogs only fed on English blood and it is hinted that they are the ghosts of Bonny Prince Charlie's hunting hounds.

Of course the most famous fictional hellhound tale is *The Hound of the Baskervilles*, written in 1902 by Sir Arthur Conan Doyle. It is the most famous case of the legendary Sherlock Holmes. In the novel a killer plays on the local myth of a spectral hound as part of his twisted scheme. Though the story is, ultimately, a straight mystery with no supernatural elements, it was written in the style of the late-nineteenth-century gothic horror stories. The various film versions of *Hound* also go for shocks and frights to keep the viewer wondering whether this is a ghost hound or not.

MONSTER DOGS IN POP CULTURE

There have been a lot of film versions of *The Hound of the Baskervilles*, including the classic 1939 version with Basil Rathbone and Nigel Bruce, which is the favorite of most fans of the Holmes series. However, the 1959 Peter Cushing/Christopher Lee version holds up nicely, and we're partial to the 1988 adaptaion with Jeremy Brett and Edward Hardwicke.

Films to avoid include the 1977 comedy version with Peter Cook and Dudley Moore; and the bland 1971 try with Stewart Granger and William Shatner.

Hellhounds on My Trail by Lincoln Renall

"As an artist, your main objective is to feed off human emotion in some way or form; and one of our strongest emotions is fear of the unknown. I like to include some form of dark undertone within a painting. Folklore is an excellent starting point for illustrations because so much of it is dark, and so much of it is open to personal interpretation."
—Conceptual artist Lincoln Renall

Other hellhounds from modern storytelling include Stephen King's *Cujo*, which tells of a St. Bernard turned murderous from rabies (the 1983 movie has a far happier end than the book). *Dogs of Hell*, a 1982 film based on a script by Tom McIntyre, was a nasty little cheapie about government-trained rottweilers who escape and terrorize a town. The *Resident Evil* movies all feature

Shape-Shifters

"Tales of shape-shifters have always fascinated me, especially the extent to which these stories exist in every culture in the world. What is typical in all of these is that the folklore around were-beasts reflects the animals in that vicinity—werewolves in Europe and North America, but were-tigers in India. So what kind of were-beast stories might evolve for urban dwellers? That idea prompted me to write 'Out of the Light' (*Dark Wisdom Magazine*, U.S. July 2007 issue #11), in which a hunter of were-beasts encounters a very unique shape-shifter preying on the citizens of downtown Toronto."—Doug Smith was a John W. Campbell Award finalist for best new writer and has twice won Canada's Aurora Award.

pretty effective scenes with packs of zombie Doberman pinschers (pretty much a worst-case scenario right there). A different kind of dead Doberman appeared in the 1977 so-bad-it's-fun flick, *Zoltan . . . Hound of Dracula*[3] in which a vampire dog has some bloody fun at a vacation camp. Hellhounds of one kind or another appeared in the pilot episode of the 2005 reboot of *The Night Stalker* and in the "Prom" episode of *Buffy the Vampire Slayer*.

In print they've trotted through "The Hounds of Tindalos," a Cthulhu Mythos tale by Frank Belknap Long. In the wacky novel *Good Omens*, by Terry Pratchett and Neil Gaiman, the Antichrist has a hellhound named "Dog." Christopher Moore's novel *A Dirty Job* features a pair of them named Mohammed and Alvin. The Harry Potter books by J. K. Rowling feature a Cerberus look-alike named Fluffy as well as a shape-shifter in the form of Padfoot—the grim animal form of Sirius Black.[4]

Dogs are frequent players in the modern folklore of urban legend, though usually they're more victim than predator. One of the most frequently told stories is that of the "choking Dober-

3. Also know as *Dracula's Dog*.
4. In the Harry Potter books a person who can adopt an animal form is known as an "Animagus."

man," which began circulating in the early 1980s. According to the legend a woman comes home to find her Doberman choking and in great distress. She immediately takes him to the veterinary hospital and returns home while they tend to the dog. As soon as she steps into the house the phone rings and it's the vet telling her to leave the house immediately and come straight to the animal hospital. Perplexed, she does, and upon arrival is told that when the vets examined the Doberman's throat they found two human fingers. The police were immediately dispatched and upon entering the woman's house found a badly injured burglar hiding in a closet.

Great story, but almost certainly just that: a story. It has a lot of variations, and depending on where it's been told (and to what audience) the story often varies so that the fingers are those of a black man, or an Hispanic or any ethnic group held in fear and contempt by the storyteller.

But the story has much older roots in a thirteenth-century embellishment of the tale of Prince Llewellyn of Wales and his dog, Gelbert. The prince returned to his house to find his house greatly disturbed and his dog lying in the hallway, its muzzle soaked with fresh blood. Fearing the worst, the prince dashes into the nursery and finds the cradle of his infant son overturned and splashed with blood. In grief and rage Llewellyn draws his sword and hacks his dog to death; but then he hears his child crying and tracks the sound to an adjoining room. The baby is unharmed and nearby is a dead wolf. Now Llewellyn realizes that Gelbert[5] had loyally defended the infant from the wolf.

Again, there's no way to know if this story is true, though it makes for a powerful and tragic tale, but the Choking Doberman tale surfaced first in areas of America that had long ago been settled by Welsh immigrants.

Aside from the true hellhound, many of the world's supernatural predators either appear as a monstrous dog, or assume that shape through transformation. Among this pack of para-hellhounds

---

5. This story, though popular, is highly unlikely and probably just borrows names of historical characters. Historically speaking, Prince Llewellyn was a political adversary of a man named Gilbert, the son of Richard, eighth Earl of Clare. There is no hard evidence to support the dog-baby-wolf story, though it does make for a good yarn.

Man's Beast Friend

▶ **135,000 B.C.E.: Recovered DNA traces prove that dogs evolved from wolf ancestors.**

▶ **100,000 B.C.E.: According to research by UCLA biologist Robert K. Wayne, some wolves and early dog species began to be domesticated at this time. Genetic research verifies that dogs evolved only from wolves, not from coyotes or jackals as had been previously believed.**

▶ **13,000 B.C.E.: Eurasian wolves are domesticated**

▶ **12,000 B.C.E.: The first travelers to North and South America bring domesticated dogs with them. Dog DNA pre-dating Columbus is recently discovered in Latin America and Alaska.**

there is the Malaysian Engbanka, the Belgian Kluddie, the Otgiruru of Namibia, the Qigirn of the Eskimo, the Sukuyan of Trinidad, the Upor of Poland and its close relative, the Upyr of Russia, the fierce Barghest of Great Britain, the Transylvanian Murony and several Filipino monsters, including the Asuang, the Pugut, and Bagat.

MONSTER DOGS IN FOLKLORE

Adlet: Among the Inuit peoples of Canada and Alaska there is an ancient legend of a race of bloodthirsty were-dogs called the Adlet. The Adlet race began as the hideous offspring of an unholy union of an Inuit woman and a monstrous red dog that was very likely possessed by a demon. This blasphemous sexual encounter bred creatures that were half human and half dog. The Inuit mother essentially gave birth to a "litter" of five of these creatures. Aghast at what she had brought into the world, she bundled them onto rafts made from whalebone and animal hide and set them adrift in the frozen Arctic waters.

The infant dog-creatures did not perish from the cold, however, but rather crossed the ocean and came ashore on the banks of one of the European countries (the legends don't specify which).

According to the mythology of the Inuits this pack of vicious monsters became the progenitors of all of the white races of Europe, which explains why there are so many tales of monsters and shapeshifters in white European culture.

Either the tale of the mother setting them adrift is wrong, or the Adlet somehow managed to return, but there have been reports for centuries of Adlet attacks—monstrous doglike creatures who attack hunters or villagers and feast on their flesh and blood.

Barghest: The Barghest is the "hound" behind *The Hound of the Baskervilles* (1901). In legend it is a monstrous hound that came out of the shadows to chase victims down country lanes. At times it has been reported baying in the forest near a home where someone is doomed to die. The howl of the Barghest can be heard on the moors and in the fields in the dead of night.

In some Yorkshire tales this hellhound actually chases down its prey and kills them with savage teeth, though when the bodies are found the marks have mysteriously vanished. In the West Country the hound's baying is enough to freeze the heart. In southern England the hound is more omen than predator, but is still counted as an evil creature in league with the powers of darkness.

Beast of Bray Road: This is an upright cryptid of the Bigfoot variety first reported in the late 1980s (see listing in Part 3). We mention it here only because some conflicting eyewitness reports and their corresponding cryptozoological theories speculate that the "upright" monster might have been a large dog standing on its hind legs with its forelegs propped on a tree branch or other object that, at a distance, gave it the appearance of a biped.

Beast of Gevaudan (also **Le Bête de Gevaudan**): The Beast of Gevaudan stands as one of history's most documented and believed monsters. Resembling a large wolf, the beast terrorized the Auvergne and South Dordogne regions of France between the years 1764 to 1767, and is believed to have killed nearly one hundred people, mostly women and children. Witnesses who lived to tell of the creature described it as roughly wolflike, but as large as a cow and with a huge barrel chest, a prehensile tail, and a mane of fur around its head and shoulders. The beast was said to be able to leap thirty feet in a single bound, and would sometimes pounce the life out of its victims.

This was not some piece of rural folklore that could be easily dismissed. The number of deaths was shocking and eventually the beast came to the attention of King Louis XV, who ordered that the creature be tracked down and killed.

Theories abound as to the exact nature of the monster. Certainly it could be any of a number of wild predators, a hyena or other canine not native to France, but brought back from distant lands by travelers or a circus. After the first few killings it was unlikely anyone would step forward to claim ownership, and therefore responsibility, for the monster.

Cryptozoologists speculate that it might have been some hyperthyroidic mutation of either a dog or a wolf; a mix of a large hunting dog and a wolf; or perhaps the last lingering member of an otherwise extinct species such as the monstrous Dire Wolf (*Canis dirus*). Or it could be a remnant Mesonychid, an order of predatory mammal that bore a resemblance to wolves and which became extinct during either the Paleocene or Eocene ages. Though wolflike in appearance, Mesonychids were actually more closely related to both Artiodactyla (goat-like mammals) and Cetacea (whales and their kin).

Whatever the beast may have been, its three-year reign of terror did come to an end, though no hunter was ever able to put the creature's head on his trophy wall.

Black Shuck (also called **the Doom Dog**): This is a brutish ghost dog reported in the coastal areas of Essex, Norfolk, and Suffolk. Like most British Hellhounds the Black Shuck has fiery eyes that radiate real heat and it is as large as a full-grown horse. Depending on who is telling the tale (and what they might have been drinking before the encounter), the Black Shuck sometimes walks on all fours, sometimes floats on the mist, and sometimes just moves through the air without apparently moving its body. Mostly it looks like a normal, if large and red-eyed, dog; at other times it's just a hulking body with no visible head. Though the Black Shuck has been encountered on lonely roads, places of executions, and at crossroads, its regular haunt is the graveyard.

Dire Wolf vs. Werewolf—Who Will Win?

According to Tom Demere (Curator of Paleontology, San Diego Natural History Museum), the extinct Dire Wolf was a pack animal 5 to 10 percent larger than the modern gray wolf, had powerful jaws and dentition that allowed it to crush bones and process slices of meat, and was an endurance runner. Thriller writer Janice Gable Bashman asked experts how the Dire Wolf would stack up when pitted against a werewolf:

▸ "The werewolf would have the upper hand. The reason—intelligence. The mixing of the qualities of a wolf and human create a formidable creature with the weapons of a wolf and the intelligence of a human—a lethal combination. After all, supernatural creatures are just that . . . super."—Jeremy Heft, wildlife biologist, Wolf Education and Research Center

▸ "Monsters in fiction and film such as werewolves are tougher, because they don't suffer the constraints of physics. In real life, animals can't move the way monsters do."
—Blair Van Valkenburgh, Professor, Department of Ecology and Evolutionary Biology, UCLA

▸ "The werewolf is a primal killing machine. There is no reasoning with the beast; it's wild, feral, and powerful beyond imagination. That's what makes it so frightening—one cannot expect to beg for one's life or reason with a werewolf on the hunt. It would have to be a pack to take a werewolf down and somehow I think the werewolf would still win."
—L. A. Banks, author of the Crimson Moon Rising series

Cadejo: In folklore, as in life, things are seldom black-and-white; however, when it comes to the Cadejo, a monster dog from the legends of Salvador, Nicaragua, Costa Rica, Honduras, Guatemala, and southern Mexico, they really are. If you see a white Cadejo good fortune is heading your way; if you see a black one, you're pretty much screwed. The white one will protect you through an otherwise dangerous journey; the black ones eat you.

In both cases the creature is the size of a cow, with shaggy fur, cloven feet, and burning eyes.

The creature gets its name from the Spanish word *cadena*, meaning "chain," because the monster is often depicted dragging a long chain behind it.

Legend has it that there are three distinct types of black Cadejo.[6] One—the worst of all—is a true incarnation of the Devil and encounters with Old Scratch just don't end well unless it says Spotless Saint on your birth certificate. The second kind is a flesh-eating monster—which isn't much better in the short term since you still die, but the long-term advantage is you don't get dragged down to hell. The third kind is a half-breed offspring of the first two (and, yes, this puts a new spin on bestiality). Though this last kind is frightening and dangerous, a strong or well-armed man can kill it.

Cerberus: Monsters beget monsters, and in the myths of ancient Greece whole family trees contain scores of bizarre and shocking creatures. Echidna—a half-human, half-serpent being—married Typhon—a dreaded beast with a hundred heads—and their off-spring included the Hydra, the Chimera, and the powerful guardian of the underworld, Cerberus.

Cerberus was an enormous doglike monster with three heads (or, if you read Hesiod instead of Virgil or Homer, fifty heads). The central head was shaped like a lion's, and the flanking heads looked like dogs. The monster had vast powers and aside from three sets of teeth as long as swords, a mane of writhing snakes, clawed feet, poisonous saliva,[7] and a ponderous mass, it had a whipping serpent's tail that could smash a man's bones to jelly.

Only a few heroes in all of Greek myth were ever able to defeat Cerberus: Hercules (who had to lure him out of Hades as one of his Twelve Labors); Orpheus (who charmed it to sleep with sweet music from his lyre); and the combined team of Aeneas of Troy and Bybil of Cumae (who lull it to sleep with a magic cake). Everyone else was apparently far less successful.

---

6. The Cadejo, and similar legends, are nicely recounted by author Simon Burchell in his book *Phantom Black Dogs in Latin America* (Heart of Albion Press, 2007).

7. Historically when Cerberus's poisonous saliva dripped to the ground it gave birth to the plant aconite, more commonly known as "wolfsbane."

Dante also wrote about Cerberus in his *Inferno*: "Cerberus, a monster fierce and strange, with three throats, barks doglike over those that are immersed in it. His eyes are red, his beard greasy and black, his belly wide, and clawed his hands; he clutches the spirits, flays and piecemeal renders them. When Cerberus, the great Worm, perceived us, he opened his mouth and showed his tusks: no limb of him kept still. My guide, spreading his palms, took up earth; and, with full fists, cast it into his ravening gullets. As the dog, that barking craves, and grows quiet when he bites his food, for he strains and battles only to devour it: so did those

Church Grim by Dennis Marcello

squalid visages of Cerberus the Demon, who thunders on the spirits so, that they would fain be deaf."

Church Grim (also **Kirk Grim** in Scotland, **Kyrkogrim** in Sweden, or **Kirkonwäki** in Finland)**:** It's unclear whether the Church Grim is a great black dog that sometimes takes the form of a small, hunchbacked human, or the other way around. In either case, the creature appears in both English and Scandinavian folklore and is believed to be a protector of churches. However, it is commonly believed that the Grim is the penitent spirit of a sinner who rings church bells and does other service as part of its centuries-long penance for a life of terrible sin.

In other legends, the Grim is believed to be the ghost of a black dog deliberately buried on church grounds so that it would rise from the grave as a guardian spirit.

Cu Sìth (also **Cusìth**)**:** A hellhound of the Scottish highlands that is as big and strong as a bull and has fiery eyes. Unlike most monster hounds of the United Kingdom, the Cu Sìth is dark green rather than black, and has long shaggy hair like that of Highland cattle.

Despite its size, the Cu Sìth is an absolutely silent hunter. However, it sometimes announces its presence—or boasts of a kill—by uttering three immensely loud barks that can be heard for miles and even far out to sea. Some folktales insist that this bark was its way of giving fair warning that it was coming, which gave villagers the chance to hide their womenfolk. The Cu Sìth, whose name means "fairy dog," was believed to capture women and carry them off to a sìthean (fairy mound), to serve as wet nurses for the daoine-sìth (fairy children).

A variation of the Cu Sith, called the Cooshee, appears in the game Dungeons & Dragons. In myth there is a feline version of this monster called, appropriately enough, the Cat Sith.

Cŵn Annwn: In Wales there are very old legends of the "Hounds of Annwn," the spectral hunting dogs that rode out with the Wild Hunt. Annwn is a spiritual realm of fairy, and depending on who is telling the tale, the Hunt and its dogs are either benevolent (and really indifferent to the human world) or they are bloodthirsty and vicious and prey on humans. One should note that after the set-

Fairytales

 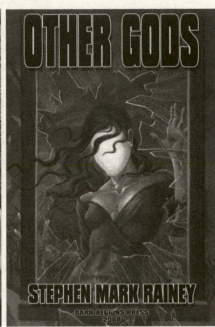

Stephen Mark Rainey

"Fairy tales are part of the first stimuli children get and those things always leave an impression—particularly since many fairy tales are full of vivid imagery that is often tinged with darkness. Fairy tales and folklore have common allegorical roots in that they put inventive faces on things we don't understand; so we seek to romanticize or otherwise put into terms other than what they truly are. Most adults at least rationally put all that behind them, but for many, I think a certain fascination remains for the workings of pure imagination—hence an appreciation, at least for some, for the truly extraordinary." —Stephen Mark Rainey is the author of *Other Gods* (Dark Regions, 2008) and *Blue Devil Island* (Thomson Gale/Five Star, 2007).

tling of Christians in the Celtic lands much of the fairy world was suddenly deemed to be Satanic and evil.

The Hounds are most commonly heard on the eves of St. John, St. Martin, Saint Michael the Archangel, All Saints, Christmas, New Year, Saint Agnes, Saint David, and Good Friday; though other tales say that they most often appeared on the Solstices and the Equinoxes.

Many believe that the Cŵn Annwn served another and more regular purpose, which was to escort the souls of the newly departed on their journey to the other side of death (be that heaven, hell, or some fairy realm). In the darker versions of the folklore, the Cŵn Annwn are frequently seen in the company of a haglike witch called Matilda of the Night (Mallt-y-Nos) who was always up to no good.

The Wild Hunt

The Wild Hunt and the hounds appear in a lot of variations in Celtic countries, and if you sniff around enough you'll encounter strikingly similar stories in accounts of Gabriel Hounds of England and the Yell Hounds of the Isle of Man. The Wild Hunt itself has its roots in even older folktales of Northern Scandinavia and Germany, and in all of the stories a group of supernatural hunters go out as a band, racing across the landscape and sometimes across the sky itself, ostensibly hunting for game but more often hunting for human women. Seeing the Hunt was believed to be very bad luck and would foretell of plague, war, or famine to come. Being in the path of the Hunt was pretty much a ticket to the boneyard for anyone except the very bravest or cleverest of warriors; and even then a surviving warrior might be bundled off to become one of the immortal huntsmen. In some of the many hundreds of variations of the Wild Hunt tale, the band is composed of faerie folk of the very worst kind; and yet in other tales the Hunt has an aspect of nobility. There is little consistency. When looking at the roster of the Hunt as it stretches across history and national lines, its members have included everyone from King Arthur to Satan. Even Gods like Odin occasionally rode out with the faerie horde.

Dip: In Catalonia[8] there are very old tales of a monstrous hell-hound called the Dip that is both a servant of the devil and a blood-drinking vampire. As with many creatures from Catalan folklore, the Dip is lame in one leg and the limp is the only thing that allows potential victims to outrun it.

Gwyllgi: A gigantic spectral mastiff from Welsh legend, often called the Black Hound of Destiny. It is generally encountered on dark country roads and terrifies unsuspecting travelers with fiery red eyes and a breath like the fumes of hell.

Gytrash: A giant spectral hound from northern England that preys on travelers. This creature can apparently shape-shift and has been known to take the appearance of a donkey or horse, though usually it appears as a hound. The Gytrash is either subject to moods, or there are different kinds of them that have different dispositions, because in some tales the creature leads lost travelers back to the correct path while in other tales it leads them astray and then eats them.

The variation of this monster reported in Lincolnshire and Yorkshire is always hostile, according to legend, and this version (or perhaps subspecies) has eyes that burn like hot coals. The author Charlotte Brontë wrote a compelling scene about the Gytrash in Chapter 12 of *Jane Eyre*.[9] "As this horse approached, and as I watched for it to appear through the dusk, I remembered certain of Bessie's tales, wherein figured a North-of-England spirit called a *Gytrash*, which, in the form of horse, mule, or large dog, haunted solitary ways, and sometimes came upon belated travelers, as this horse was now coming upon me. It was very near, but not yet in sight; when, in addition to the tramp, tramp, I heard a rush under the hedge, and close down by the hazel stems glided a great dog, whose black and white color made him a distinct object against the trees. It was exactly one form of Bessie's Gytrash—a lion-like creature with long hair and a huge head . . . with strange pretercanine eyes . . ."

8. An autonomous community of the Kingdom of Spain.
9. This appears in each of the many concurrently published editions of *Jane Eyre*.

North Country Hellhound: In the late eighteenth and early nineteenth centuries there was a rash of animal killings in the mountainous country between Northern England and Scotland. Hundreds of sheep were found dead, their throats torn out and their bodies drained of blood. At the scene of each killing the farmers and investigators found numerous prints like those of a very large dog. Now, up to this point the story is gruesome but not actually weird, because wild dogs do roam those mountains and hungry dogs have certainly been known to dine or a sheep or two. But here's the kicker: according to paranormal investigator Charles Fort,[10] the sheep were drained of blood but none of their flesh was eaten, and there was not enough blood on the ground to explain the total exsanguination. Hounds that kill just for blood? Yeah, that's creepy. No solution to the mystery has ever been found.

In the latter part of the twentieth century this story resurfaced during the investigation of similar animal killings, particularly cattle mutilations and the desiccated victims of El Chupacabra, the Goat Sucker (see listing).

Old Bull: In the Wharton State Forest, part of the vast Pine Barrens of New Jersey, there is a very old Lenni Lenape legend of a vengeance hound named Old Bull. In the story, Hessian soldiers fleeing defeat by General Washington and his troops hid out in the pine forests of New Jersey. Some of them married women of Royalist families while others took Lenni Lenape women as wives. One soldier, whose name is variously given as Friedrich von Lossburg or Gunter von Bünau, married a Native American woman and settled down to carve out a small farm. The soldier had with him a huge old hunting dog named Bull who had come all the way over from Wiesbaden with him. One day when the former soldier was out hunting, a party of Colonial soldiers happened upon his farmhouse. They raped and murdered the Hessian's wife and set his house ablaze. Seeing the smoke, the Hessian hurried home and when he saw that his house was burning he ran inside to try and save his wife; but he succumbed to the smoke and died. Bull sat outside and howled for three full days and nights

---

10. Reported in *Lo!* by Charles Fort, published by Gollancz of London, 1923.

and then the grief-stricken and exhausted dog crawled onto the blackened cinders of the house and died.

That night was a full moon and the loyal hound's ghost rose from the ashes—his fur smeared black with soot—and set about hunting for the murderers.

One version of the story says that Bull tracked down the soldiers and tore them to pieces and now guards the place where his master is buried; another version says that the soldiers made it safely back to Washington's army and escaped the dog's wrath, but that the hound now hunts down their descendants. According to the cautions given with the tale, if a person encounters this fearsome hound, it's important to close your eyes and say: "Guter hund."

Good dog.

Old Bull will pass by and leave you unharmed.

While the story of Old Bull is not nearly as famous as that of another local monster, the famous Jersey Devil (see Chapter 3), it's a fascinating story that echoes many vengeance tales from Western and Central Europe. We first heard the story from a "Piney"[11] who claimed descent from the same Lenni Lenape village. It was, appropriately enough, told around a campfire and Jonathan learned about Old Bull almost a year before he first heard of the Jersey Devil around the time he was eight years old. Sadly we were unable to find anyone in that area who still remembers the full story of Old Bull, and most of the variations Jonathan encountered where the same ones he learned as a kid. "Perhaps Old Bull has finally found a quiet place to take his rest, or maybe myths have shelf lives just like books. In either case, I do remember one black night in late September, under a fingernail moon and a sky littered with stars, where I stood by the edge of the woods and heard a distant howl. A dog's howl.

"Sure, there are a lot of farms in Jersey, and there are a lot of people who own big dogs, and a lot of dogs howl. But to me, deep down, that will always be the howl of Old Bull. I believed it then

11. "Piney" is an often derogatory term used to describe some of the residents of the Pine Barrens, particularly those from poor and undereducated families. Oddly, several of these folks with whom I became friends during my many summers camping in Bel Haven Campground in New Jersey used that term to describe themselves, and they seemed to take pride in the label.

with all my heart, and now . . . well, I'll continue to keep an open mind and if I encounter something big and canine in the Jersey pines, I just may try closing my eyes and saying, 'Guter hund.' "

Shunka Warak'in: Among the Ioway native peoples the Shunka Warak'in is an ancient legend of a wolflike creature that will attack humans as well as animals. Spotted frequently on the Great Plains by Native Americans and settlers as well during the late eighteenth and well into the nineteenth centuries, the Shunka Warak'in was known for sneaking into a campsite or village to hunt for dogs. Its name even means "carries off dogs."

The Shunka Warak'in had oversized forelegs and shoulders, giving it a stature more like a wild boar than a dog. When one of these creatures was killed it supposedly cried out in a voice that was eerily human.

There is a long-standing rumor that a settler killed one at the end of the nineteenth century and mounted it before donating it to a tiny museum located in a grocery store in Henry Lake, Idaho . . . but the specimen has since vanished.

Waheela: A lupine cryptid that has been reported many times in the Northwest Territories of Canada, particularly in the Nahanni Valley. Ivan Sanderson (1911–1973), the noted naturalist and cryptozoologist, believed that the Waheela might be a surviving example of a kind of "bear dogs" known as amphicyonids, which lived during the Late Eocene to Late Miocene. The creature was believed to be a solo hunter, which is one of the many reasons this creature bears some striking resemblance to the Inuit legend of the Amarok.

Yardley Yeti: Since early fall of 2005 there have been a number of sightings of a strange doglike creature roaming the fringes of various Bucks County, Pennsylvania, towns. The creature looks like a mix of dog, jackal, and kangaroo, and was dubbed "The Yardley Yeti" by newspaper columnist J. D. Mullane[12] (Bucks County *Courier Times*). Other

---

12. And, no, this creature does not fit the profile of a Yeti, which is a manlike hominid found in the frozen peaks of the Himalayas; but Mullane liked the way it scanned with "Yardley," and now the nickname is stuck to the legend.

The New Folklore

 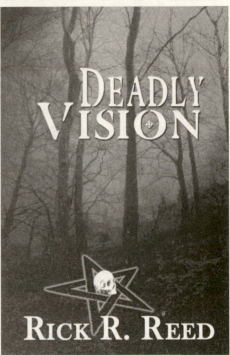

Rick R. Reed,
photo by Mike Smarro

"I agree that urban legends are the new folklore, since urban folklore has its roots in the very same kind of behavior around which older folklore grew: the telling of stories, the verbally passing it on, the changes and embellishments the tale goes through as it's passed from one mouth to the next ear. I think most urban legends are told rather than written and I believe that's how folklore originally started as well." —Rick R. Reed is the author of *Deadly Vision* (quest, 2008) and *Orientation* (Amber Quill, 2008).

folks are calling it the Lower Makefield Lurker (or Lower Makefield Monster), the Bucks County Boggart, and the New Hope Hyena.

Lower Makefield Police Chief Ken Coluzzi said that his department had fielded several reports about the creature. Chief Coluzzi told Jonathan: "The greatest part of this job (law enforcement) is the unknown. We say that it's the greatest show on earth. Just when you think you have seen and done it all—bam another bizarre encounter occurs. When I first overheard the conversations about a sighting of a mutant doglike creature I just laughed. Then the reports started coming in. Officers were called to various locations within my township to take reports of people who claim to have spotted it. They did not know what it was. Some called it a cross between a dog and a hyena. Others said a wolf dog, and others said it was a sick looking foxlike creature. Others said a coyote."

Now here's where this story gets even weirder . . . Jonathan has not only seen it, he's taken photos of it. Considering that he writes books about strange creatures, it seems wonderfully appropriate that he got a chance to not only see the thing, but to photograph it. Jonathan and his wife, Sara Jo, were visiting the Michener Art Museum in New Hope, Pennsylvania, on October 30, 2005. "We had our camera with us (a Minolta D-Image digital). In the parking lot we saw a very odd-looking creature moving among the parked cars.

"It was brownish, with some gray, with an unhealthy-looking coat. The creature moved very quickly. It was never aggressive in any way. It didn't even take notice of us other than to continue moving away from us. It moved out of the parking lot and across the tracks of the Ivyland–New Hope line before finally disappearing into some brush. It made no sound, and didn't even react when I made some noise to try and attract its attention," Jonathan says. "At a guess I'd put it at about thirty-five pounds, give or take."

After seeing the photos, Chief Coluzzi observed: "When I viewed the pictures you sent me I was truly amazed. It appeared to me to be a mix of all the descriptions. Whatever it is or turns out to be, I hope our suspicious creature likes us."

If it's a dog . . . then it is the weirdest mutt Jonathan ever saw. If it's a fox, then the critter has been popping steroids.

Various website postings have included speculation that it's a cougar (not a chance); that it's an unknown species of fox (doubtful); that it's a coyote (maybe); that it's a dog (possibly—but a dog of what species mixed with what other species?).

TV reporter Don Polec (ABC/Action News Channel Six in

Philadelphia) also saw the creature a couple of years ago, though the one he described was bigger (German shepherd–sized) and gray. Polec said: "It's noteworthy when you almost hit a creature with your car . . . that you can't identify. When it dashed across the road in front of me and into the woods, I was at a loss as to what it was. The best I can do is say it was a quadruped, gray in color, about the size of a large German shepherd, skinny, really ratty looking, body parts that seemed oddly out of proportion, too large for a fox, legs too long for a coyote or dog, head too small for its size, and really in need of some grooming and big dish of Alpo."

Though the animal he describes is similar to the one Jonathan and Sara Jo saw, his was gray and much larger. Then in December 2007 Jonathan saw another version of the Yardley Yeti. This one was as big as Polec's, but was a pale gray-white, with even longer ears and a lean body suggestive of a whippet or greyhound, but it still had the characteristic marsupial face and down-tilted shoulders.

On various cryptozoology websites, such as www.cryptomundo.com, the leading theory is that the creature is a red fox with mange, but when we showed the pictures to veterinarian and exotic animals expert Adam Denish, DVM, he said that it was definitely not a mangy fox. In fact, he told us, "Frankly, I don't know what it is."

So . . . the mystery continues.

3 THEY HOWL

Werewolves and Wolf-Men

THE BIG BAD

Depending on which source you rely on, the name werewolf is either of Old English origin (wer: man; wulf: wolf), or (more probably) Norse, from the phrase *varg-ulfr*, which is further derived from *vargr*—a term variously meaning "outlaw" or "evildoer" and "ulf" meaning "wolf." There are a lot of spins that can be put on that, and the way in which the word is interpreted is crucial, because not all werewolves are the same.

In the broadest sense, the werewolf is a human who transforms into a wolf through magic, a curse, or by some other unknown means. The modern take on the werewolf legend indicates that most folks believe that werewolves are generally unthinking creatures who transform during the three days of the full moon and

Lycanthropy

 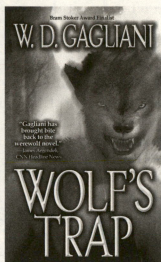

William Gagliani,
photo by J. Radzium

"My novel *Wolf's Trap* (Leisure) utilizes some of the familiar trappings of lycanthropy (werewolf) lore to tell a North Woods noir crime story. Werewolves can be found throughout European folklore to the current day, and between the Dark and Middle Ages, hundreds of people were tried and executed as lycanthropes. It now appears that cases of lycanthropy were either unknown or undiagnosed illnesses such as porphyry, or mental illness, or cases of revenge in which a malicious accusation was aimed at some enemy. However, belief in the ability of some humans to alter their shapes is shared by so many cultures that, as with vampirism, it may make one think twice before dismissing the possibility. In creating the background for my novel, I tried to imply that European werewolf lore and rituals could be crossed with Native American totemism, a dash of voodoo, and other magick could be tossed in, and the resulting hybrid might look like our traditional movie werewolves. Even though it's likely that the werewolf's aversion to silver was a Hollywood invention, I liked using it—a bit like a lycanthrope's Kryptonite." —W. D. Gagliani's fiction has appeared in anthologies such as *Dark Passions: Hot Blood 13*, *Robert Bloch's Psychos*, and *More Monsters From Memphis*.

run around eating people; but this doesn't really square with the folklore.

First off, many of the werewolves of myth and legend retained their human intelligence, and often even the power of speech, when in wolf-shape. Not all werewolves are savage, and not all of them are evil. It's not even accurate to say that most werewolves in folklore are lycanthropes—beings who physically transform from human to wolf. As I said . . . a lot of it's in how the story is interpreted.

When viewed from a purely scientific perspective, it's likely that no werewolf actually transformed and that the concept of a man becoming a savage animal was a way of trying to make sense of savage behavior. This becomes very clear when reading the transcripts of the werewolf trials of Europe (notably Italy, France, and Germany of the fourteenth through seventeenth centuries). Evidence given in these trials—both eyewitness and confession—clearly indicate that a person acted like an animal, hunted humans

Preparing for Horror Roles

David Fine

"Even before I became an actor my whole life has been a sort of research laboratory for the darker side of human experience . . . from at least the age of twelve when my father gave me a copy of *The Encyclopedia of Murder*, and before that with my fascination with horror films. I was at the Saturday matinee double feature on a weekly basis . . . usually horror . . . at the good old college theater in Swarthmore, Pennsylvania." —Actor David Fine has appeared in dozens of films, including *The Pursuit of Happyness*, *Rent*, *Dog*, and *Lonely Joe*.

as prey, killed without mercy, occasionally consumed their flesh and/or drank their blood, and then tried to cover their tracks by attempting to conceal the corpse or lay false trails to deflect legal attention. To our ancestors of a few hundred years ago this was the behavior of a person who had become possessed of a monstrous and animalistic spirit. To our modern minds, given over a century of psychoanalysis and forensic psychology, these are the actions of a totally different kind of monster: a serial killer. No less dangerous, but all too real.

Even the concept of cycling attacks—whether it's a lunar cycle or some other pattern—fits the profile of a serial killer.

This idea is not news. The Reverend Sabine Baring-Gould (1834 to 1924), an English biblical scholar, novelist, and historian, posited an early version of theory in his nonfiction work, *The Book of Werewolves*,[1] though as the phrase "serial killer" had not yet been coined, he doesn't use that term. His meaning is clear, however, and most scholars and psychologists tend to agree with him.

The famous novel *The Werewolf of Paris* by Guy S. Endore (1933),[2] was based on one such case, involving a sergeant in the French army, Francois Bertrand, who robbed a number of graves and cannibalized the corpses before being apprehended in 1840.

Werewolves

"The werewolf, to me, is more frightening in what its endurance as an archetype says about humanity. In my novel the main character becomes a werewolf in part when his primal urges take over in response to a traumatic event in his life. In essence, he loses control of his emotions—he is driven by his rage instead of reason. This is more frightening than the vampiric archetype, because it says we are one step removed from monsters ourselves." —Christopher Fulbright is the author of *Of Wolf and Man* (PublishAmerica, 2003).

---

1. First published in 1865.
2. This was also the basis for the 1935 film *The Werewolf of London*.

There are some competing theories that the violent actions of people labeled as werewolves were the result of a variety of medical maladies ranging from chemical imbalances, tumors, and other brain disorders to rabies and porphyry—diseases that can cause paranoia and hallucinations as well as psychotic behavior. And some folks are just plain crazy.

However, not all werewolves from folklore are psychotic madmen. The *Epic of Gilgamesh*[3] (a real historical king of Uruk in Babylonia c. 2000 B.C.E.) makes mention of a lycanthrope in the character of Enkidu, a wild man created by the sky god Anu. Enkidu and Gilgamesh are initially adversaries, but after the hero defeats the werewolf they become great friends[4] and share many epic adventures together. Enkidu is intelligent and honorable and becomes a valuable companion to the hero-king.

Various cultures believed in animal possession and would symbolically invite this by wearing animal skins during rituals and while in battle. In the excavated ruins of Catal Huyuk in Turkey (formerly Anatolia), eight-thousand-year-old cave paintings clearly show hunters wearing the skins and heads of animals, suggesting either a real or psychological link with animal predation methods. Another classic example of this were the Viking Berserkirs,[5] who covered themselves with animal skins (bear, wolf, etcetera) and they fully believed that the spirits of these animals then entered into them and imbued them with animal cunning, power, and a predatory joy of the kill. They were the fiercest of fighters, totally unflinching, absolutely committed to battlefield murder. They were extraordinarily strong, resistant to injury, and filled with such a battle rage that just the presence of them on the battlefield was often enough to make enemies break and run.

The Berserkirs were not evil—they believed that Odin, king of the Norse gods, allowed them to become one with their animal

3. The oldest known story that has survived, twelve clay tablets in cuneiform script.

4. Technically Enkidu's savage nature is tamed by a temple prostitute named Shamhat, but that paves the way for his friendship with Gilgamesh.

5. Also spelled *Berserker* and *Berserkr*.

spirits, and so when they fought it was with the belief that their chief god was very much on their sides. This combination of intense psychological belief and religious fervor turned them into the deadliest kind of battlefield fanatics. Often Viking attack forces would place a dozen Berserkirs in the forefront of an advancing line to break the enemy formations, and this they did with a complete passion for battle and a fury unmatched by anything human or animal.

In Greek myth, the tale of Lycaon gives another early example of—and another twist on—the werewolf story. The story has several variations, but in the most popular version Lycaon was the corrupt king of Arcadia and, along with his fifty evil sons, was a tyrant and a fiend. When Zeus came to visit him, Lycaon offered the king of the gods a meal in which cooked human flesh was the centerpiece. What was apparently a delicacy on Lycaon's table was not at all to the liking of Zeus, who in a fit of righteous rage transformed the king and his sons into wolves. The moral, apparently, that if someone acts like an animal then they are an animal.

Early Greek and Roman scholars believed that the Neuri, a tribe living in what is now modern Poland, were all werewolves. The Greek philosopher Herodotus (c. 484–425 B.C.E.) mentions them in his *Histories*, Book IV:[6] "It seems that the Neuri are sorcerers, if one is to believe the Scythians and the Greeks established in Scythia; for each Neurian changes himself, once in the year, into the form of a wolf, and he continues in that form for several days, after which he resumes his former shape." The Roman geographer Pomponius Mela (birth and death dates unknown) likewise wrote about them in his *De Chorographia*[7]: "There is a fixed time for each Neurian, at which they change, if they like, into wolves, and back again into their former condition."

Olas Månsson, known in popular history as Olaus Magnus (1490 to 1557), a Swedish ecclesiastic and writer, wrote extensively of mass lycanthropic transformations in his *Historia de Vent*: "In Prussia, Livonia, and Lithuania, although the inhabitants suffer

6. Written 440 B.C.E.
7. Published in 43 C.E.

Fury of the Werewolf by Eldred Tjie

considerably from the rapacity of wolves throughout the year, in that these animals rend their cattle, which are scattered in great numbers through the woods, whenever they stray in the very least, yet this is not regarded by them as such a serious matter as what they endure from men turned into wolves. On the feast of the Nativity of Christ, at night, such a multitude of wolves transformed from men gather together in a certain spot, arranged among themselves, and then spread to rage with wondrous ferocity against human beings, and those animals which are not wild, that the natives of these regions suffer more detriment from these, than they do from true and natural wolves; for when a human habitation has been detected by them isolated in the woods, they besiege it with atrocity, striving to break in the doors, and in the event of their doing so, they devour all the human beings, and every animal which is found within."

And there is the most famous werewolf case in history, that of Peter Stubbe (a.k.a. Peter Stube, Peeter Stubbe, or Peter Stumpf), known as the werewolf of Bedburg,[8] who was executed for savage

Werewolf on the Hunt by Kelly Everaert

crimes in 1589. After being tortured on the rack, Stubbe confessed to having practiced black magic since he was twelve years old, and claimed that the devil had given him a magical belt that enabled him to metamorphose into the likeness of a greedy devouring wolf. Stubbe, who sometimes went by the name of "Ubel Griswold" (literally "wolf of the gray forest"), claimed to have killed and eaten animals and humans for twenty-five years. The court, appalled by these crimes, sentenced him to having his skin torn off by red-hot pincers before being beheaded.

Strangely, there are addendums to this legend suggesting that Peeter Stubbe was arrested several more times in different places around that part of Europe over the next fifty years. Each time he confessed and was executed. Either someone was playing fast and loose with the facts, or the relating of accurate news was taking a beating via oral storytelling, or something very, very weird was happening in that part of Germany.[9]

The Beast of Gevaudan mentioned earlier in this chapter is another strange case that may (or may not) be related to the mythology of the werewolf.

The werewolf exists in many places under many names: Albania (*oik*), Armenia (*mardagayl*) France (*loup-garou*), Greece (*lycanthropos*), Spain (*hombre lobo*), Mexico (*hombre lobo* and *nahual*), Bulgaria (*varkolak*), Turkey (*kurtadam*), Czech Republic/Slovakia (*vlkodlak*), Serbia/Montenegro/Bosnia (*vukodlak* вукодлак), Russia (*vourdalak*, оборотенъ), Ukraine (*vovkulak, vurdalak, vovkun*), Croatia (*vukodlak*), Poland (*wilkołak*), Romania (*vârcolac, priculici*), Macedonia (*vrkolak*), Slovenia (*volkodlak*), Scotland (*werewolf, wulver*), England (werewolf), Ireland (*faoladh* or *conriocht*), Germany (*werwolf*), the Netherlands (*weerwolf*), Denmark/Sweden/Norway (*Varulv*), Norway/Iceland (*kveld-ulf, varúlfur*), Galicia (*lobisón*), Portugal (*lobisomem, lobishomen*), Lithuania (*vilkolakis* and *vilkatlakis*), Latvia (*vilkatis* and *vilkacis*), Hungary (*Vérfarkas* and

8. Bedburg is a town in the Rhein-Erft-Kreis, North Rhine–Westphalia of Germany.

9. Jonathan Maberry's novels *Ghost Road Blues* (2006), *Dead Man's Song* (2007), and *Bad Moon Rising* (2008) are inspired in part by this legend.

Farkasember), Estonia (*libahunt*), Finland (*ihmissusi* and *vironsusi*), Italy (*lupo mannaro*) . . . and the list goes on and on.

THE WEREWOLF VARIATIONS

In folklore there are three distinct types of werewolves. The first is the true werewolf, a person who transforms completely into a wolf and, though it maintains its human intellect, its powers are no different than those of an ordinary wolf.

Misfiring Movie Monsters

"Three sad things happened, one in the mid-1990s, a time when horror was at pretty much an all-time low, which was the self-referential horror movie, á là *Scream* and the like. It was this new breed of horror movie that recognized the conventions of the past and started to reference them with sort of a wink at the audience, but then started just mindlessly repeating the very thing it was attempting to spoof in sequel after sequel. The second sad thing that happened (in the early years of the twenty-first century) was an attempt to either re-create movies from the seventies—not specifically in the sense of a literal remake (although to be sure that has happened more than is forgivable) but in the respect of filmmakers going for "the style" of a *Texas Chainsaw Massacre* or *Last House on the Left*, without actually capturing the soul of what made those movies great. The third bummer was a tendency of younger filmmakers to take an existing monster and sort of hip-ify it—now we no longer have just werewolves and vampires. The werewolves are these totally unconvincing video game CGI creations, and the vampires are sleek, badass *Matrix*-looking characters who know kung fu and sling nickel-plated pistols like characters out of a John Woo movie. Again, nice idea, but by removing all the mystery from the monster, it no longer works." —Adam Huddleston wrote, directed, coproduced, and starred in the independent horror feature *Sullen*.

The second are the serial killers like Peeter Stubbe and his more modern colleagues Jeffrey Dahmer, Ed Gein, and Ted Bundy.

The third are wolf-men, creatures who only partly transform so that they have many wolflike characteristics such as fur, a lupine face, and a snoutful of fangs, as well as clawed hands and feet, but who walk upright on two legs. Popular fiction and the movies make use of this kind of monster.

Among the supernatural werewolves there are two additional subgroups: wolf-man and the true werewolf. The true (and far more common) werewolf completely transforms into a wolf. It possesses the natural speed, cunning, strength, and ferocity of that animal, but only in those levels typical of a natural wolf. The wolf-man is a creature that possesses qualities of man and wolf: generally walking upright, wearing human clothing, and possessing some degree of human intelligence. It is the wolf-man which is endowed with unnatural power, not the werewolf.

Most of the werewolves seen in movies tend to be of the wolf-man variety, though in the film *An American Werewolf in London* the creature was a little of both: a gigantic wolf, larger than any normal wolf and far more powerful.

The method by which someone becomes a werewolf (of either species) varies from folktale to folktale. Many stories influenced by the early Christian church hold that a person may become a werewolf when his ability to keep his sinful nature in check has failed and the animal that lurks inside all men is released. In other tales, it is curse that brings out the wolf. Beginning in the early 1800s, the story changed so that it was the bite of another werewolf that began the transformation. This theme is now endemic to all werewolf film and fiction.

In 1941, Lon Chaney, Jr., created the classic role of the tortured Lawrence Talbot in the film *The Wolf Man*. Film and fiction have changed the folkloric beliefs so radically that the pervasive beliefs nowadays come almost exclusively from pop culture, and *The Wolf Man* set several standards for what has become the new werewolf folklore: the werewolf sees a pentagram in the palm of its next victim; it is vulnerable to silver (and is in fact beaten to death by a silver-headed walking stick); it is the werewolf's bite that transmits the curse; and only the death of the last werewolf breaks the bloodline. These themes have all been picked up and used by other films in much the same way that the crosses and other trappings of the novel and movie *Dracula* have been adopted.

According to folklore, the werewolf is not particularly hard to kill, no more difficult than an ordinary wolf. It cannot pass on its curse through a bite or a scratch. However, the bite can cause a lingering sickness much like that of a poisonous snake, and death is the most common result.

There are two links from the past that have carried over into fiction that may have more solid connections to the ancient beliefs: wolfsbane and silver.

In medieval times, silver was considered the purest of metals, although this speaks more to its color rather than any knowledge of metallurgy. Something so essentially pure was believed to be a proof against evil, and it apparently severed the connection between the physical body and the demonic spirit inhabiting it.

Theoretically, silver should have worked like an antidote to werewolfism, but there are no reported cases of it being a benign cure. Instead, a person had to be killed by silver—or silver had to be involved in the killing—for the demonic possession to be broken. Although this did little to help the cursed person while they were alive, it did prevent them from being damned in death.

Wolfsbane has been used for centuries in herbal medicines, and it exists in a variety of species. It is used to treat bites from poisonous animals and this is very likely the basis for the belief that it cures a person of the poison from a werewolf's bite. Unlike garlic, wolfsbane does not drive off a werewolf, as is suggested by the movies.

Paranormal romance author Margaret L. Carter shared an interesting observation on werewolves with us: "Stephen King proposes that all monsters ultimately symbolize the fear of death. While I agree that there's a lot of truth in that thesis, the monsters of myth and folklore incarnate other, subsidiary meanings, too. The werewolf represents the beast within us. The prospect of its breaking out frightens us. Yet, if the transformation is involuntary, it also liberates us—without conscious guilt—to obey impulses civilization requires us to suppress. Ghosts and vampires represent the fear of death but also the yearning for the beloved dead to return.

In another layer of meaning, revenants are traditionally viewed as malevolent because of our dread that the returned dead will remember the ways we mistreated them during their lives (even if we loved them). Vampires, of course, also represent the wish to overcome death and live on indefinitely, as well as the symbolism of power and intimacy involved in consuming a vital bodily fluid."

One fact never touched on in the movies is that in many cultures, werewolves and vampires are not only linked but also overlapping creatures that possess similar qualities. And in quite a few cultures, when a werewolf dies it can come back from its grave as a vampire, which is a truly terrifying thought.

Most popular fiction has it that a person cursed with werewolfism will only transform into a monster during the three days of the full moon, and that the transformation is totally outside their control.

Folklore differs from this in most cases. Transformation is not generally believed to be beyond the werewolf's control, but rather a deliberate act. In most legends around the world, a person may become a wolf or a wolf-man (depending on the species of werewolf) by deliberate choice. Most often, this choice is based upon an evil nature and a desire to do great harm.

The concept of a werewolf transformation occurring only during the full moon most likely dates back to 1250 C.E. It can be traced to the writing of a Norseman named Kongs Skuggsjo, who related the tale of how St. Patrick prayed to God to punish some men who heckled him, or "howled" him down, when he attempted to convert them to Christianity. God bestowed an ironic punishment: the men were condemned to howl like wolves at each full moon. Skuggsjo's story does not say that the men actually became wolves or engaged in werewolf predation, but it is the most likely link between werewolfism and the full moon.

Most legends do mention that werewolves often hunt by moonlight, not necessarily the light of the full moon. The Venerable Bede wrote of this, in 731 C.E., as did Gervaise of Tilbury in 1214. This does not mean that daylight keeps a person safe from werewolf attacks, as the creatures can also transform and hunt by the bright light of the sun.

Modifying the Werewolf Myth

  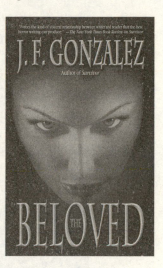

J. F. Gonzalez, photo by Cathy J. Gonzalez

"*Shapeshifter* is a werewolf novel, yet it wasn't the first of my novels that was inspired by or influenced by folklore. That honor would go to *Conversion*, my first attempt at a novel. *Conversion* was a vampire novel, and with that I basically not only learned how to write a novel, I didn't really contribute anything new to the vampire mythos. With *Shapeshifter*, however, I had a bit of an edge in the fact that not many people were writing werewolf novels at the time. Therefore, I thought I could do something different with that old archetype. As things turned out I relied on the old myths to get me through the character development of my werewolf and was able to play around with him a bit. For example, I did away with that old silver bullet and crucifixes standby, but I kept the full moon myth intact with some difference. My werewolf is affected by the lunar pull, yet he has the power to control it." —J. F. Gonzalez is the author of several novels of horror and suspense including *Shapeshifter* (Leisure, 2008), *Clickers* with Mark Williams and *Clickers II: The Next Wave* with Brian Keene (both Delirium, 2008).

WEREWOLVES IN POP CULTURE

The very first cinema big bad wolf was *The Werewolf* (1913) a silent Canadian film (now lost, alas) directed by Henry McRae in which a Navajo witch woman transforms her daughter into a wolf in order to attack invading white men. An actual wolf was used in the transformation sequence. Two years later Reliance-Mutual Studios released *The Wolfman*, but it, too, was lost. Other silent werewolf films include *The Wolf* (1915), *Le Loup Garou* (France, 1923), and *The Wolf Man* (1924). *The Werewolf* (1932, Germany), directed

Wolf-Men of the Movies by Allen Koszowski

by Friedrich Feher, was the first "talkie" featuring a werewolf. The film was based on the Alfred Máchard novel *Der Schwarze Mann*.

The Werewolf of London (1935) was the first of Universal's werewolf films and one of the best of all time. In the story, Dr. Wilfrid Glendon (played by Henry Hull) is a botanist who is bitten by a werewolf (played by Warner Oland), and once back in England transforms into a monster himself. The film is intelligent, moody, and entirely watchable even three quarters of a century later.

The Wolf Man (1941) is still the most famous werewolf film of all. Lon Chaney, Jr, stars as the tragic Larry Talbot. He is bitten by a werewolf played by Bela Lugosi, and survives to carry the curse himself. This film introduces the link between werewolves and wolfsbane. Joe Johnson directed the 2009 remake with Benecio Del Toro in the Lawrence Talbot role, Anthony Hopkins as his father; and Emily Blunt as the gal who brings out the animal in him.

The Larry Talbot wolf-man also appeared in a number of other films, including *Frankenstein Meets the Wolf Man* (1943), which is the direct sequel, *House of Frankenstein* (1944), *House of Dracula* (1945), and one last time in *Abbott and Costello Meet Frankenstein* (1948).

1946's *She-Wolf of London*, starring June Lockhart (later of *Lost in Space*) was something of a dud, and really spent more time trying to build mood than explore the concept of lycanthropy.

In the 1957 flick, *I Was a Teenage Werewolf*, horrific transformation is used as a metaphor for puberty and teen angst. Even so, the film, starring a nineteen-year-old Michael Landon as the unfortunate victim of the werewolf curse, is pretty good (if unintentionally funny).

A personal favorite of ours was *The Curse of the Werewolf* (Hammer Films, 1961), which, although campy and talky, gave us one of the more frightening werewolves in the form of the young and muscular Oliver Reed. In this film's mythology a person can become a werewolf as a result of being the offspring of a raped woman, apparently perpetuating the evil seed of the rapist father.

1981 is regarded by many werewolf film experts as "the year of the werewolf," because it gave us three landmark films: *An American Werewolf in London*, *The Howling*, and *Wolfen*. The first two films broke new ground for a number of reasons, but particularly

Ravenous

"With *Ravenous* I did research into actual wolves. I ended up covering some stuff I already knew, but learned some new things as well. I became rather disturbed by the fact that I was writing about monsters, when in fact wolves are gentle, affectionate, intelligent, extremely social creatures that have been demonized over the centuries by myth and superstition. It bothered me that I was contributing to that—if, indeed, I was—but I told myself that my creatures were not fully wolves, they were a combination of wolves and humans, and the human side was dominant, making these creatures vicious. I decided that in *Bestial*, the sequel to *Ravenous*, I would address that fact. So in *Bestial*, I have a character from the first book who is turned, but rather than letting her human instincts lead her, she gives in to the lupine side of her new nature and becomes a very different creature. She is still a werewolf, but more noble than the rest of the pack, and she actively resists the vicious, raping, bloodthirsty werewolves that have taken over Big Rock.

"When I wrote *Ravenous*, I knew going in that somehow I had to work in sex. The werewolf myth as it's been handled in the past has never really been very sexual on the surface, but to me, the connection has always been obvious. The very word 'wolf' has long been used to refer to horny men out to get laid. A werewolf is a person who is overtaken by his animal side, the beast inside him. That's not sexual? That's the definition of sexual! So I decided to spread the werewolf condition through a sexually transmitted virus rather than a bite. I've gotten some criticism for my use of rape in the book. But these are people who have become mostly animals and are driven by instincts, urges, not reason. They have two things on their minds—eating and fucking. Being ravenous monsters, they don't ask politely, they simply take. Rape seemed to me to be a natural behavior for these creatures. I worked hard to make the rape scenes as ugly and unpleasant as possible—I didn't want anyone to confuse that for erotica, because it's not, it's violence. But still, there are those who thought I went too far and I've taken some flak for it. I also lost the connection between the werewolf transformation and the full moon, simply because it's a pain in the ass to write around that. It's too limiting."

—Ray Garton is the author of *Live Girls* and *The Loveliest Dead*.

because of the revolutionary use of special effects that made the transformations believable—replacing the old method of merely doing quick cuts from one stage of transformation to another. In these films we saw muscle and bone change, we saw skin sprout hair, and we saw fangs grow. It was scary as hell. This was before CGI and it was unlike anything the moviegoing audience had experienced.

An American Werewolf in London blended black comedy with real shocks, and the film explored the curse of werewolfism and its implications for both the werewolf and its victims. (The 1997 sort-of-but-not-really a sequel, *An American Werewolf in Paris*, had more expensive special effects and did a lot less with them.)

The Howling, based on the excellent novel by Gary Brander, explored the concept of werewolves living in a structured community, much like a wolfpack.

Wolfen was the third monster-wolf film released that year and is technically not a werewolf film at all. It's really an exploration of the possibility that a subspecies of wolf continued to evolve until they were as smart as humans but with all of the animal instincts and skills of wolves. The movie is (rather loosely) based on a novel of the same name by Whitley Strieber, and though the adaptation doesn't quite match, the story in the film is equally compelling.

Stephen King put his own spin on the werewolf legend, first in the 1983 illustrated novel, *Cycle of the Werewolf*, which featured stunning artwork by Bernie Wrightson, and then in King's own 1985 film adaptation, *Silver Bullet*. The film earned little critical or commercial support, which is a shame because it's a damn fine (if slightly sentimental) werewolf flick that explores issues such as the power of compulsion, the nature of inner strength, and the bonds of family.

Though *The Howling* was a pretty powerful film, the sequels—many of which are sequels in name only—kind of suck. The only one worth mentioning is *The Howling III* (1987), an odd but interesting entry that deals with a species of marsupial werewolf in Australia. Worth catching mostly for its efforts to think outside the Hollywood box.

Werewolves went mainstream with Mike Nichols's *Wolf* (1994), starring Jack Nicholson as an aging doormat of a man who

The Appeal of the Classic Monster

Harry Shannon, photo by Yossi Sasson

"I suspect the classic monsters—vampires, werewolves, and so on—continue to endure precisely because they have endured. Joseph Campbell once wrote that myths were myths precisely because they are true, meaning in a powerful metaphorical sense. So perhaps the werewolf expresses our violent, predatory self, the vampire our selfish sexual narcissism, the demon our hatred for limits and obligations to others. A forensic psychiatrist I admire wrote a book titled *Bad Men Do What Good Men Dream*.[10] That says it very well, in my opinion." —Harry Shannon is the author of a number of horror short stories and novels, including *Night of the Beast, Night of the Werewolf*, and *Daemon*.

becomes a business and sexual tornado after getting bitten by a werewolf. The film also stars James Spader as his rival (in business and predation) and Michelle Pfeiffer.

10. Robert I. Simon (American Psychiatric, 1995).

Werewolfism as a metaphor for puberty was explored a few more times, with varying success. *The Company of Wolves* (1984) starring Sarah Patterson and Angela Lansbury was an adaptation of three variations of the Little Red Riding Hood folktale ("The Company of Wolves," "Wolf-Alice," and "The Werewolf") from feminist author Angela Carter's 1979 short-story collection *The Bloody Chamber*.[11] The film is elegant and surreal, though not at all targeted at the horror crowd.

2000 saw the release of *Ginger Snaps*, which—much like Stephen King's *Carrie*—used horrific storytelling elements to hammer home the powerful and often traumatic effects of puberty and the onset of menstruation. In this film a Goth teenager named Ginger (played by Katharine Isabelle) is bitten by a wolf on the eve of her first period and then begins changing in extreme and dangerous ways. The two 2004 sequels, *Ginger Snaps: Unleashed* and *Ginger Snaps Back: The Beginning*, though interesting, lack the power of the first film.

One of the very best werewolf films was released direct to video in 2002 and sadly went almost completely unnoticed. *Dog Soldiers*, directed by Neil Marshall and starring Kevin McKidd, Sean Pertwee, and Liam Cunningham, tells the story of a squad of British soldiers training in the lonesome Scottish hills who stumble upon a ferocious family of werewolves. Bloody, action-packed, and entertaining, it tops the list of all-time great werewolf movies, equal to *An American Werewolf in London* and *The Howling*.

2002 also gave us *Le Pacte des Loups* (*The Brotherhood of the Wolf*), an art-house action film based on the Beast of Gevaudan[12] in France between 1765 and 1767. The movie combines horror, court intrigue, and martial arts into a visually stunning film experience.

Pitting werewolves against vampires made *Underworld* (2003) a box-office smash and turned a leather-clad, gun-toting Kate Beckinsale into an action-film fanboy's dream. This movie takes a twisted version of Romeo and Juliet as Kate Beckinsale's vampire falls for a werewolf while everyone on both sides are gearing up

---

11. It was first published in the U.K. by Vintage and won the Cheltenham Festival Literary Prize.
12. See entry in Part 2.

Killers from Fact to Fiction

Peter Straub, photo by Jerry Bauer

"About midway through the writing of *The Throat* (Random House, 1994), the Jeffrey Dahmer case exploded into view, and soon I was stunned and riveted by the similarities between Dahmer and my primary villain. Both were serial killers who had been born in Ohio, done their first murders there, served in the military, then later located in Milwaukee (in the novel, the city's called Millhaven, but it's still Milwaukee) and killed many, many people, sometimes enjoying a bit of cannibalism. It felt as though I had invented the guy. This excited me so greatly that almost instantly I invented a new character named Walter Dragonette, whose crimes and methods deliberately echo Dahmer's. Millhaven, already overstocked with serial killers, had acquired a new one, and this guy was even more lurid than his predecessors." —Peter Straub is the *New York Times* best-selling author of *Lost Boy, Lost Girl* and *In the Night Room.*

for an all-out war. The sequel, *Underworld: Evolutions* (2006), deepened the story but failed to catch the fun of the first film.

In 2004 Christina Ricci—formerly Wednesday of the *Addams Family* movies—took a swing at modernizing the werewolf film in Wes Craven's *Cursed*, but the movie was a dud with critics and audiences. The same year Julian Sands starred in *Romasanta: The Werewolf Hunt*, one of the few films to attempt to tie the werewolf curse with serial killers, but it was direct to video and largely overlooked.

Between *Underworld* films Kate Beckinsale made another try at the werewolf genre in 2004's hugely disappointing *Van Helsing*, costarring Hugh Jackman. It was hoped that the film would launch a major franchise, but it overused CGI effects and as a result made the monster look too fake, thus spoiling any real chance at suspense.

2006's *Wild Country*, a low-budget Scottish werewolf film, flew completely under the radar in the United States but managed to nab a few decent reviews despite uneven acting and poor effects. Unlike many of the bigger-budget films, this little werewolf flick actually moves along at a respectable pace and is quite enjoyable if you can find a copy on DVD.

Skinwalkers, a 2007 film starring Jason Behr and Rhona Mitra, was released theatrically but bombed. Although it had a lot of advance buzz, the result was disappointing. Lots of pretty people shooting guns and an attempt to build a "chosen one" mythology that fizzled nearly from the beginning.

Another box-office bomb was *Blood and Chocolate*, supposedly based on Annette Curtis Klause's young adult novel of the same name, but it seems the name is the only thing the screenwriters actually used. The story deals with the loup-garoux (sic) society of werewolves living in secret in our world. The novel placed the loup-garoux in an alternate reality. They should have stuck to the book.

Though some werewolf movies are based in whole or part on novels, as with King's *Cycle of the Werewolf*, Brandner's *Howling*, Strieber's *Wolfen*, and a handful of others, much of the body of werewolf fiction remains unmined by Hollywood, and as a result it's often overlooked by the mainstream audience. That's a shame, too, because there's a whole library of good, solid, scary as hell werewolf novels out there that deserve more attention than they're getting.

One of the earliest fictional werewolves appeared in the poem "Bisclavret," written in 1198 by Marie de France, which presents a noble baron who can transform into a wolf but because of the treachery of his wife is trapped in wolf-shape. The tale was popular and was reworked into "The Lay of Melion," where we again see a knight transform into a wolf using a magic ring, and that once he's off in lupine form his wife steals his ring and takes off with another man. Melion, still a wolf, stows aboard a ship bound for Ireland, his wife's homeland, and through a series of violent adventures—and the timely help of wise King Arthur—is able to recover his ring and restore himself to human form. Both versions of the tale were presented as *lais* or "lays," derived from the Celtic word for song, a form of medieval French and English romance literature comprised of short rhyming tales—usually six hundred to one thousand lines—of love and chivalry that frequently involved some aspect of the supernatural.

"Guillaume de Palerme" (William of Palerno),[13] a French romance poem written circa 1200 by Yolande, daughter of Baldwin IV, Count of Flanders, tells of a foundling named Guillaume who is brought up at the court of the emperor of Rome. Guillaume falls in love with the emperor's daughter Melior, although she has been promised in marriage to a Greek prince. The young lovers cloak themselves in bearskins and flee to the woods, where they are protected and provided for by Alfonso, a Spanish prince and Guillaume's cousin, who is also a werewolf. He is a very noble and benign werewolf who was transformed by a spell from his evil stepmother. In return, Guillaume takes it on himself to defeat the stepmother and her husband the king, Alfonso's father. He succeeds and the enchantment is broken, allowing Alfonso to ascend to the throne of Spain. Alfonso marries Guillaume's sister and everyone lives happily ever after.

These early werewolf stories seldom had anything to do with the phases of the moon or a curse. The transformation was typically accomplished through use of a magic device (belt, ring, hat, or something similar), and the werewolf could not only transform at

___

13. The English translation and retelling was commissioned in 1350 (approximate) by Humphrey de Bohun, 6th Earl of Hereford, and written by a poet known only as William.

will but also often retained full intelligence and character while transformed.

By the nineteenth century, epic poems had largely given way to short stories and novels as the source of fanciful storytelling. One of the first of these Victorian Gothic werewolf tales was "Hughes The Wer-wolf," a short story written by Sutherland Menzies and serialized in 1838. It deals with a Kentish family that had been accused of werewolfism. The last remaining member of the family decides to perpetuate the myth by pretending to be a werewolf. This key passage from the story[14] reveals the truth behind the legend:

> This chest, which had evidently remained long unopened, contained the complete disguise of a were wolf—a dyed sheep-skin, with gloves in the form of paws, a tail, a mask with an elongated muzzle, and furnished with formidable rows of yellow horse-teeth.

While the story deals with a pseudo-werewolf, it might be closer to the truth if the theory that werewolves were actually serial killers is accurate. The story also contains some insight into pack behavior, which also shows up in the history of serial killers. Consider this passage:

> Witchcraft, larceny, murther (sic), and sacrilege, formed prominent features in the bloody and mysterious scenes of which the Hugues Wulfric were the alleged actors: sometimes they were ascribed to the father, at others to the mother, and even the sister escaped not her share of vilification; fair would they have attributed an atrocious disposition to the unweaned babe, so great, so universal was the horror in which they held that race of Cain!

As with the Manson family and their murders, the killings were a team effort. This has become a storytelling subgenre that includes *The Texas Chainsaw Massacre, The Hills Have Eyes,* and the novel *The Girl Next Door* by Jack Ketchum (Warner Books, 1989) and the 2007 film of the same name.

---

14. From the September 1838 issues of *The Lady's Magazine and Museum.*

The Girl Next Door

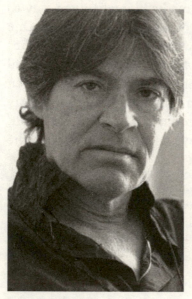

Jack Ketchum

"Gertrude Baniszewski, her children, and her children's friends tortured and murdered sixteen-year-old Sylvia Likens in the basement of their home in Indianapolis, Indiana, in 1965. There was a photo of Gert in Jay Robert Nash's *Bloodletters and Bad Men* that haunted me for years, as did her story—violence toward a young woman orchestrated by a much older woman, with half the neighborhood either directly culpable or turning a blind eye. I decided to explore that story in novel form. When my mother died and I returned to my family home in New Jersey to settle up her affairs I realized I could set my novel there, on what was then a dead-end street when I was growing up, back in the 'innocent' 1950s."
—Jack Ketchum is the award-winning author of *Off Season*.

And, as is often the case, the real-world monsters are sometimes far more frightening than their fictional counterparts. Consider Ed Gein, the psycho killer who was the inspiration for *The Texas Chainsaw Massacre*. When the police arrested him and investigated his house they found human skulls mounted on the corner posts of his bed, skin fashioned into a lampshade and used to upholster chair seats, breasts used as cup holders, human skullcaps apparently in use as soup bowls, a window shade pull consisting of human lips, and other horrific items.

Another significant mid-nineteenth-century lycanthrope tale was 1857 novel *Wagner The Wehrwolf* by W. M. Reynolds, in which an old man agrees to serve John Faust for the last year of his life in return for youth, wealth, and beauty. Unfortunately the youth comes with a curse: he becomes a werewolf. A more recent

Preparing to Play Leatherface

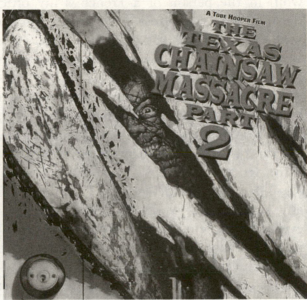

Bill Johnson

"*For Texas Chainsaw Massacre 2* the values of the character I portrayed, Leatherface, was anarchistic to his family's values of old; '. . . turned traitor for a piece of tail . . .' " accuses Bubba's older brother, Dreighton Sawyer, played by Jim Siedow. Unlike many productions of stage plays or films, this film production, *TCM2* had the screenwriter, L. M. Kit Carson (also a producer) on set (revising and rewriting the entire time we filmed) who was very collaborative, so 'research' was done through talking with Kit Carson (and also Tobe Hooper, who was a contributing writer/Sawyer family historian) in order to examine and illuminate the special world of that screenplay. When *TCM2* was released in 1986, it was rejected as a horror film. Reviled. Despised as too bloody and violent, a gratuitous slasher movie, nothing redeeming; but nowadays *TCM2* is accepted, welcomed, cherished, even, and also considered kind of lightweight in the violence and gore aspect." —Bill Johnson's Hollywood film credits include Leatherface, a.k.a. Bubba in *Texas Chainsaw Massacre 2* and Oliver Stone's *Talk Radio*.

story is Guy Endore's 1934 classic *The Werewolf of Paris*, which was actually largely based on a true story of a ghoul (not a werewolf) in the person of a French army officer named Francois Bertrand who was arrested for digging up and eating corpses. A year after the book was published, it was made into a film, *The Werewolf of London*, but with such significant story changes that it bore little resemblance to the novel.

The TV series *Dark Shadows* featured a werewolf in the form of heartthrob Quentin (played by David Selby), and the character became so popular that he shared most of the latter seventeen of the run of thirty-three Paperback Library novels inspired by the show, written ostensibly by Marilyn Ross (a pen name for Dan Ross). For most of the series (TV and novel) Quentin was a good guy, and even his werewolf aspect somehow did the right thing even if for the wrong reason. The soap opera show, however, delved into the darker aspects of his curse and some of his lupine actions were quite reprehensible.

Much of the more recent werewolf fiction has appeared either in the young adult market or in paranormal romance.

The young adult, or YA, books, often present werewolves as dangerous but not evil, suggesting a parallel to the real-world bad boys who can go out of control but are not corrupt by nature. Stephenie Meyer's novels *Twilight*, *New Moon*, and *Eclipse*[15] feature a teenage werewolf named Jacob "Jake" Black,[16] a character originally intended for a small expository role but whose part in the series quickly grew as both author and readers bonded with the good-guy lycanthrope.

In the Demonata series[17] of books by bestselling author Darren Shan, we meet Grubbs Grady, a young werewolf fighting against demons.

Eileen Wilks has an ongoing series of dark fantasy novels with a werewolf theme: The World of the Lupi, featuring Lily Yu—a Chinese American sensitive who works for the Magical Crimes Divi-

---

15. All published by Little, Brown Young Readers.
16. Portrayed in the 2008 feature film by Taylor Lautner.
17. Little, Brown Young Readers.

The Psychological Werewolf

"Both of my books—*Ivy Cole and the Moon* (Nedeo, 2005) and *Luna* (2008)—are about werewolves, and I drew on the medieval myths of lycanthropes as well as what can only be called the 'new folklore,' which mainly evolved through the movie industry. I think human beings are fascinated by the beast within themselves. On a psychological level, a werewolf can be interpreted as the inner id, our civilized nature gone feral. There is a sensual lure to the idea of man reverting to beast; hidden within us all, isn't there just a little of the wild man yearning to be set free? And isn't that idea, perhaps, the scariest of them all—that a wolf lurks in the deep corners of the most common of characters?" —Gina Farago is a Winner of the New York Book Festival Award and top finalist for the Compton Crook, IPPY, and Benjamin Franklin awards.

sion of the FBI in a world where werewolves and magic are commonplace. Books in the series include *Tempting Danger* (Berkley, 2004), *Mortal Danger* (2005), *Blood Lines* (2007), *Night Season* (2008), and *Mortal Sins* (2009).

In Carrie Vaughn's fantasy novels, the main character is Kitty Norville, a werewolf who hosts *The Midnight Hour*, a popular radio phone-in show. In the first book, *Kitty and the Midnight Hour*, she slips up on the air and more or less "outs" the werewolf community, which sparks anger from the other supernaturals as well as the religious right. This theme is continued in *Kitty Goes to Washington*, in which she faces a McCarthyist persecution. Other entries include *Kitty Takes a Holiday* and *Kitty and the Silver Bullet*. Other entries in the paranormal romance/dark fantasy werewolf subgenre include *Dancing With Werewolves: Delilah Street, Paranormal Investigator* (Juno, 2007) by Carole Nelson Douglas.

WEREWOLVES IN FOLKLORE

Airitech: In the mythology of the Goidelic Celts (the Irish, Manx, and Scots) there is a legend of the great and terrible Airitech, a monster who dwelled sometimes in our world and sometimes in the supernatural world. Airitech had three lovely daughters who were actually lycanthropes and at will, or at the bidding of their father, they would transform into murderous werewolves.

Cas Corach, the son of Caincinde, a heroic bard whom the Book of Lismore (1512–1526) called ". . . the best musician of Erinn or Alba" confronted the three werewolf daughters of Airitech. The young hero lulled them into a romantic stupor with the sweet music of his harp, and then killed them, thus ridding the region of their predatory evil.

Amarok: A ferocious wolf from the legends of the Inuit, but unlike normal wolves, this monster is a solo hunter who targets anyone who dares to hunt alone and at night.

Enkidu: The Epic of Gilgamesh makes mention of a lycanthrope (werewolf) in the character of Enkidu, a wild man created by the sky god Anu. Enkidu and Gilgamesh are initially adversaries, but after the hero defeats the werewolf they become great friends and share many epic adventures together.

Farkaskoldus: The Farkaskoldus is an interesting twist (and blend) of the vampire-werewolf relationship. Resisting classification as either vampire or werewolf, and embracing characteristics of both, the Farkaskoldus is usually an unnaturally resurrected spirit that returns to seek revenge. When a wronged person dies (usually a shepherd who has been abused or unfairly treated in life) he is resurrected as blood-drinker—not a thirsty vampire but instead a bloodsucking werewolf.

The majority of legends hold that once the Farkaskoldus has gotten whatever justice is desired, its spirit will be able to rest and it will return to the grave, never to rise again. In some folktales the Farkaskoldus, once freed of its compulsion to seek redress, will begin attacking anyone until it is hunted down and killed.

The Farkaskoldus can be killed by ordinary means—a sword,

gun, or even clubs—but it is a fierce fighter and cannot easily be overcome. The safest method for disposing of the monster is to have a large group of armed men with torches and hunting dogs herd it toward a clearing where a bonfire has been prepared. Once in the clearing the men can overpower it using nets, ropes, or sheer numbers, then bind the creature to a stake and light the bonfire.

Lobishomen: The sinister Lobishomen is another Brazilian vampire that preys mainly on women. Like the Jaracacas, this creature seldom kills its victims. Instead it draws only enough blood to nourish itself. However, its bite creates a kind of infection that turns the woman into an insatiable nymphomaniac. As a result she often becomes a sexual vampire, preying on men other than her husband and destroying the sanctity of her marriage vows. In this way the Lobishomen accomplishes its evil purpose.

Portugal has a legend of a Lobishomen that is often overlapped with the legend of the Bruxa: vampire witches who attack children to suck their blood. In some areas where the Portuguese settled in Brazil, the Lobishomen is regarded more as a werewolf than a vampire.

In werewolf fiction, the herb wolfsbane is commonly cited as a protection against lycanthropes, much as garlic is used against vampires. The same holds true in the folklore of the Lobishomen. Wolfsbane is planted on graves to keep the dead from rising as werewolves. In cases where a witch is suspected of being a werewolf, the herb is crushed into a paste with sweet onion and smeared around doors and windows.

Most sightings of the Lobishomen describe a small creature, hunchbacked and scampering on stumpy legs. Its face is horrifying, with pale and bloodless lips, jagged black teeth, jaundiced skin, and stiff bristling hair like that of a jungle ape.

Disposing of a Lobishomen is fairly tough, because it is clever and elusive, but it has one often fatal weakness in that it has no head for alcoholic beverages. Leaving cups of strong wine will get it drunk, at which point it can be overcome by several strong men, crucified to a tree, and then stabbed to death. The corpse is then burned.

In centuries past, it was believed that a knife or sword that had been used to kill a Lobishomen was tainted and had to be melted down or otherwise destroyed. But in the ninth century the belief sprang up that such weapons had become imbued with special powers and were kept as talismans, often hung over thresholds to send a clear message to other evil creatures: Keep out!

Loup-Garou: The French word for "werewolf," these creatures seem to have invaded the United States along with early French settlers.

The werewolf and the vampire are closely linked in many cultures. In Byelorus, when a werewolf is killed it comes back as a species of vampire called a Mjertovjec. The Loogaroo of Haiti are witches who shed their skins at night to become vampire/werewolf hybrids. The Romanian Pryccolitch is a vampire/werewolf hybrid. The Portuguese Lobishomen is regarded by many scholars to be as similar to a true werewolf as it is to a vampire. In Greece, when a wronged person is killed (a common source for vampire legends) it is reborn not as a vampire but as a werewolf called a Farkaskoldus.

A werewolf is any person who changes into a wolf or wolflike creature. In folklore this was something that happened by force of will, but in more recent fictional accounts (books and movies) it is related to a curse and only happens during the three days of the full moon.

The name is probably derived from *vargulf*, a Norse expression meaning murderer or predator. In fact, many of the accounts of early "werewolf" attacks were closer to the murderous methods used by human serial killers. The Greek term lycanthrope (wolf-man) is also commonly used. More general terms for the metamorphosis of people into animals include shape-shifter, turnskin, or turncoat.

Most European cultures have stories of werewolves, including Greece (lycanthropos), Russia (volkodlak), England (werewolf), Germany (werwolf), and France (loup-garou). In northern Europe, there are also tales about people changing into bears. In European mythology, the legends of berserkers may be a source of the werewolf myths. Berserkers were vicious fighters dressed in wolf-or bearhides. They were apparently immune to pain and in battle were vicious killers, slaughtering their opponents with the single-mindedness of wild animals. In Latvian mythology, the Vilkacis was a person who had been changed into a wolflike monster, though the Vilkacis was occasionally benevolent.

Many of these legends came to American shores with visitors as early as the Vikings, and more steadily with the colonists. Of the European werewolf legends, the Loup-garou, or d'Loup-garou (pronounced loo-guROO) is by far the most common, especially among the Cajuns of Louisiana.

One common Cajun legend is used to frighten children into good behavior. A Loup-garou lives deep in the swamps of Louisiana and comes out when the moon is full. According to local stories, this creature is "the meanest, smelliest, ugliest monster." It can smell when a child has been mean, comes to their house, and "eats bad lil' girls an' boys—from d'tip o'dey hair to dey baby toenails."

The Loup-garou can be killed in any number of ways, from firearms to burning, but it's easiest to ward it off with a charm made by a priest or priestess of vodoun.

The Loup-garou is not confined to the bayous and swamps of Louisiana. In Vincennes, Indiana, legends of the Loup-garou suggest that a person can be cursed to transform into a wolf, cow, horse, or some other animal. Once under the spell of this demonic spirit, the unfortunate victim becomes an enraged animal that roams through the fields and forests at night. The curse only lasts for a specific span of time, usually 101 days. During the day, the Loup-garou returns to his human form, but will afterward be plagued with poor health and depression.

The only way for the Loup-garou to be released from the curse is for someone to recognize him as a human that has transformed to an animal, then somehow draw blood from him while in his transformed state. This is difficult and dangerous and is usually only possible while the creature sleeps. However, the curse states that even if the spell is broken neither the victim nor his rescuer can mention the incident, even to each other, until the original 101 days are over. Otherwise they will both suffer even worse enchantment.

Vincennes, Indiana, has been the center of more than a century of werewolf legends. Even today there are plenty of people who look closely at any animal acting strangely, and make the sign of the cross to ward off the possible Loup-garou lurking within.

Vilkacis: The Vilkacis ("wolf's eyes") is a malicious Latvian creature whose nature combines elements of werewolf and vampire. Latvian folklore is uncertain how a person is transformed into such a monster, but curses and sinning against the gods of the Latvian pantheon play a major role. Quite a few folktales suggest that when a person sleeps, the darker side of his personality sometimes "escapes" as a Vilkacis and goes running free in the dark, often taking nightmarish shape. In Latvia this kind of astral projection is called "running with the wolf."

Luckily it is no more difficult to kill a Vilkacis than an ordinary wolf, though this creature is smarter and more cunning. If the Vilkacis is killed, then the sleeping person dies as well.

When the Vilkacis appears it hunts randomly in the forests around its own home or village. If a person catches the Vilkacis while sleeping and encircles it with rose petals, the Vilkacis is then subject to that person's will and can be made to sniff out buried treasure. In some stories the Vilkacis will lead someone to treasure without being forced to do so, but will take pleasure in the corruption this sudden wealth often brings to the villager's life.

The Vilkacis belongs to the same lower level of Latvian mythological beings as Dievini, Ragana, Pukis, and the shape-shifting and devious Vadatajs.

 THEY HIDE

Cryptids and the Science of Cryptozoology

SOMETHING IS OUT THERE

There are some pretty weird things out there, and we're not talking about vampires and werewolves or creatures from myth. No, our own physical world has its fair share of very strange things. You've heard of some of them: Bigfoot, El Chupacabra, the Loch Ness Monster, the Jersey Devil; but there may be many dozens of these unknown animals.

So . . . what are they?

Some of these animals may be UMA's (Unidentified Mysterious Animals) that, due to lack of physical evidence, spoor, or DNA, resist scientific classification in the known biology. A second classification includes all of the legendary creatures such as the Cyclops, Pegasus, Harpies, and similar monsters from myth. Still others are relicts,[1] surviving examples of species believed to be extinct or so close to extinction that living examples are rarely found. The common horseshoe crab (which is actually more closely related to a spider or tick than a crab), is a surviving example of the family limulidae, and are descended from eurypterids (sea scorpions). They evolved during the Paleozoic Era (540–248 million years ago) and all of their close relatives have long since become extinct while they remain virtually unchanged. Another more exotic example is the coelacanth, a large fish believed to have become completely extinct over sixty million years ago; and yet one was netted in December of 1938 by Hendrik Goosen, the captain of the South African trawler *Nerine*. Since then living populations of them have been sighted (and caught) in the waters around Indonesia and South Africa.

But there is a third group of unknown animals, the cryptids, for whom we do not have a clear understanding of whether they exist or not. Like UMAs, cryptids (which means "unknown" or "hidden" animal) rarely leave physical evidence and any continued belief in their existence is based on eyewitness reports of varying credibility. There's even a science to locate and classify them: cryptozoology, a term coined by Bernard Heuvelmans (1916–2001)[2] for his 1955 book, *On the Track of Unknown Animals*. Heuvelmans was one of many scientists, explorers, hunters, and others who felt a compulsion to know the truth about the things people have reported seeing in forests, in lakes, on mountains, and in their own backyards.

---

1. Relict refers to biological artifacts; relic refers to human artifacts or remains.

2. Originally published 1955, republished in English by Kegan Paul, 1995.

Andy Jones, *Dragon Alley*

"I tend to take a shred of an idea from something I have read or seen in a film, and run with it. More often than not the inspiration has been some old tale rather than a new monster myth. The old ones are the best, as they say. Like dragons—they are elegant, majestic, vicious, solitary, beautiful, ugly, everything!"

Andy Jones is a freelance fantasy/horror/sci-fi artist living in North Wales. He has done artwork for several books, magazines, and independent films.

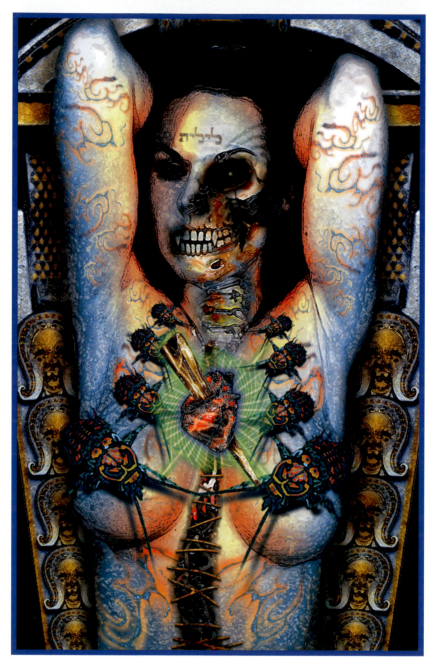

Bill Chancellor, *The Mara*

"I take beautiful women and transform them into frightening creatures. Why I do this . . . I'm not entirely sure. Some deep part of me is struggling to make a statement about the nature of beauty versus ugliness in the world, and how often they are aspects of the same thing."

Bill Chancellor has done art and design work for Warner Brothers, Disney, Hanna-Barbera, the Superman/Batman licenses, and many others. His art has also appeared in *Vampire Universe* and *The Cryptopedia*.

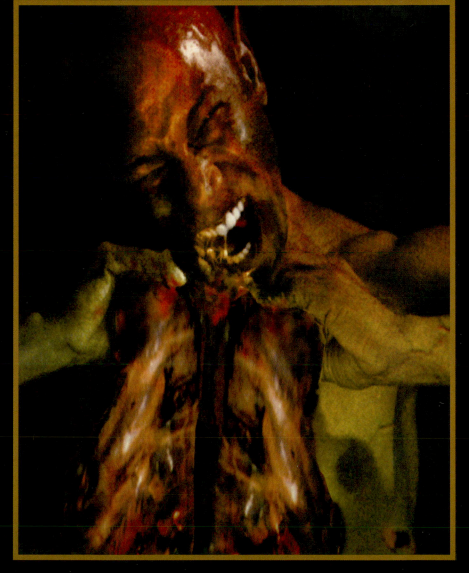

Brom, *Foul Things*

"My novel *The Plucker* (Abrams Books, 2005) was inspired by the classic childhood fears of boogies beneath the bed. I still, to this day, make sure my feet do not get to close to the under-bed."

Brom is an internationally renowned artist and author of the illustrated novel; he has done art for Michael Moorcock, Terry Brooks, R. A. Salvatore, TSR, White Wolf, DC, Dark Horse, World of Warcraft, Tim Burton's *Sleepy Hollow, Galaxy Quest, Ghosts of Mars, Scooby-Doo,* and *Van Helsing.*

Caniglia, *Flesh Eater*

"For me, folklore has always been a combination of two elements, mythical and religious stories, which have both been handed down for centuries and altered to fit personal and cultural agendas. There are moral and deeply psychological meanings in the subtext of all stories and paintings depicting folklore. Folklore seems simple, but for those willing to dig deeper, there are layers and ideas below the surface that can provide great insights and real warnings."

Caniglia is a successful contemporary figurative painter and illustrator. His work is in private collections and museums around the world.

Hervé Scott Flament, *Realms of Faerie*

"For *After the Hunt* I wanted to create a menacing and bloody atmosphere presaging something dark and undefined in uncontrollable and slow gestation . . . the death of the great goddess Nature."

Hervé Scott Flament is an artist of France's renowned *fantastique* movement. His work has appeared in galleries, books, and magazines.

Jason Beam, *Red Riding Hood*

"There are a few interpretations of the tale of Red Riding Hood, and all the ones I have read seem to regard a woman's sexuality—with references to casting off the red cloak as a sign of womanhood, to the sexual predator symbolism of the wolf, and so forth. I decided that in my 'grown-up' version of Red Riding Hood, it seemed much more natural to place her (model Christy Hemming) in a position of control rather than venerability. And Kevin Roberts' photography really gave her an air of sensual dominance. Sure, it's not a traditional interpretation of the story, but half of the fun is spinning your own take on it."

Jason Beam is a digital artist whose work has appeared in galleries worldwide and on a variety of movie posters, DVD packaging, and book covers.

Mike Bohatch, *Harpy*

"I've always enjoyed monster lore. We've seen it all countless times, but it still manages to deliver. While many of my pieces tend to distort images of myth and legend, folklore is a root for building a visual relationship with the viewers."

Mike Bohatch is a professional artist whose work has appeared in numerous publications and CD packages worldwide, and just about every horror medium in the genre.

Ric Frane,
Dark Seduction

"I love all the classic Universal horror movies. And I've always loved Hammer Films, particularly *Horror of Dracula.* I still try to imagine an audience seeing the blood-covered face of Dracula hissing in color for the first time. Vampires have always been a favorite of mine. Even when I was little, I used to draw Dracula. Now this was before the whole big vampire thing started. But now I paint mostly female vampires."

Ric Frane is a professional artist and illustrator known world-wide for his erotic pinups, many of which are horror themed.

Cryptozoology refers to the scientific search for unknown and nonsupernatural animals believed or purported to exist but which have not yet been included in the official fossil record of known creatures. Generally cryptozoologists search for the more sensational megafauna[3] cases, such as Bigfoot, rather than new species of beetles or flies. As a result, their work is often dismissed by more conventional biologists. Mainstream scientists dismiss cryptozoology with the same thoughtless disdain with which they pooh-pooh parapsychology and the hunt for UFOs. And just between us, blind disbelief is not supposed to be a part of the empirical process. Maybe those folks don't want to believe, or are just so stubborn that they need a carcass or measurable data before they can accept even the possibility of reality. Good thing Columbus didn't share that view—or Archimedes, Galileo, or other more open-minded thinkers.

Despite the criticism, the cryptozoologists persist, however, and in recent years their work has received some validation and support from the general public and from the media. Documentaries on the hunt for cryptids have become a staple of cable TV, ranging from the Sci-Fi Channel to the Discovery and National Geographic networks.

The search for unknown megafauna has also received some credibility sabotage from within. It turns out Roger Patterson and Robert Gimlin actually fudged the legendary Bigfoot film footage in 1967; and Christian Spurling's world-shaking 1934 photo of the Loch Ness monster was similarly faked. That kind of sensationalism (or, if you're in a tolerant mood you could call it "prankishness") does real harm to the progress of serious research. Even so, there are plenty of scientists and researchers out there in the field using sound scientific methods to prove—and in many cases disprove—the existence of cryptids.

Consider how few of the world's many animals were known to science even a century ago, and how many new species are discov-

3. "Large animal," the term in biology used to describe any animal weighing more than 40 kg.

ered every year. It puts a lot of egg on the faces of those who mock cryptozoology out of hand. Consider that two hundred years ago the first explorers to claim to have encountered a webfooted, egg-laying aquatic mammal with a duckbill and a poisonous sting were not believed. And yet the duck-billed platypus exists. As do the giant squid, mountain gorilla, and the okapi—all of which were considered myths for years. In May of 2005 a new species of long-tailed tree monkey (highland mangabey) was discovered in Tanzania, East Africa. The following February a section of previously unexplored Indonesian forest was penetrated to reveal entirely new species of butterflies, frogs, giant rhododendron, and a type of honeyeater bird that was previously unknown to science. In March 2006, National Geographic News broke the story of a new shark species (dubbed *Mustelus hacat*) discovered in Mexico's Gulf of California. In June of that year a team from Hebrew University in Jerusalem excavated a cave and discovered six previously unrecorded species of animal: four seawater and freshwater crustaceans and four terrestrial species of invertebrates. And the real jackpot was the discovery by an international team of scientists of hundreds of rare and previously unknown and ultrarare plants and animals in the mountain rain forests of New Guinea. The scientists discovered new species of birds, four new species of butterflies, egg-laying spiny anteaters, tree kangaroos, twenty new species of frogs, and a number of plants, including giant flowers.

We may have mapped the human genome, but we're nowhere near through with our inventory of what walks, crawls, slithers, hops, swims, flies, or grows in this big old world of ours.

Given the frequent discovery of new species, it's a marvel that people can still be so closed minded about the possibility of other new species.

One of the frequently used arguments against the possible existence of a creature such as Bigfoot is that there has been no physical evidence recovered. Granted, we don't have a forensic workup on the big hairy guy, but consider how much evidence we have on the neanderthal. For a species that existed for hundreds of thousands of years, there are remarkably few skeletal remains, and no complete skeletons. Turns out that scientists have just sorted out the fact that neanderthals were cannibalistic and very likely ate their own dead. That's not exceptionally rare in animal species, and there are cultures that still like to munch on a relative or rival.

Given all of this, why is it so difficult to accept the possibility of even stranger creatures out there? Who knows what ancient species somehow dodged the evolutionary bullet or which unknown animals are just waiting to be discovered?

In this section we'll meet several kinds of cryptids, divided into two groups: those on land (including flying cryptids) and those found in lakes and oceans.

Fear in Film

"The mutant characters in Alexandre Aja's *The Hills Have Eyes* (2006) speak to a folkloric fear of nature's monsters (Celtic faerie tales, Native American myths, etc.). My character, Goggle, was a spiritual creature that lived closer to the earth than his family members. My whole backstory dealt with his connection to the earth and its mysteries.

"Film is a much more visceral art form than novels or plays. Film can affect an audience on a molecular level. It becomes part of the audience. Literally. A scare in a movie theater is far more effective because (a) it's larger than life (literally) and (b) the visual is much more dependent on an audience completely giving themselves over to the experience. Film is far more emotionally manipulative. And fear is an emotional reaction. Which is why films that don't work feel so offensive to fans. And a good one will haunt them forever. They become real memories. A part of the viewer. No other art form has this effect."

—Ezra Buzzington is an actor with over thirty films to his credit including *Fight Club* (1999), *Ghost World* (2001), and *The Prestige* (2007).

Achiyalatopa by Geff Bartrand

"As an artist I have a lot of freedom with folkloric monsters: I can change
the mythology behind them to come up with some new kind of twist or give
them a new look or combine them to become even more powerful
and horrific. The possibilities are endless as long as you keep pushing the
envelope of your creativity."—Geff Bartrand regularly illustrates stories
for *Black Ink* horror magazine.

CRYPTIDS AROUND THE WORLD

Achiyalatopa: The Zuñi Indians of Western Nevada have legends of
a gigantic bird-monster with feathers made from sharpened spikes
of flint. Though immensely powerful and massive (its body weight
is necessary to counterbalance the stone knives that make up its

quills), the Achiyalatopa is not an evil predator. Quite the reverse, in fact, as the Achiyalatopa taught many secret and holy skills to the Zuñi. Even today, archeologists frequently find Zuñi altars that bear carvings of this ancient creature.

Adule: This large canine cryptid was frequently reported in North Africa over the last couple hundred years and was reported to have had supernatural powers, including shape-shifting abilities. However, it's since been debunked and the sightings are now believed to have been poor eyewitness reports of wild canines.

Ahool: This giant, batlike cryptid from the rainforests of Java gets its name from its distinctive cry, "AhhhOOOoool!" Eyewitness reports claim that the Ahool has a simian head, a strong body covered in gray fur, clawed hands, and a ten-foot wingspan. Based on pure description it's likely that the Ahool is actually the more common wood-owl of that region. Uncertain lighting in the sun-dappled (or moonlit) forest can play a lot of tricks on even the most skeptical observer.

Almas: The Almas are another of the world's many as yet unclassified species of hominids.[4] For five hundred years they have been spotted in the wastelands of Siberia, the Caucasus and Pamir Mountains of central Asia, and the Altai Mountains of southern Mongolia. Unlike either the shorter hominids such as Ebu Gogo or towering wild men like the Yeti, the Almas are approximately the same height and general build as regular humans, though with longer arms and, like their cousins of both statures, covered with coarse reddish-gray hair. They are not aggressive and generally disregard humans, and when approached will melt away into the forests or snowy wastes. For additional research on this elusive creature, we recommend *Still Living?: Yeti, Sasquatch and the Neanderthal Enigma* by Myra Shackley (W. W. Norton, 1983).

Alom-bag-winno-sis: Among the Abenaki Indians of New England there is a legend of a water monster that delights in upsetting boats

4. Hominids are manlike creatures. A thorough discussion of these creatures can be found in *Vampire Universe* by Jonathan Maberry (Citadel Press, 2006) and *Forbidden Archaeology: The Hidden History of the Human Race* by Michael A. Cremo and Richard L. Thompson (Bhaktivedanta, 1996).

and drowning people. The Alom-bag-winno-sis glides along beneath the water, sometimes in the form of a sea snake, sometimes in the form of a dwarfish human, and then surges up beneath the canoe of a fisherman or river traveler and overturns the canoe. The Alom-bag-winno-sis often chooses spots where the water is already turbulent, hoping that the rapids and the surprise dunking will be enough to cause pain, injury, or drowning.

Altamaha-ha: Though the South Atlantic does not have quite as many monsters as the South Pacific, there are still quite a few cryptids plying those waters, including the Altamaha-ha, which is seen most often around the scattered islands of South Georgia and the South Sandwich Islands. These islands are territories of the United Kingdom, but the waters are ruled by a thirty-foot-long sea monster that has a serrated ridge running along its back, rows of powerful dorsal fins, and a tapered mouth like that of an alligator packed with rows of conical teeth. Despite this fierce armament, the Altamaha-ha appears to either be placid in nature or timid and tends to shy away from contact with humans.

Aniukha: Deep in the icy wastes and frozen forests of Siberia, there is a legend of a small but deadly predator called the Aniukha. Perhaps the most rare and least documented of Europe's many cryptids, the Aniukha nonetheless appears in occasional folktales, especially among exiled Jews sent to Siberia during and after the era of Joseph Stalin (1879–1953).

This creature has been variously described as being as small as a praying mantis or as large as a squirrel. It runs on all fours like a woodland mammal, but can also stand erect and leap great distances, much like a cat. The Aniukha has a pale body covered in scales with patches of sparse gray or dark brown fur. Its face is like that of an emaciated cat, with huge dark eyes, ears that rise to tufted points, and a short snout filled with very long hollow teeth.

Aremata-Popoa and **Aremata-Rorua:** Polynesian cultures depended on water traffic. Boats of all kinds would ply the waters between the thousands of islands in the South Pacific, engaging in trade, exploration, and occasionally a bit of warfare. For the most part the seas were the allies of these ancient peoples, but within the seas there were evil forces as well as good. Two very destructive demons of the oceans were Aremata-Popoa, whose name means "short wave," and Aremata-Rorua, whose name means "long wave." As implied by their names, these water demons manifest themselves as aspects of the water through which the Polynesians sailed. Aremata-Rorua would send large, often massive, waves against the boats, swamping them, striking them amidships (pooping them), or overwhelming the fragile craft by knocking it on its beam ends. Aremata-Popoa is slyer and uses short, choppy waves to knock the boat back and forth, turning it at right angles to the waves so that it gets pooped or pounded to pieces. Wise sailors try and appease these water demons by singing prayers and spreading offerings of flowers on the water before setting out for any journey onto the deep blue sea.

Atakapa: The Atakapa (Attakapa, Attacapa) nation of Native Americans, including the subgroups Akokisas and Deadoses, occupied the coastal and bayou areas of southwestern Louisiana and southeastern Texas until the early 1800s. Atakapa means "eaters of men" in Choctaw, but the question has been raised whether the Atakapas were cannibals for subsistence or ritual. Some legends have it that the Atakapa were not merely cannibalistic humans but some species of supernatural predator, possibly a ghoul or a type of flesh-eating vampire. Unfortunately most of what is known of the Atakapa comes from European accounts, which were rarely accurate nor sympathetic to any Native American peoples of the time. One exception is Jack Claude Nezat's self-published book, *The Nezat And Allied Families 1630–2007* (Lulu 2007), and in this case the author is a descendant of the Atakapa people.

Atlas Bear: An extinct subspecies of the brown bear that was the only bear native to Africa and which is believed to have become extinct in the late nineteenth century. However, occasional sightings are reported, suggesting that the creature may not have been hunted to extinction.

Ba'a' (also **Chequah**): Most North Americans think that the Thunderbird is just a sporty muscle car, but for centuries the Comanche of Texas believed in a great bird, similar to an eagle but as large

Preserving Folklore

 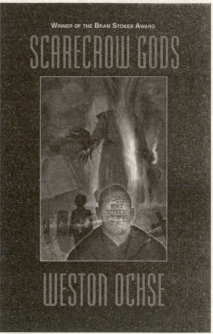

Weston Ochse,
photo by Enzo Giobbe

"In Southern Arizona we have a Folklore Preserve. Within it are the preserved tales of many of the peoples from the area, including Native Americans, miners, African American infantrymen (a.k.a. Buffalo Soldiers), and the many other odd and different groups that comprise the population of this Sonoran Desert area. Their tales have been captured for preservation and study, so that each succeeding generation can understand the texture of the people's lives and the beliefs that stitched the fabric of their existence. Without this preservation, the peoples of the area would soon become two-dimensional historical figures, lacking everything that made them. Within the Folklore Preserve is the official Arizona State Balladeer—Dolan Ellis. Through song and verse he passes along much of the folklore, keeping the words alive, so that visitors can experience and take with them the folklore of the peoples." —Weston Ochse is the Bram Stoker–winning author of *Scarecrow Gods* (Delirium, 2008).

and predatory as a pterodactyl. They called the creature Ba'a', and in their stories this creature brought thunder and rain and could conjure destructive hurricane-force winds with its wingbeats. Also known as Chequah by the Potawatomi of Michigan and other Native peoples, the thunderbird was believed to have a wingspan of about twenty feet and when standing on the ground towered to eight feet. Its talons could cleave rock and its beak could snap a canoe in half. The Ba'a' was said to be capable of snatching a man or elk off the ground and carrying this meal away with him. In many stories it is described as looking like an eagle but one of enormous size; in other stories it is a kind of hawk, an owl, and some have described it as being composed of fire and lightning.

The most recent sighting of this monstrous bird was by three

Ba'a by Jonathan Maberry

boys playing in their backyard back in July of 1977. The boys claimed that two gigantic birds swooped down on them, and one of the boys was grabbed by the shoulders and lifted off the ground. Though he was later dropped, he was traumatized for many years by the incident.

If the Ba'a' exists, cryptozoologists speculate that it may either be a surviving subspecies of pterodactyl or, more likely, a surviving teratorn (*Teratornis merriami*), a gigantic bird supposedly extinct since the Pleistocene age.

Barmanou (also **Barmanu**): The Barmanou (literally "big hairy one") is a hominid believed to live in the most remote mountain passes of Pakistan and Afghanistan. The creature is large, hairy, and bipedal and is most often spotted by shepherds. At the beginning of the twenty-first century serious expeditions were launched to try and locate the creature. One of the foremost researchers on the subject, Dr. Jordi Magraner, was assassinated in Pakistan in 2002, and since 9/11, all serious investigations into the creature have been shelved due to ongoing war in the region.

Beast of Bodmin Moor: Around the world there are a number of reports of great hunting cats causing trouble in places where they have no reason to be. These ferocious felines are lumped together in the lexicon of cryptozoology under the heading ABCs (Alien Big Cats)—and in this case "alien" refers not to extraterrestrial but from other places on earth, or perhaps other historic eras.

Such is the case with the Beast of Bodmin Moor, a mighty hunting predator believed to be the culprit in a variety of attacks, including the mass slaughter of livestock in rural areas. In 1995, less than a week after Britain's Ministry of Agriculture released a statement that there was "no verifiable evidence" of hunting cats loose in the U.K., a little boy found the skull of a young male leopard on the bank of a stream. And in the late 1990s, large, feline pawprints were examined around Bodmin Moor by officials from the Newquay Zoo.

Beast of Exmoor: A large hunting cat frequently reported in Exmoor, Devon, and Somerset in the United Kingdom. In 1983, Eric Ley, a farmer in South Molton, claimed that the beast had slaughtered over one hundred of his sheep in just three months—a tally that suggests that the beast hunts for pleasure, since it could not possibly have consumed that many sheep in that time. The running theory is that the Beast was a black leopard or cougar released into the countryside following the passing of a law forbidding owning of predatory animals (except for zoos). If so, then the animal is likely to have died decades ago—since cats of that type generally live between twelve and fifteen years. This case is one of a very few of the British big cat stories to yield actual physical evidence: puma hairs were recovered and analyzed by police labs.

Beast of Riber: Another of Britain's mysterious big cat cryptids, this one believed to be hunting livestock in the vicinity of Riber in Derbyshire. The animal was sighted in 2001, and the mauled body of a lamb was found surrounded by unusual animal pawprints. The pawprints measured four inches across, six inches long, and one and a half inches deep. That's no house cat.

Behemoth: The Behemoth is a monster from Biblical legend[5] and was supposed to be so huge that it could swallow, in one gulp, all the waters that flow from the River Jordan in a whole year. The Behemoth has incalculable strength and can shake the whole world when it moves.

Bergman's Bear: In Kamatchka Peninsula in Russia there have long been legends of a gigantic bear called the God Bear, and the tales were often so outlandish that they have become part of folklore. Then, in 1920 Sten Bergmen, a zoologist from Sweden, discovered a pelt from a bear as of then unknown to science. Unlike the normal bears of that region, this specimen had short hair.

Bessie (also **South Bay Bessie**): A lake snakelike cryptid of approximately thirty-five to fifty-five feet in length that has been spotted off and on since 1817 in and around Lake Erie, Pennsylvania. Unlike many of her cousins around the world, sightings of Bessie have increased significantly in recent years, particularly over the last three decades, and in 1992 three people were killed when Bessie allegedly attacked their sailboat.

5. Job 40:15–24.

Big Bird: In a weird example of life imitating art, when a gigantic bird was spotted in the Rio Grande Valley it was given the nickname of Big Bird—after the daffy character from *Sesame Street.* Unlike the child-friendly yellow bird of TV, the Big Bird of the Rio Grande looks much like a giant bat, standing five feet tall, with great leathery wings and a face like a night ape. Aside from a few scattered sightings, this particular unidentified flying object has managed to stay off the radar of cryptozoologists.

Bishop-Fish: Sea monsters come in all sizes, from tiny water sprites to leviathan, and their appearance can vary from beautiful mermaids to monsters so hideous that the very sight of them is lethal. Some sea monsters are not so much overtly threatening as simply very strange, as in the case of the Bishop-Fish. Also known as a "Sea-Bishop," this creature bears a strange resemblance to a mitered cleric with a shaved head, reminiscent of a Catholic monk, a fishlike body, and a draping of scales that—from a distance— appears to be a cloak, like a cardinal or bishop might wear. Over the centuries a couple of these creatures have been captured, and one was reputedly brought before the King of Poland, who desired to keep it as a pet. However, some bishops in the King's court saw the creature and when it noticed them it gestured to them in a way that suggested an intelligent being pleading for its life. When the bishops appealed to the King for its release, the creature made the sign of the cross, an action later repeated as it was released back into the sea.

Black Tiger: For centuries there have been legends in India of a great black tiger, but zoologists dismissed them as unproven and probably the invention of a romantic writer. Then in October 1992 the hide of a pseudo-melanistic[6] tiger was obtained from a hunter in South Delhi and, when measured, was eight and a half feet long. Just where this hunter (who was also a smuggler and therefore not particularly forthcoming) bagged this specimen is uncertain, but it

6. Melanism is a genetic condition resulting in increased amount of black or nearly black pigmentation on skin, hair, or feathers. Pseudo-melanism in tigers is a defect in their natural marking in which their stripes are darker and broader so that they partially or totally obscure the yellow body hairs.

at least provides proof that the black tiger is not just a product of literary whimsy. The hide of this great brute is on display at the National Museum of Natural History in New Delhi.

Blobs (also **Globster**): Blobs are the nickname given to any of the several masses of unknown tissue washed up on beaches around the world, and particularly in Bermuda, New Zealand, and Tasmania. Scientists often refer to any as-yet-unknown beached carcass as a Globster; but the Blobs are a subgroup because of their more unusual nature, and because they have been much more difficult to ultimately classify. These Blobs can range in size from as small as eight feet across to as big as thirty feet; they lack skeletons, and they have very tough and stringy flesh. Some Blobs have a thin coating of hair, and many are roughly cylindrical in shape.

These rare forms of Blobs have become moderately famous in the world of cryptozoology. One such creature, known as Bermuda Blob, was discovered in 1988 by Teddy Tucker. When Tucker attempted to cut the seemingly gelatinous flesh, he said it was like "trying to cut a car tire." This Blob also had five stumped appendages that might have been limbs or perhaps foreshortened tentacles. The Tasmanian Globster, discovered by Ben Fenton, Jack Boote, and Ray Anthony near the Interview River in western Tasmania in 1960, was twenty feet long,[7] eighteen feet wide, and appeared to have a slitlike mouth. Sadly, neither creature lingered long enough for adequate samples to be taken for lab analysis. They either decomposed or were washed away by tidal waters.

Blue Tiger (also **Maltese Tiger**): Since 1910 there have been a number of sightings throughout the Fujian Province of China of a great hunting cat whose pelt was a striking Maltese blue in color. American Methodist missionary Harry R. Caldwell saw one and initially thought he was seeing a man wearing unusual blue garments, but then realized that it was indeed an animal. He attempted to shoot the creature, wanting to preserve its hide for scientific posterity, but there were a couple of children playing nearby and he couldn't risk their safety, so he withheld his shot.

7. From an account in *The Mercury* (Hobart), March 9, 1962.

Boobrie: In Scotland there are legends of a strange birdlike creature called the Boobrie—a beast with black wings, claws like human hands, black eyes that have a piercing stare capable of driving a man insane, and a large bill as long as a sword.

The Boobrie is not a fishing bird, but instead prefers a diet of land animals, and when hungry enough will attack a boat transporting livestock. Legends tell of them tearing through wooden rails and ripping apart nets and then flapping off into the night with a full-grown hog skewered on its beak. Some tales also tell of the Boobrie tearing apart a sailor or fisherman who tried to stop it from stealing the livestock.

Brosne: A sixteen-to-twenty-foot-long lizardlike lake monster with luminous skin living in Lake Brosno frequently reported by residents of Benyok (a few hundred miles from Moscow, Russia). The Brosnie has been reported off and on for over 150 years, but only one photo of Brosnie has been published, and the picture is so badly blurred that it is nearly useless as evidence. And, yes, it's annoying that so many photos of these cryptids are blurry.

Bunyip: The Bunyip is a creature of Aboriginal myth with some of the qualities of a hellhound and is often described as being as big as a moderate-sized calf. It lives in ponds and other spots where the waters are calm. For the most part it leaves people alone, but if its home or its territory is disturbed, the Bunyip can turn quite spiteful and savage.

The name "Bunyip" comes from the Aboriginal word for "spirit," and the Bunyip is an immortal and supernatural creature. The creature appears in the Aboriginal dreamtime stories and has been described in a variety of different ways: from a feathered creature not unlike an otter to a beast with flippers and walrus tusks.

Buru: The Buru is a cryptid infrequently spotted in the valleys between the Sub-Himalayas in India that sounds remarkably like a sauropod. According to the Apa Tanis, the people of that region, the Buru was a lizard that walked on two legs, had vestigial forelegs,[8] a large tail that acted both as support when standing and

8. In some reports its forelegs are small but quite developed, like those of a mole.

a counterbalance when running, and had a large head with a big mouth filled with rows of sharp teeth. Its back was covered with shingled rows of armor plating, and its hide was a mottled blue-black in color except for its stomach, which was pale.

Caddy (also the **Sea Hag**): A giant sea creature spotted in 1920 in the waters of Cadboro Bay, near Vancouver Island, B.C., and seen frequently since. Described as a large serpentine beast forty to fifty feet in length, with a ridged or knobbed spine and flippers shaped like those of a humpback whale, though not as large. When first spotted, the creature was called "the Sea Hag," a nod to the legends of the Old Hag known to appear in the dreams and folklore of many nations; but over the years the creature has come to be called "Caddy" and, like many lake monsters, is fondly regarded as a kind of local mascot. Caddy bears a striking resemblance to Ogopogo, a cryptid known to haunt nearby Lake Okanogan, and may be of the same species or even the same creature.

Canvey Island Monster: In August 1954 a man was walking along the beach of Canvey Island in the Thames when he spotted a large mass covered in seaweed. Under the weed was a creature that, at first look, seemed to be a sea creature, but further examination revealed that it had hind legs like those of a biped. Each leg ended in a reptilian foot shaped like a horse's hoof but with five toes and a concave arch. The creature was about thirty inches tall and had reddish-brown skin. Its head was soft, as if either it had no skull or its skull had softened through decomposition. It had protruding eyes, sharp little teeth, and slits on its throat that appeared to be gills. Despite the presence of legs, the creature had no arms or upper-torso fins.

Cartazonon: Folkloric unicorns are often a far cry from the symbols of beauty and innocence we see in Disney movies and fantasy novels. In India and parts of Northern Africa, for example, there is a subspecies of unicorn called the Cartazonon that is decidedly aggressive and will kill anyone who tries to capture it, and will even attack humans and animals for no apparent reason. The African variety is particularly aggressive toward lions, and legends tell of the Cartazonon attacking a whole pride of lions and slaughtering them. The Cartazonon has reddish-yellow hair and a long and flowing mane. Its horn is very long and as black and shiny as basalt. No one has ever managed to capture one of these creatures alive, and considering how vicious and powerful they are, few have even bothered to try.

Catoblepas: In Greek myth there are many hundreds of creatures ranging from totally benign to absolutely malevolent. Many creatures are neither and are only threats when provoked, as with the case of the Catoblepas. The creature was described as a bull-like monster with an oversized head, a scaly body over which grew a long mane, and bloodshot eyes that were perpetually cast down. Its name, in fact, translates as "that which looks downward."

Champ: Lake Champlain touches on parts of New York, Vermont, and Quebec and is the home to "Champ," one of the few lake monsters apparently caught on film.[9] That footage showed a creature with a thick body and a long tapering neck reminiscent of a plesiosaur. Since the plesiosaurs became extinct about sixty-five million years ago, the footage is a bit startling. The legend of Champ dates back to the Iroquois Indians who lived in that region, though in their tales the creature was a great horned monster. More recent sightings, however, do not describe horns of any kind. Reports of the monster started showing up in newspapers around 1873, when it was spotted by men laying railroad track near the town of Dresden in New York. The workers claim to have seen the head of an "enormous serpent" rise up from the water and look at them. The men, wisely, fled. In August of that same year a small tourist ship was reported to have struck the creature and nearly capsized. The reports in the paper following the collision claim that passengers saw the creature on the surface of the water thirty or so yards from the ship. Showman P. T. Barnum put up a $50,000 reward for the "hide of the great Champlain serpent to add to my mammoth World's Fair Show," but never had to pay out the reward.

Chupacabra: Throughout Latin America there have been countless reports of a strange creature—or race of creatures—that viciously

9. A famous photo of Champ that was taken on July 5, 1977, by Sandra Mansi.

attack livestock and drink their blood and other vital fluids. Because goats were among the first victims of this beast, the monster earned the nickname El Chupacabra, which translates as "sucker of goats." The Chupacabra is a bizarre being that has three or four powerful claws on each hand, a ruff of tall spines running from skull to tailbone, mottled skin, and a voracious appetite. The monster's face has been variously described as being like that of a kangaroo, a baboon, or a giant rat. In some reports the creature also has leathery wings, much like the Jersey Devil. There have been Chupacabra sightings and video evidence as recently as August of 2008, when a supposed Chupacabra was caught via the dashboard camera of a Texas lawman. However, this creature that reportedly "ran like no dog I've ever seen," according to the witnesses, ran

El Chupacabra by Kevin Bias

like "every dog we've ever seen" to the authors, so it's going to be a difficult call.

The earliest sightings of the Chupacabra were in Puerto Rico beginning in the early 1990s, but there are constant animal slaughters to this day associated with the Chupacabra. From 2000 to 2004 there have been nearly four thousand cases of unexplained animal mutilations in that small island territory. But the Chupacabra is not confined strictly to Puerto Rico. There have been sightings and mutilations all through Latin America. The official explanation in Puerto Rico is that packs of dogs are responsible for the attacks, or perhaps a panther or other big hunting cat illegally owned and released into the woods. As no traces of dogs or hunting cats have been found near the scenes of goat slaughters, this theory holds no more water than the dozens of other explanations floated by various groups. The Chupacabra sightings began shortly after a series of UFO sightings in the region (mostly over Mexico), and some fringe groups insist that aliens have—intentionally or accidentally—released an extraterrestrial predator animal that is now breeding and attacking terrestrial animals. This idea was explored briefly in an episode of the TV series, *The X-Files* (1993–2002). In UFO circles such creatures are referred to as Anomalous Biological Entities (ABEs).

Another theory is that crocodiles are behind it all, despite the fact that many of the killings are far inland and away from waterways. This idea carries a little weight because of the lurid tales of the "Vampire of Moca," the name given to an unknown "monster" attacking livestock back in 1975. As it turns out, the vampire in question was actually a few crocodiles that strayed out of the swamp. But even then, they weren't as far away from the water as many of the Chupacabra have been. It is an interesting coincidence that the Vampire of Moca events also followed a spate of UFO sightings.

Con Rit: In Vietnam and surrounding countries, there is a legend of a particularly frightening cryptid called the Con Rit, whose name translates as "centipede," which is unfortunately an accurate description. The Con Rit, however, is not the kind of insect you can crush under your heel. The creature was sighted repeatedly in

Conspiracy Folklore

 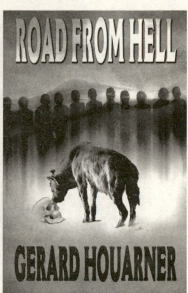

Gerard Houarner,
photo by Brian Addison

"Folklore is not limited to the supernatural world, but can be rooted in pseudoscientific psychic research and even popular interpretations of scientific and military research (experimental planes flying in and out of military bases, etc.). There's a set of beliefs born from 1950s postwar stress made real by nuclear weapons and the Cold War that have established themselves as modern folklore. The whole UFO and alien-abduction theme strikes me as part of the evolutionary line coming from the old fairyland and elves tradition. Conspiracies are huge, at least in postwar America, like Area 51 and black helicopters, Men in Black, Camp Hero at Montauk Point, and provide a rich source of monsters and boogeymen. Chris Carter documented the kind of folklore I'm talking about in the *X-Files*. As a writer I like to fish these kinds of waters for material because it gives me a very different perspective on the human condition and some pretty weird story material." —Gerard Houarner was married at a New Orleans voodoo temple and is the author of *Road From Hell*, as well as the anthology/collection *Dead Cat's Traveling Circus of Wonders and Miracle Medicine Show*.

Folklore for Filmmakers

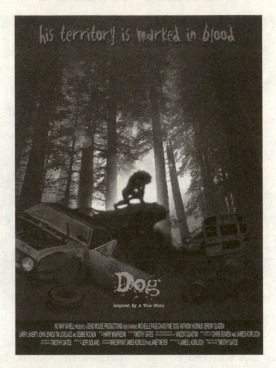

"The Abominable Snowman, Bigfoot, the Chupacabra—they're all such interesting and enduring figures. I guess that most of my scripts/films have a bit of folklore to them. The title character in the last movie I scripted, *Dog* (2008), has been compared to the werewolves of myth; and my latest, *Ritual Season* (2009) is steeped in Celtic fact and folklore. In the beginning, it was the simple story of a serial killer, but I eventually added a supernatural element, which completely changed the dynamics of the story. Folklore provides incredible richness for the storyteller." —James Korloch has been an actor and special makeup effects artist for more than twenty years. He wrote the screenplay for the werewolf film *Dog*.

1883, and Tran Van Con, a native of Along Bay, Vietnam, claims to have seen the corpse of a dead Con Rit washed up on the beach. He measured the carcass and recorded that it was three feet wide and a staggering sixty feet long.

Devil Bird (also **Ulama, Maha Bakamuna**): The Devil Bird of Sri Lanka and India is one of the rare cases of a cryptid being moved from the limbo of folklore and onto the solid ground of the verified fossil record. This creature has been frequently sighted in the deepest and most inaccessible jungles of the mountain regions of India.

Dobhar-chú (also **Dobarcu, Doyarchu**, and **Dhuragoo**): Dobhar-chú is the Gaelic name for a lake monster unlike Nessie or the standard saurian cryptids. The Dobhar-Chu earned its name ("water-hound") because it roughly resembles a dog, though it has a longer and sleeker body and teeth like an otter. From tooth to tail it measures about eight feet and is covered in thick white fur. The Dobhar-chú, however, is neither a playful otter nor man's best friend. This cryptid is a man-eater and there is quite a record of it attacking humans without provocation.

Ebu Gogo: In the mythology of the Flores people of Indonesia there is a longstanding series of tales of a race of diminutive humanoids known as the Ebu Gogo, who were reported to be only a few feet high. The name "Ebu Gogo" is rather chilling when translated from the Flores language. Ebu means "grandmother," but Gogo means "one who eats everything." This combines to "Grandmother Who Eats Everything," and refers to a creature of omnivorous tastes. The Ebu Gogo will eat plants, animals, fish, and, in a pinch, human flesh.

In the folklore of the region the Ebu Gogo were given many of the same qualities as elves—magical natures, prankish personalities, a strange language, and so on—and any question of their reality was routinely dismissed as hogwash (at worst) or popular myth (at best). However in one of those all-too-rare moments of science and superstition coming into agreement rather than colliding, scientists have begun to think that the Ebu Gogo are, in fact, real. When Professor Richard "Bert" Roberts of the University of Wollongong investigated reports of a race of diminutive people, he was quoted[10] as saying: "They are described as about a metre tall, with long hair, pot bellies, ears that slightly stick out, a slightly awkward gait, and longish arms and fingers—both confirmed by our further finds this year." Along with other scientists he searched for physical evidence and has, in fact, uncovered bits of hair and other artifacts in places where the Ebu Gogo are believed to have lived. Roberts does not, however, insist that the creatures still exist, though, like many of his colleagues, he is leaving that open to the findings of continued investigation.

El Dientudo: Throughout the rural areas of Argentina, especially in the dense forests surrounding Buenos Aires, there is the legend of a horrifying monster called El Dientudo, which translates as "The Big Teeth."

This aptly named creature is a flesh-eating and blood-drinking predator. It is vaguely manlike in appearance, covered completely in thick matted hair, stands seven or eight feet tall, and reeks like rotting flesh.

Emela-Ntouka: One of the more fascinating cryptids, this monster has been sighted in and around the Likouala swamp regions in the Republic of the Congo. Emela-Ntouka is the Lingala phrase for "killer of elephants," which eloquently describes the ferocity of this hulking, amphibious monster described as being as large as an elephant but with an armored tail more reminiscent of a Nile crocodile. It has a snout ending in a hooked beak and a single large horn sprouting from its forehead. Its huge footprints indicate sharp, clawed toes. Despite its fearsome appearance, the Emela-Ntouka is said to be an herbivore, but when confronted it shows a far more aggressive side. There are eyewitnesses who claim to have seen the Emela-Ntouka disembowel a bull elephant and trample a lion to death.

Ennedi Tiger (also **Tigre de Montagne**): This critter is a sabertooth cat reported in the lands east of Chad in Africa. Residents and travelers in the region have reported two distinctly different types: land

10. From a news story reported in the Telegraph.co.uk on October 28, 2004.

On the Odd Disappearance of King Kong

King Kong by Ken Meyer, Jr.

"I was commissioned to do a King Kong piece. I wanted to experiment with a technique based on the work of the great illustrator C. F. Payne.[11] Basically, you use many media you wouldn't normally use together—watercolor and oil, for example. But the layers are separated by a spray fix. Each layer is supposed to be as finished as you can get it, so it sounds very time consuming, but I think of each layer as a new underpainting, adding new depths to the painting with each layer. It worked well with this piece, as I got it done on time and the client liked it fine. The bad part of the story is, at the next San Diego ComiCon, it was stolen. So, in a way Kong has become one of those 'missing monsters' of our new folklore."

—Ken Meyer Jr. has done artwork for McGraw-Hill, Sony, *Computer Edge* magazine, Marvel Comics, Image Comics, Caliber Comics, Wizards of the Coast Games, White Wolf Games, *Penthouse* magazine, RAINN organization, Tori Amos, American Cancer Society, Bell Helmets, and more.

---

cats who hunt in the mountains (called Hadjel, Gassingram, or Vossoko), and those who live in and around lakes (called Mourou

11. Chris Fox "C. F." Payne is an American illustrator and caricaturist whose work has appeared in *Time*, *Sports Illustrated*, *Rolling Stone*, *Mad*, *Esquire*, and *National Geographic*.

N'gou, Mamaimé, or Dilali). Sabertooth cat species (such as the Megantereon and Afrosmilus) are believed to have become extinct 500,000 years ago. However, sightings of the Ennedi Tiger persist.

Ferla Mohr (also **Brenin Llwyd**, **Big Gray Man**, **Grey King**): A creature resembling King Kong is not the sort of thing you'd expect to find loitering around the mountain passes of the Scottish Highlands or the more remote forests of Wales, yet legends of a twenty-foot-tall gray-furred gorilla have persisted for centuries. Known as Ferla Mohr in Scotland, Brenin Llywd in Wales, and a number of other names, the creature's nature varies from legend to legend from an overgrown hominid to a supernatural king of some elder faerie race.

Fouke Monster (also **Boggy Creek Monster**): The Fouke Monster of the Texarkana region of Arkansas has often been described as Bigfoot's nasty cousin, and that's not that far from the truth. Unlike the shy and docile Bigfoot, the Fouke Monster is reputed to be vicious and predatory, and is anything but shy. In 1997 there were over forty sightings of the creature, and at least a couple of dozen a year since.

The creature has been spotted hundreds of times since the first sightings back in the late 1860s, and several times over the years it has chased residents. Luckily there are no deaths reliably tied to the monster.

Like many of the larger hominids, the Fouke Monster stands about seven to nine feet tall, is covered with coarse wiry hair, and has a roughly simian face. At one point a good-quality plaster cast had been made of the creature's footprint, but in the late seventies that useful piece of evidence was destroyed in a fire at the service station where it had been on display. Despite the frequent sightings, most cryptozoologists dismiss the Fouke Monster as an elaborate hoax. The residents of that region, however, beg to differ.

Garkain: The Aboriginal people of the Northern Territories of Australia have folktales about a variety of giant and smaller hominid races. Some of these creatures are considered to be leftovers from the days of the Neanderthal, and some of have a more supernatural origin. These creatures terrified the Aborigines in ages past. Legends tell of giants, pygmies, apemen (similar to Homo erectus, or the Java Man), and the bloodthirsty vampiric creatures called the Garkain. Garkains lived in remote areas, inhabiting caves and rock shelters on higher plateaus. They hunted in the swamps, hiding in the rushes and feeding on reptiles and insects.

Giglioli's Whale: This as-yet-unconfirmed species of whale was first reported by Enrico Hillyer Giglioli (1845–1909), an Italian anthropologist and zoologist who spotted one 1,200 miles off the coast of Chile in 1870. He was not able to take specimens, however, and did not have ready access to camera equipment. The creature swam alongside the ship for half an hour, which allowed Giglioli to record a great deal of information. Giglioli estimated the whale's length at sixty feet, with two large dorsal fins (each over six feet high), and long curved flippers. Of the known whales in the fossil record, only the Rorqual comes close, but that species does not share the same fin and flipper design. A similar type of whale was spotted off the coast of Scotland a year later. In the twentieth century—in 1983—French zoologist Jacques Maigret saw one of them in the waters between Corsica and the French mainland. Though these sparse sightings have not lead to a verifiable discovery, the whale has been provisionally named *Amphiptera pacifica.*

Goatman: There is something very peculiar about in the backwoods of the United States—a creature that is part man and part goat. Unfortunately, witness accounts seem to differ as to which part is which. Spotted from Washington, D.C., all the way to west Texas, the Goatman has been described by some witnesses as a great brute of a man with a huge black goat head set on his muscular shoulders; while others claim that the head and upper torso are that of a man but that he walks around on a gnarled pair of hairy goat legs. The former image fits some artistic representations of The Horned God, Goat of Mendes, Baphomet, or the God of the Witches (take your pick), and suggests an earthly manifestation of a satanic creature. Most often referred to as Baphomet, this image first came to public awareness during the persecution and trials of the Knights Templar, when the once-exalted knights had been brought down[12] with accusations of devil worship and paganistic rituals. The latter image brings to mind the satyrs of Greek myth who were companions to both Pan and Dionysus. In either case, cryptozoologists have long wondered what they are doing in America. Most witnesses claim that the creature was the size of an ordinary man, though a few more hysterical reports claim that the thing was gigantic, towering twelve to fifteen feet high.

Hibagon (also **Hinagon**): Japan has its own domestic version of Bigfoot, with sightings beginning in the early 1970s. Known as the Hibagon, this apelike hominid is of the shorter variety, barely topping five feet, with a face that is more human than simian (though not much). It has bulky shoulders and a slumped posture, but walks upright. Castings of Hibagon footprints have been taken and these are grossly out of proportion to its stature: the prints are six inches wide and ten inches long!

Ilimu: Among the Kikuyu tribe of Kenya, there is an enduring legend of a shape-shifting monster called the Ilimu. It is not a human being cursed to be a monster, like the European werewolf, but a demon that possesses animals and shape-shifts into the likeness of a man. This creature appears in one form or another in legends from many African nations, including Ghana and Uganda. In 1898, two lions in Uganda were suspected of being Ilimu, and were responsible for the deaths of more than 130 people involved in the building of a bridge across the river Tsavo. The lions hunted together using deceptive tactics and trickery uncommon to animals, and over the course of their two-month reign of terror everyone—even the Europeans supervising the construction—came to believe that there was something supernatural about them. Big-game hunters eventually brought the lions down, but only after the lions had foiled their traps time and again. The incident was made into a movie, *The Ghost and the Darkness* (1996), starring Michael Douglas and Val Kilmer.

---

12. This was part of Philip IV's plot to use the wealth of the Templars to rebuild his sagging economy.

The Jersey Devil by Kate Landis

Incanyamba (also **Howie**): In South Africa there is an ancient legend of a lake monster called the Incanyamba, and the descriptions suggest a beast startlingly similar to a plesiosaur—the group of aquatic dinosaurs that generally have long necks and flippers. The plesiosaurs were a very hardy group and their tenure on earth began at the beginning of the Jurassic Era and ended, as far as we know, during the Cretaceous, with the big K-T Extinction.[13]

13. More formally known as the Cretaceous-Tertiary Extinction Event, this was an extinction of species that occurred about 65.5 million years ago which most scientists believe was the result of a meteor striking the earth.

Jersey Devil: One of the most enduring of American legends, with thousands of sightings dating back more than two and a half centuries and more occurring every year. Stories of the Devil's origins vary dramatically, but there are two versions of the story that are told most often. In the first version, a woman called Mrs. Shrouds[14] of Leeds Point, New Jersey, had twelve children and was so frustrated by her hard life she swore that if God wouldn't help her provide for a dozen hungry kids, if she ever got pregnant again that child would be fathered by the Devil himself. That is, apparently, one of those things a person shouldn't say, because she certainly got pregnant again and shortly after she gave birth the child transformed into a misshapen monstrosity with goatlike legs, a human torso, bat wings, and an elongated snout variously described as similar to that of a wolf, horse, fox, or crocodile. When Mrs. Shrouds tried to suckle the infant, it spread its wings and escaped up the chimney.

In the second most common story, a young girl from Leeds Point supposedly fell in love with a British soldier during the Revolutionary War. Naturally the local townsfolk felt that she betrayed her country and laid a curse on her that any child that came from that union would be a devil. This, too, ended badly. Since the birth of the Jersey Devil, it has been spotted by politicians, dignitaries, forest rangers, police officers, and thousands of travelers. Even Joseph Bonaparte (brother of Napoleon) saw it while living in exile in America. In the nineteenth century, a naval officer, Commodore Stephen Decatur, who was engaged in artillery testing at the Hanover Iron Works in Hanover, New Jersey, fired at and hit it, but the creature flew away, apparently uninjured. The commodore claimed that the creature he saw was at least nine feet long from head to tail.

Kasai Rex: Another of Africa's many reptilian cryptids is the Kasai Rex, but unlike the more docile lake monsters, this beast is a bipedal predator built along the lines of a Tyrannosaur. The creature has a black hide streaked with red stripes and some witnesses claim to have seen it hunting and killing rhinos and hippos.

14. In some versions of the tale she is called Mother Leeds or Abigail Leeds.

Shape-Shifting Lemurs

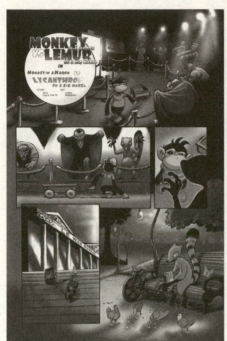

Monkey vs. Lemur by Ken Lillie-Paetz

"I think I try to throw some element of folklore into most of my writing (usually in the form of reference to artifacts or particular esoteric rituals). I have always been obsessed with folklores and for some reason lemurs, though unfortunately there isn't much lemur folklore. That is why the work I am proudest of is my five-page wordless comic-book story "Monkey in a Wagon vs. Lemur on a Big Wheel," for it allowed me to finally combine folklore and lemurs and introduce the dreaded Were-Lemur."
—Ken Lillie-Paetz is the author of the comic-book series *Open, Elsinore* and *Monkey in a Wagon vs. Lemur on a Big Wheel* (with cocreator and artist Chris Moreno).

Though there have been eyewitness reports and even news stories (in Rhodesia and elsewhere), cryptozoologists have tended to largely discount this as a hoax.

Killer Badger (the **Beast of Basra**): Though this sounds like a Monty Python skit, the killer badger is an enduring myth in the region around Basra in Iraq. Local legend has it that a yard-long carnivore with a gray and black pelt and a face like a lemur has boldly attacked both livestock and animals. The locals accused the occupying U.S. military of having released a strange mutant creature, and though you wouldn't think such a claim would even be acknowledged, the level of outrage was so high that UK military spokesman Major Mike Shearer had to issue an official statement: "We can categorically state that we have not released man-eating badgers into the area." He managed to keep a straight face, too. As it turns out, reflooding of marshland originally drained by Saddam Hussein drove various animals into Basra, including the Ratel, a particularly vicious animal also known as a Honey Badger. So . . . this is one of those cases where a cryptid just turns out to be a little-known animal. Even so . . . killer badgers?

Kingstie: Since 1817 fishermen on Lake Ontario have been reporting the presence of a thirty-to-forty-foot-long serpent, black or dark brown in color, with a fierce head and glaring eyes. One witness was so adamant that he swore to his account under oath and before a magistrate. Since many of the sightings have been near Kingston, Ontario, the creature has been dubbed "Kingstie." The most significant recent sighting, reported in 2001, was by two men diving the wreck of the *George A. Marsh*, a coal ship that sank in 1917. They said that the creature was gliding along the bottom near the ship, and at first they thought it was some kind of cable, but then it turned toward them, swam to within thirty feet, and then turned and swam away very fast. Because the serpent was between them and the ship, they were able to approximate its length and put it at twenty-five feet. They reported that it appeared to be curious but not aggressive.

Kongamato: Though the register of world cryptids includes plenty of lake and land monsters that appear (at least according to witnesses) to be holdovers from the age of the dinosaurs, there are only a few reports of flying dinosaurs. One of these rarities is the Kongamato, a probable pterosaur that has been variously described as a gigantic bat, a great vulture, or a creature closely resembling a pterodactyl. The Kongamato has been seen throughout the sub-Saharan region of Africa, where the Kaonde tribe of Zambia claim that it attacks humans. Its name even means "overwhelmer of boats."

In his 1923 book, *Witchbound Africa*,[15] author and adventurer Frank H. Melland conducted interviews with Kaonde natives and recorded their descriptions of the beast.

Kung-Lu: Whereas the vast Himalaya are home to the docile Yeti (see entry later in this chapter), the lower mountain passes are the hunting grounds of a similar race of giant hulking monsters, the Kung-Lu. Both are gigantic manlike creatures covered in fur, but the similarities end there. The name Kung-Lu means "great hulking thing." There are ancient tales of wild tribes of Kung-Lu sweeping down on villages and slaughtering everyone before drinking their victims' blood and eating their flesh. Also known as Dsu-The, Ggin-Sung, or Tok, the Kung Lu sometimes hunt solo, often stealing a human child for their meal.

Lake Van Monster: A monster found in Turkey's Van Lake, which stands as the most frequently sighted sea monster in the world, and also one of the most recent. First spotted in 1995, the creature was caught on film in 1997 by twenty-six-year-old local man, Unal Kozak. The video footage shows what is believed to be the creature's head, partly submerged, and a single piercing black eye glaring out of the water. The footage was shown on CNN and other news services and has become something of a classic for cryptozoologists. Since 1995 there have been well over one thousand sightings of this monster.

Leech Monsters of the Great Blue Hole: Belize, a favored diving spot in Central America, has a culture built around the sea. Aside from sportfishing, island tours, and diving, there is also active trad-

15. *In Witch-bound Africa: An Account of the Primitive Kaonde Tribe and Their Beliefs* by Frank H. Melland; J. B. Lippincott Publishers, 1923.

Sea Monster by Allen Koszowski

ing in folktales of monsters from the deep that prey on unwary swimmers and fishermen. Most of these tales center around an off-shore atoll called the Great Blue Hole, just off Lighthouse Reef. Seen from the air it looks just like a vast blue hole in the ocean floor that was formed about 15,000 years ago, during the last Ice Age, when glaciers from the north trapped so much water in their vast frozen expanses that the sea level in these areas was lowered by more than 350 feet. Over the centuries freshwater flowed through the limestone deposits, forming huge caverns, and the col-lapse of the roof of one of these formed the Great Blue Hole. The result is a creepy sinkhole full of dark blue shadows that is con-siderably deeper than the surrounding shallow waters.

Leviathan: Like Behemoth, the Leviathan is a gigantic fire-breathing monster from biblical legend[16] that was so vast and dreadful that its "teeth are terrible" and "out of its mouth go burn-ing lamps, and sparks of fire leap out." Leviathan has impervious armor and even if peppered by arrows it would not so much as twitch to acknowledge it. Some Bible scholars assert that Behe-

16. Job 41:1–34.

The Hunt for Nessie

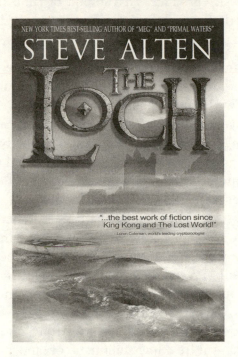

NEW YORK TIMES BEST-SELLING AUTHOR OF "MEG" AND "PRIMAL WATERS"

STEVE ALTEN

THE LOCH

"...the best work of fiction since King Kong and The Lost World!"
— Loren Coleman, world's leading cryptozoologist

Two weeks before bestselling author Steve Alten was supposed to turn the manuscript for *The Loch* in to his publisher, he was contacted by Bill McDonald, a forensics investigator who had been studying Loch Ness since 1993. McDonald needed to get to Loch Ness immediately; his local contacts were urging him to come quickly because there had been a number of rare land sightings (that December). A deal was struck for the exclusive, and McDonald returned with shocking new evidence, including "slide tracks" of an animal that he estimated to be fifty to sixty feet long! Then, a few months later, Bill was tracked down by two American students who had gone to the UK on spring break in March. They claimed they had hired a local to take them around by boat. On a shoreline they spotted a dead deer that had been bitten in half and mauled. As if that wasn't enough, lodged in its exposed rib cage was the remains of a shed tooth that must have come loose during the attack! Everything's on video. You can see it at www.SteveAlten.com.

moth is male and Leviathan is female, but God ordained that they were not able to reproduce. At the end of time the Leviathan is destined to battle Behemoth to the death, and the loser's flesh will be fed to the righteous.

Loch Ness Monster (also **Nessie**, **Niseag**): Nessie, the Loch Ness Monster of Scotland, is the world's most famous lake monster. It is also the one with the longest track record of sightings, with glimpses of Niseag (Nessie's Celtic name) going back as far as 565 C.E., when Saint Columba saw the creature shortly after attending a funeral for a man purported to have been killed by it. The most famous encounter, though, took place in 1933, when a couple, Mr. and Mrs. Spicer, saw the creature cross the road right in front of them. The creature had an animal carcass clutched in its jaws and paused to look at them before taking its meal and slipping back into the chilly waters of the loch. There have been hundreds of sightings as well as very well-organized scientific investigations, but despite some rather questionable photos and some curious sonar readings, no hard evidence has yet been found. Even so, belief in the existence of Nessie is very strong, and not just among cryptozoologists—quite a few scientists, oceanographers, and biologists have stepped up to defend the possibility that the monster could really be there.

Lofa: Many of the blood drinking or flesh-eating monsters of North America, especially those whose sightings continue into modern day, seem to be variations of what most people would refer to as Bigfoot. Among the Chickasaw of Oklahoma (the reservation to which they were transplanted), and their ancestors in what is now Mississippi, there is a story of a race of intelligent beast men called the Lofa.

Loveland Frog (also **Loveland Lizard**): Since 1955 there have been a number of sightings of strange batrachian[17] cryptids in and around the back roads of Loveland, Ohio. In the initial sightings the creatures were described as being about as big as a medium-sized dog,

17. Any of the vertebrate amphibians without tails, such as frogs and toads.

and were able to stand erect on their hind legs. At full height they stood about four feet high, and probably weighed about sixty pounds. The beasts appear to be amphibious, with froglike faces and glistening, leathery skin. It's doubtful that kissing this frog will turn it into a fairy-tale prince.

MacFarlane's Bear: This is very likely a little-known and now-extinct species of bear once found in the Northwest Territories of Canada. According to naturalist Robert MacFarlane, who spotted one of the creatures in 1864, the bear was enormous and covered with a thick yellow fur. The body of one of the creatures was recovered in 1918 by Dr. Clinton Hart Merriam, who classified it as a new species and genus: *vetularctos inopinatus*. However there is some strong scientific speculation that these creatures may have been a genetic cross-breed of polar and grizzly bears.

Mahambo: The Congo has seen a fair amount of cryptid action, both historically and recently, and one of the most enduring legends is of a gigantic crocodile called the Mahambo. Reported to be at least fifty feet from tooth to tail, the Mahambo favors the more remote swamps and is particularly foul-tempered and aggressive. There are accounts of it lunging up from river bottoms to swallow an entire canoe or raft. No physical evidence has ever been collected, though there are numerous sketches from eyewitnesses. Skeptics insist that the Mahambo is nothing more than a Nile crocodile that has grown larger through the telling of the tale. The Congolese beg to differ. Cryptozoologists argue that the Mahambo may be a surviving member of a line of giant prehistoric crocodiles called the Sarchosuchus Imperator, which weighed a massive eight tons.

Malawi Terror Beast: Some of the world's cryptids are truly "unknown," and that certainly applies to a creature that killed three people and seriously injured sixteen others in the Dowa district of Malawi, a small African nation. These were savage attacks in which the monster crushed the skulls of the victims and then devoured their genitals and intestines. The survivors of the attacks lost limbs, ears, eyes, and other body parts. Though a rabid hyena was shot and killed by a posse, not everyone accepts that animal as the culprit.

Mamlambo: You have to appreciate any monster whose name means "brain sucker," and the accounts of this monster from the residents in the region of Bisho in South Africa were not simply dismissed by the government. After nine people were killed in the area surrounding the Mzintlava River Bridge, Ezra Sigwela, the Minister of Agriculture for the Eastern Cape region, made a plea to the South African Eastern Cape legislature to help track down this monster. Sigwela ordered conservation officers to hunt the monster down. However, the hunters were unable to locate the creature.

Mapinguari: Accounts of the hairy Brazilian cryptid known as the Mapinguari tend to vary more often than they agree. In some cases the creature is a kind of giant sloth, docile in nature, which lives high in the branches of trees. In other reports the creature walks upright like a man. In all cases, however, the creature is described as being covered in dense, long hair (sometimes brown, often reddish). In the more recent sightings it has a horselike snout and large, square teeth. Most accounts state that it exudes a foul body odor. In both cases the Mapinguari is said to utter a strange, loud call that is eerily human in pitch and tone. Many cryptozoologists have speculated that the Mapinguari is probably a holdover from the Megatherium, or giant ground sloth, a species believed to have become extinct more than eight thousand years ago. In the dense remoteness of the rainforest, though, anything is possible.

Megalania Prisca (also **Mungoongalli**): A saurian cryptid spotted occasionally in Australia and New Guinea that resembles a modern Komodo dragon, but which is considerably larger. Weighing in around half a ton and stretching twenty-five to thirty feet from snout to tail, the Megalania Prisca is a significant predator. Variously reported for decades, it was first reliably sighted by two men, a farmer and a scientist named Frank Gordon. Gordon, a herpetologist, claimed that the creature he saw was at least thirty feet long, possibly longer, and that it ran off into the woods. Cryptozo-

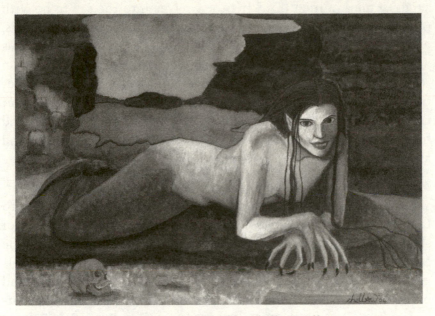

Levanya the Mermaid by Shelley Walker

"In old stories mermaids are dark, predatory creatures, and the folklore surrounding them talks of people being taken or drowned, so I took that and ran with it and came up with Levanya—a cross between a mermaid and a vampire."
—Shelley Walker is a professional fantasy and Gothic fantasy artist.

ologists have labeled the creature a Megalania, believing it to be a surviving example of the documented Megalania prisca, a kind of giant goanna that lived in what is now Australia between 1,600,000 to 40,000 years ago, during the Pleistocene Age.

Mermaid: Mermaids appear in the folklore of every seafaring nation and very often tales of them are strikingly similar. Generally mermaids are described as intensely beautiful women from the waist up and fish from the waist down. Like sirens, the mermaids use compelling calls and swim in a very suggestive way—though, considering they are half fish, one wonders what it is they are suggesting. Around the world there are thousands upon thousands of tales of men throwing themselves into the sea to be with one of these creatures, only to find that they, unlike the mermaids, can't breathe underwater. Often, they discover that the mermaids are carnivores. In a number of tales the mermaid is seen lying on rocks and combing her hair with one hand while holding a silver mirror with the other. The flash of the mirror is often what catches the eye of the ship's lookout. The mermaid of myth and folklore bears no resemblance at all to the lovely, gracious, and affable versions so often presented in film.

Minhocão: The Minhocão of the jungles of South America is a fearsome brute of a worm, running to more than seventy feet, with tentacles (or perhaps feelers) on its head and a durable coating of shiny black scales. First spotted in the mid-nineteenth century, the Minhocão is thought to be a burrower and its underground tunnels are believed to be the cause of the collapse of roadways and bridges. The first scientific article discussing the creature was written by French naturalist Auguste de Saint-Hilaire[18] (1779–1853) and published in 1847 in the *American Journal of Science*. In the article, Saint-Hilaire explained that the creature's name was derived from "minhoca," the Portuguese word for earthworm. In 1877 a German zoologist, Fritz Müller, who claimed to be an actual eyewitness, published an article in the *Zoologische Garten* in which he described the creature as ". . . a strange animal of gigantic size, nearly one metre in thickness, not very long, and with a snout like a pig, but whether it had legs or not he could not tell . . . whilst calling his neighbours to his assistance, it vanished, not without leaving palpable marks behind it in the shape of a trench." Müller documented the trenches allegedly left by the Minhocão, and his accounts are disturbingly convincing.

Mngwa (also **Nunda**): In the East African country of Tanzania there are tales of a catlike creature the size of a donkey called the Mngwa. Its name implies its nature: Mngwa means "strange one." The creature has calico fur and leaves marks like those of a leopard, only much larger. Bernard Heuvelmans, the father of crypto-

---

18. Auguste de Saint-Hilaire, "On the Minhocão of the Goyanes." *American Journal of Science*, 1847; 2:4.

zoology, held to the belief that the Mngwa was a subspecies of *Profelis aurata*, or Golden Cat, which are generally medium-sized feline predators found in Central and West Africa. However, during a hunt for the Mngwa following some attacks on natives, hair and print samples were taken and they did not match any known cat.

Mokele-mbeme (also **N'yamala**, **Guanérou**, **Diba**): In the Likouala swamps and Lake Tele in what is today known as the Republic of the Congo[19] there have been reports and sightings of a ferocious monster known as "Mokele-mbeme," which translates as "one who stops the flow of rivers." This mighty beast will kill to defend its territory, but apparently it is an herbivore. The Mokele-mbeme is a brute roughly the size of a young elephant, with a thick rounded body, four trunklike legs, a tail like that of a crocodile, and a long tapering neck with a head relatively small compared to its body. This description suggests some sort of dinosaur, but what a sauropod would be doing sixty-five million years past the point of its extinction suggested by fossil record is anyone's guess.

Mòrag: Loch Mòrag is the deepest of Scotland's many lakes, and these chilly waters are the home of that nation's other sea serpent. Unlike Nessie, this lake takes its name from the monster rather than the other way about. Mòrag is an Anglicized version of the Gaelic "Mhorag," meaning "spirit of the lake." Mórag is a saurian water creature, roughly thirty feet long from head to tail, with three ridged humps on its back; its hide is a mottled brown, with some highlights of purple and black. It has been spotted scores of times since 1887, with at least thirty of those sightings coming from sober, credible witnesses.

Mothman: Point Pleasant, West Virginia, is a quiet little town, but it's also the home to a very shocking and strange cryptid called the Mothman. Researchers are not quite sure if the Mothman is a true cryptid, a supernatural being, or perhaps something otherworldly. The creature is tall, vaguely humanoid, with fiery red eyes and large wings. It actually does look something like a blend of human

---

19. Not to be confused with the Democratic Republic of the Congo, which is a separate nation.

and moth. It was first sighted in November of 1966 by two couples, Roger and Linda Scarberry and Steve and Mary Mallette, who were out taking a drive. Just as they were passing by an old World War II munitions factory (they made TNT there), they spotted a pair of glowing red lights. Curious, they stopped to investigate and found that the red lights were the eyes of a bizarre creature. The creature was huge and menacing, and the couples fled in terror—but the Mothman took flight and chased them for a while.

Back in town they reported the sighting to Deputy Millard Halstead, who investigated but found nothing. That evening there was a strange poltergeist-like attack at the Scarberry house, which many believed was related. The following night a group of armed residents went Mothman hunting. They found nothing, but a woman waiting back with the cars during the hunt confronted the creature. She locked herself and her child in her car and claims that the Mothman peered in at her through the windows.

The Mothman was seen several more times around the TNT factory, but there were no direct attacks.

Here's where the story gets even stranger. Shortly after the first sightings of the Mothman the town was visited by strange men in dark suits and unmarked cars—the infamous Men in Black. The men asked a lot of questions but provided no information as to who—or indeed what—they were. Since then the sightings have fallen away, but the theories have grown in number and scope, ranging from demons to aliens. Several significant books have been written about the Mothman, including the seminal *Mothman Prophecies* by John Keel (Saturday Review Press, 1975). The story was updated and made into a film in 2002 with Richard Gere.

Mukade: In the rich folklore of Japan, most things are not what they seem. An ordinary bat might be a thousand-year-old monster, a cat may be a vampire, and a centipede may be a terrifying, man-eating monster the size of a mountain. This monstrous centipede—known as Mukade—was over thirty meters long and scaled much like a Chinese dragon. Its entire length glowed as if a brightly burning lantern was hidden behind each ornate scale, and its fiery eyes could boil a man's blood just by looking at him. Mukade lived near Lake Biwa and invaded the underwater palace of one of the

The Folklore of the City of Angels

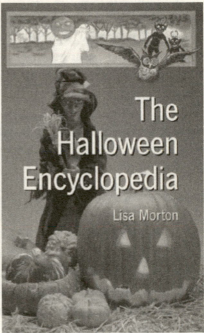

Lisa Morton

"I love the folklore of my hometown, Los Angeles (and yes, it really does have a long and fascinating folkloric history). One nearby lake, Elizabeth, was believed by the early Californios to hold its own water monster; the San Gabriel Valley, just to the east of L.A., is supposed to be home to a creature called 'La Japonesa,' the spirit of a cat-woman brought from Japan by early Spanish traders; and according to a 1930s engineer named G. Warren Shufelt, a race of 'serpent people' lived beneath the streets of downtown Los Angeles in tunnels lined with gold!"
—Lisa Morton is a Bram Stoker Award winner and author of the nonfiction books *The Halloween Encyclopedia* (McFarland, 2003) and *A Hallowe'en Anthology* (McFarland, 2008). She is also the screenwriter for *Meet the Hollowheads* (1989), *Tornado Warning* (2002), and *Blood Angels* (2004).

legendary Dragon Kings, and the creature's ferocity was so great that even this powerful magical realm was being destroyed. Even the Dragon King of Lake Biwa was no match for Mukade, but the clever and resourceful samurai hero Hidesato was able to slay the monster by dipping an arrowhead into his own saliva (to make it slippery) and then shooting it into the brain of the monster. The arrow struck home and went deep and Mukade was destroyed. The Dragon King was so grateful that he used his sorcery to give Hidesato an enchanted bag of rice that could never be emptied, thus ensuring that the samurai and everyone in his clan would never know hunger. Thereafter Hidesato was known as "Lord of the Rice Bale."

Ogopogo (also **N'ha-a-itk, the Lake Demon**): Ogopogo is a plesiosaur-like creature believed to live in and around Lake Okanagan in British Columbia, and is similar in many ways to Caddy of Cadboro Bay. Stories of this monster date back to the Okanekane Indians, where the monster was originally a man possessed by a demonic spirit that drove him to commit murder. The gods of the tribe exacted a peculiar punishment on him, transforming him into a sea monster so that he would forever be near his people but unable to rejoin human society. The transformed creature was called N'ha-A-Itk, which can be variously translated as "water god," "lake demon," or even "sacred creature of the water," though he is more popularly known as Ogopogo.

Onza (also **Cutlamiztli**): A giant cryptid hunting cat from the Sierra Madre of Mexico. Known as Cutlamiztli by the Aztecs, the Onza[20] was a larger, longer, leaner feline than either the jaguar or the puma. In the 1930s a group of hunters shot and killed an Onza, thinking it just another predator cat. They took no trophies from it and only later, after they had returned and told of their hunt, did they realize that the beast they shot was unknown to science. Without physical evidence, however, the scientific community labeled their claims as ridiculous. Some years later a large cat was shot and its body brought back for study, and for a while was widely believed to have come from a true Onza, but forensic test-

20. Onza is based on the Latin word, Unica, meaning "cheetah."

Familial Horrors

Yvonne Navarro

"My family is old Kentucky, so I'm sure I have more references in all these books and stories than I can recall. However, two stories come to mind. 'For Love of Mother' (originally published in *Narrow Houses*, vol. 2 of *TouchWood*) and 'Revelation' (unpublished) immediately come to mind. 'For Love of Mother' deals with an old Kentucky superstition about how someone dies if you wall up a doorway, while 'Revelation' is about yet another Kentucky superstition that enables a woman to know who she's going to marry. Both are very poignant, emotional stories."
—Yvonne Navarro is the author of twenty novels and has won, among others, the Bram Stoker Award and the Rocky Mountain "Unreal Worlds" Award. She has written horror, science fiction, suspense, and all points in between, including novelizing such films as *Aliens: Music of the Spears* (Spectra, 1996), *Hellboy* (Pocket Star, 2004), and others.

ing proved that it was indistinguishable from a normal puma. Though this finding deflated many cryptozoologists, there are others who shrug it off and agree that, yes, *that* cat may have been a puma, but that the Onza is still out there. This belief is supported by the discovery of several partial skulls of an unknown predator cat. One such skull was given to Richard Greenwell, the secretary of the International Society of Cryptozoology, two Mexican ranchers gave another to Greenwell and colleague Robert Marshall (author of a noted work on the Onza), and a third was found in the collections at the Academy of Natural Sciences in Philadelphia. The hunt continues.

Orang-Bati: The Indonesian island of Seram plays host to yet another giant batlike cryptid, the Orang-Bati, who has been blamed for the abduction and murders of a number of small children. The Orang-Bati looks essentially human, though it has fierce red skin, a whipping tail, and gigantic wings. Only a few Westerners have reported sighting the monster, and in their accounts the creature had short black fur and the torso of a woman. In both cases the Orang-Bati has a face like an ape. Scientists have theorized that the Orang-Bati may in fact be a species of monkey-eating bird called the Philippine Eagle (*Pithecophaga jefferyi*), a fierce avian predator that is one of the largest birds in the world, with a wingspan of six feet.

Orang Pendek: In Sumatra there is a strange creature that may be the world's only were-ape; or if not a were-ape, then yet another of the world's many species of ape-human hybrids such as the Sasquatch or Kung-Lu (see Tibet). The Orang Pendek stands about five feet tall and is covered in dark hair. European settlers tried to convince the natives that what they were seeing were simply orangutans, but the descriptions really didn't match. Orangutans have shaggy orange hair and are quite docile on the whole. The Orang Pendek's fur is short and brown, and their behavior has often been reported as savage. Both creatures are highly intelligent, but the Orang Pendek apparently have their own language.

Ozark Howler: This cryptid is a hairy bearlike monster that howls like a wolf and has horns. It has been variously described as walking on two legs or four, and the prints that are believed to belong to the creature bear close (but not exact) resemblance to those of a big hunting cat.

Queensland Tiger (also **Tasmanian Tiger**, **Tasmanian Wolf**, **Tassy**): One of the more famous cryptids is the Queensland Tiger, a catlike predator infrequently spotted in the rainforests of Queensland, Australia. The tiger is a medium-sized striped marsupial rather than an actual feline and has been sighted for thousands of years by the Aborigines and for over four hundred years by Europeans who settled on that continent.

Pua Tu Tahi: Not all sea monsters are serpents or dinosaurs, as seen with the Pua Tu Tahi of Tahitian folklore. This deadly creature is a kind of demon who rises to the surface and shape-shifts into a knob of jagged rock in order to tear the keels out of fishing boats. The nature of the monster is even suggested by the translation of its name: "Coral Rock Standing Alone."

Ropen: The Ropen is one of the many giant winged cryptids haunting the world, this one making its home in the jungles of Papua

Pua Tu Tahi by Allen Koszowski

New Guinea. First spotted by missionaries following World War II, the Ropen was described as having the basic body structure of a bat, though it is much larger than any ordinary bat; a long tail with a delta-shaped tip; and a beak filled with needle-sharp teeth. The Ropen was most often seen in the vicinity of New Britain and Umboi, located in the Bismarck Archipelago. Local legend has it that the Ropen is a carrion creature and feasts on putrefying corpses, though some claim it will attack the living if approached.

Santu Sankai: The Santu Sankai (translated as "Mouth Men") are savage monsters from the dense forests near Kuala Lumpur. These hideous creatures appear to be a kind of werewolf and like wolves, they often attack in packs. They are fierce predators, hunting animals and humans alike for blood and fresh meat.

Sasquatch (also **Bigfoot**): All over the world there are stories, legends, and myths about strange manlike creatures living wild in the mountains and deep forests. From Russia to Australia, from China to the Pacific Northwest, there have been sightings of these ferocious wild men every year. Some of these creatures appear to be benign (especially those living at higher altitudes) whereas others are bloodthirsty predators. Perhaps the most famous of all of these humanoid monsters is Bigfoot, more formally known as Sasquatch. This creature roams the forests of Western Canada, all the way down to Northern California. For centuries, Native Americans have told tales of hairy, manlike predators. Sightings among the European American population date back only to the 1960s. On October 20, 1967, Roger Patterson and Bob Gimlin shot footage of what was purported to be a "real" Bigfoot. Although the film has been analyzed thousands of times and generally discredited as a hoax, sightings persist. The Sasquatch is often described as being about seven to ten feet tall, with a face similar to a Neanderthal, but markedly more simian. The creature has powerful, sloped shoulders and long arms, and its body is completely covered with fur or hair that can be brown, black, red, or white. Casts have been made of supposed Bigfoot tracks, and these feet range from twelve to twenty inches. The creature's weight has been estimated at five-hundred pounds, half the weight of a grown horse.

The big hairy guy has been great source material for virtually every aspect of pop culture, including stuffed toys, candy, comics (Sasquatch is a superhero in Marvel, and Steve Niles and Rob Zombie even attempted a serious comic book, *Bigfoot*, released by IDW in 2005); scores of short stories and novels and a slew of movies titled *Bigfoot* released in 1967, 1970, 1987, 1995 and 2006; plus the John Lithgow comedy *Harry and the Hendersons* (1987), a clash between Bigfoot and the *Six Million Dollar Man* ("The Secret of Bigfoot," episode airdate 1975), and two dozen other screen appearances. One movie industry blogger even joked that the reason sightings have diminished is that Bigfoot got an agent and moved to Hollywood.

In 2008 a couple of guys who run a Bigfoot tour claimed to have found a dead Bigfoot, a claim that kicked off a media circus. Of course the whole thing turned out to be another hoax, but . . . what the hell, for a while we all hoped.

Shampe: The Choctaws have always had legends of great monsters and demons, and the most terrifying of all is the gigantic blood-thirsty beast called the Shampe. This creature lives deep in the forests of western North America, and only emerges from his secret lair to hunt at night. The Shampe is one of only a handful of blood-drinkers who actually fear and shun sunlight, but this is one of the creature's few weaknesses. The Shampe has supernaturally acute senses, particularly those of sight and smell. It has a shark's ability to smell blood miles away and will relentlessly stalk anyone who is injured or carrying freshly killed game. Once on the track of its prey it is nearly impossible to shake loose. One trick is for the person to drop his bloody game and leave it behind for the Shampe. Another option is to shoot something else and leave its dead or dying body behind to distract the beast.

Shíta: The Hopi people of the Southwest tell of a cannibalistic creature called a Shíta. This monster preyed on the village of Oraíbi, attacking and devouring any children it could catch. When it could not catch a child it would turn and attack any person, young or old, slaughtering and feasting on them.

Frightened and frustrated, the villagers appealed to two magical brothers from a nearby village, Pöokónghoy and his younger brother, Balö'ngahoya. The brothers asked the villagers to make each of them a special arrow, and then they went hunting. They ambushed the Shíta and allowed themselves to be swallowed whole by this enormous beast. Once inside the creature, the brothers shot their magical arrows into its heart, slaying it.

Tatzelworm (also **Alpine Tatzelworm**, **Stollenworm**): All through the Alps in Bavaria, Austria, and Switzerland there are frequent reports of a burrowing, wormlike creature about four to five feet in length that has a distinctly feline head and many short legs. Known as the Tatzelworm, which means "clawed worm" or Stollenworm ("hole-dwelling worm"), this bizarre cryptid is not just a burrower but also a predator. In 1921 an Alpine herdsman claimed that one of the monsters leapt at him. He escaped unharmed, but there are other "rumors" of Tatzelworms attacking and killed children left unattended. Similar creatures have been reported as far away as Sicily, Germany, and Portugal.

Trunko: In 1922, in the waters off the coast of Margate, South Africa, one of the strangest sea battles took place. Not between naval vessels, but between two whales and a gigantic sea monster covered in white fur that has come to be known in cryptozoology circles as the Trunko. The Trunko lost its fight and its carcass washed ashore, where it was examined and measured. The Trunko taped out at forty-seven feet and presented a number of anatomical anomalies, such as the absence of any conventional "head"; instead it had an appendage more like a trunk.

Unceglia: The Unceglia is a dragonlike monster from Lakota Sioux legend who steals people away so that no trace of them is ever found. Even well into the twentieth century the Unceglia was being blamed for inexplicable disappearances.

Veo: Not all cryptids are predators, as seen with the docile Veo, a gigantic night-hunting insect-eater. The Veo is said to be as big as a small horse, and the descriptions of it closely match that of the Giant Pangolin (*Manis paleojavanicus*), a species of scaly anteater found in equatorial Africa; however the Veo is many times as big as any living pangolin specimen. It's true that giant anteaters (*Manis paleojavanicus*) did live on nearby Java and Borneo, but not for many centuries. Cryptozoologists suspect that if it exists it may be a relict.

Vodyanoi: Mermaids and similar creatures don't just live in the depths of the oceans; around the world there are plenty of tales of half-human and half-fish creatures haunting lakes, ponds, streams, and rivers. One such is the Vodyanoi of Russia—a particularly nasty and vicious monster that lives at the bottom of any inland body of water. In the more romantic folktales the Vodyanoi lives in a submerged palace of pure crystal decorated with treasures stolen from sunken ships—but before a comparison can be made between that and Disney's Little Mermaid, consider that the Vodyanoi is a flesh-eating predator and very far from being cute. Some legends describe the Vodyanoi as looking like a bent old man with a sea-weed beard and skin as rough as fish scales, though this may only be a disguise. Many more tales describe the Vodyanoi as looking like a cross between a fish—scales, goggle eyes, lipless slash of a mouth—and a human. In either case, it possesses the ability to leave the water and walk on land in search of prey.

Waheela: In the Nahanni Valley in the Northwest Territories of Canada there are reports of a wolflike cryptid whose body structure is similar to a hyena, with short hind legs, overdeveloped forelegs, a burly chest, and thick snow-white fur. Known as the Waheela, the creature is far bulkier and more powerful than a wolf and stands nearly four feet at the shoulders. They are solitary hunters and have also been spotted in Alaska. The Native peoples of those regions regard the Waheela as an evil spirit and ascribe a variety of nasty traits to it, not the least of which is savage murder and decapitation.

Windigo (also **Wendigo**): According to folklore of Ontario, Canada (as well as Minnesota in the United States), the Windigo is a fierce predatory monster created whenever a human resorts to cannibalism. The Windigo is also known as the Cannibal Demon of the Northern Woods. Windigo stories are thematically linked to both werewolves and vampires in that both of these creatures can also be created by committing sins, and cannibalism is certainly a taboo in nearly all human cultures. During frontier days cannibalism was a bit more common (although still rare) because the heavy snows and brutal winters trapped settlers and Native Americans in the remote northern woods. Game was scarce and the will to survive strong, so a trapped and desperate person was sometimes forced to eat another human in order to survive. That was all it took for the Windigo spirit to emerge from a man's deepest inner recesses and take total command of that person, body and soul.

The Windigo has turned up in a variety of pop-culture references including Algernon Blackwood's excellent 1910 story, "The Wendigo," which introduced the creature to mainstream readers; and Stephen King's *Pet Semetery* (1989), in which an old Micmac burial ground has become the unfortunate graveyard for pets. The creature also pops up in games (*Final Fantasy*, *Dungeons & Dragons*, *World of Warcraft*, etcetera), comics (notably as a villain in Marvel Comics), and a bunch of movies including *The Lure of the Windigo* (1914), *Ghostkeeper* (1981), *Windigo* (1994), *Frostbiter: Wrath of the Wendigo* (1996), *Ravenous* (1999), *Wendigo* (2001), *Ginger Snaps Back* (2004), and in episodes of the television series *Blood Ties* (2007), *Charmed* (1998–2006), and *Supernatural* (2005).

Woolly Cheetah: A species of shaggy-coated cheetah reported in the nineteenth century but not seen since. It's possible that the examples of this animal caught (but, sadly, not preserved) two centuries ago were cheetahs with recessive genes that allowed their coats to grow wild. It appears that the genetic anomaly has corrected itself and no new examples have been seen in India or South Africa.

Yeren: The Yeren is another of the world's many strange man-beasts. It lives in China's rocky northern territories and sightings of this hairy creature have been so common for so long that in 1994 the Chinese government formed an organization to find them. The Committee for the Search for Strange and Rare Creatures is comprised of scientists in various fields (paleontology, cryptozoology, paleoanthropology, etcetera) and has sent a number of official expeditions into the hills. Expeditions have returned with artifacts such as hair samples, feces, plaster casts of Yeren footprints, and so on. Extrapolating the creature's height from the size of its footprints (which range up to sixteen inches), the creature is believed to be an average of seven feet tall.

Yeti: Though certainly native to the Himalayas of Tibet, Yeti (or some very similar species) are believed to populate the mountain regions of several Russian provinces in what was once Soviet Central Asia. Mountain climbers have reported seeing them in the Pamiro-Alai mountain range in Tadzhik as recently as 1980. The Russian Yeti are apparently as nonviolent and timid as their Tibetan cousins and may even be of the same species, whereas most of the world's other man-beasts are maneaters. The various peoples of that region of the former Soviet Union use different names for the Yeti. The Georgians call it the Tkys-katsi; the Azerbaijani call it Mesheadam; in Dagestan it is the Kaptar; the Balkas, Chechens, Kabardins, and Ungushes call it the Almasti.

5 THEY HAUNT
The Unquiet Dead

Spirits of the Dead: Specters and Vengeance Ghosts

GHOST OF A TALE

All cultures have ghost legends, and that includes our modern-day urban society. Turn on the TV and you'll either catch the millionth rerun of *Ghostbusters* or an episode of *Ghost Whisperer*; cruise over to the nonfic channels and you can go ghost chasing with the Penn State kids from *State of Fear* or the spook-chasing plumbers who are now the internationally famous *Ghost Hunters*. Most people believe in ghosts. A Gallup poll that took a cross-section of ethnicities, religious backgrounds, ages, and both sexes estimated a belief in ghosts at about 77 percent. That number is probably low. A lot of people won't admit to a belief in ghosts, but they believe all the same.

Acceptance of the possibility of ghosts generally (but not always, as we'll see) goes hand in hand with the belief in the soul. The nineteenth-century anthropologist James Frazer discussed the link between ghost beliefs and animism—the belief in the existence of souls, in humans and in all things—in his 1922 classic book, *The Golden Bough*: "If a man lives and moves, it can only be because he has a little man or animal inside, who moves him. The animal inside the animal, the man inside the man, is the soul. And as the activity of an animal or man is explained by the presence of the soul, so the repose of sleep or death is explained by its absence; sleep or trance being the temporary, death being the permanent absence of the soul . . ."

Psychologists and social anthropologists have postulated that the belief in ghosts is part of the natural human process of making the world around them more personal and less arbitrary. Personification allows for the belief in anything, and a belief in a hereafter is comforting. It's comforting, even when there's a price to pay, such as the acceptance of supernatural evil. Religious scholars often tell us that one cannot believe in God without believing in the Devil, because the two are balancing halves of a universal whole. And though this argument doesn't stand up to scrutiny even for the devout (if God is truly All, then He does not require a Devil in order to exist—it's a fundamental tenet of faith), this does allow us to believe that there is some balance to the universe. For example, if a child dies of some inexplicable illness (such as Sudden

Representing Strange Worlds

"The most comprehensive folklore I've illustrated is the world of Gary Braunbeck's Cedar Hill.[1] He has created his own panorama of supernatural creatures that hover on the threshold between the human world and the world beyond. His characters are manifestations of human emotion or ancient Indian legends or harbingers of news from the other side. On the cover of *Graveyard People*, the first Cedar Hill collection, Earthling Publications, 2003), I showed a parade of these creatures entering the town. There's a turtle with antlers on its head and a lion that wears armor. There are walking flowers with the faces of children. They carry weapons and magical charms and musical instruments. These folks are piercing that veil that separates the human world from the supernatural." —Deena Warner has illustrated dozens of books, magazine features, and CDs.

Infant Death Syndrome, which we are only now beginning to medically understand) then the belief that evil came and stole the child's life or breath is easier to accept than the concept that God allowed it or, worse yet, that these things "just happen." Having a Devil, a monster, a supernatural predator helps restore balance by providing a reason for something that is otherwise both inexplicable and unbearable.

However, something actually may be out there in the dark doing deliberate harm, and the authors of this book are not about to dismiss the beliefs of the majority of humanity (living and in previous generations) who believe that there is a larger world than the one we can currently touch and measure. Besides . . . we believe, too.

That brings up the question, however, of what does belief mean? The two authors of this book come from different religious and cultural backgrounds, and in many ways we do not share the same beliefs. But belief is there.

With our previous book, *The Cryptopedia*, we explored more than a dozen different aspects of the belief in a larger world, from div-

1. A fictional town in which Braunbeck sets many of his stories.

ination to UFOs to demonology to what is loosely called New Age. We've met thousands of folks who believe (and a smaller percentage of those who don't, but who keep an open mind). Some folks have beliefs that are—to us—pretty much "out there," just as our beliefs might be "out there" to them. The nature of belief is that it does not need to be justified to another, but only to ourselves, and justification in that regard is more intuitive than logical.

One area in which the beliefs of the largest number of people converge—as seen through our experiences at signings and interviews during research, and as demonstrated in dozens of polls done by independent organizations—is the belief that ghosts exist.

Of course, just what a ghost is opens up a whole different debate.

Some feel that a ghost is a spirit of a dead person who, for whatever reason, is either trapped on earth or has unfinished business to complete. With our own polls, the majority of folks believe that ghosts are aware of humans but not necessarily aware that they are ghosts.

Another view is that ghosts are a kind of spiritual imprint contained somehow by a structure—house, graveyard, etcetera—and that the appearance of the ghost is like a video file being played out on a continual loop. Some X-element triggers the loop to play. In such cases the belief is that there is no personality attached to the ghost and probably nothing of a supernatural nature. Perhaps the minerals in the architecture somehow act like a storage battery for the image loop. Many scientists are in this camp.

Still others believe that ghosts are an intrusion into our dimension from an entirely different world.

Some hold that ghosts are conscious spirits who know who and what they are and are interacting with the living. This would explain the pranks played by certain kinds of ghosts and the reports of conversations and interactions with the living.

And some insist that ghosts are holdovers of emotion—a burst of rage or hurt or something else equally intense—that recurs when triggered by a similar or sympathetic emotion in a human.

And of course some people believe that ghosts are here to complete unfinished business: to redress a wrong done to them in life or seek justice for the crime that put them in the grave. In this view the ghost will struggle to make itself known and try to either harm the person who harmed them or reveal the identity of their killer (or abuser if the incident led the victim to commit suicide), or to direct a living person to where their bones lay hidden so they can be properly buried and thus released.

This last view is not the most common in the modern day, at least not in America, but it's also not that rare. It is, however, a very common belief theme in ghost tales told in various religions and cultures around the world and throughout history. These spirits are called vengeance ghosts, and we'll explore these hauntings in depth later in this chapter.

Psychopomp by Allen Koszowski

There are other kinds of ghosts, of course, many of whom drift into the world of supernatural predators—some for ill, some for good, and some neutral. One of the neutral ghost types is the psychopomp, a spirit whose purpose is to guide the newly dead to the underworld or afterlife. Psychopomp even means "guide of souls." For the most part these spirits are nonjudgmental, merely doing their nine-to-five, which is ushering the dead to the next phase of existence. These creatures come in all shapes and sizes and some of them are so fierce that they are viewed as evil or threatening even though they are not. Charon, the spooky boatman who ferries the dead across the river Styx, is a prime example and the skeletal Angel of Death is another.

Positive and Negative Aspects of Death

Death is a funny thing. As a concept it is endlessly elastic and we humans almost always personify it, giving it a nature and ascribing intent to it. When a person is struggling to survive injuries sustained in an accident, the doctors or EMTs declare that they won't let death win—as if death is vying for the soul of the dying person. If a person is taking a reckless risk, we say he's defying death; if someone survives a nearly fatal situation, we see it as cheating death. When someone dies we shout at death to "be not proud,"[2] and yet if a person is dying horribly with no hope of recovery we view death as merciful.

With the rise of Judeo-Christian belief—and particularly with medieval Christian teachings—the Angel of Death became a monster that often sought to do harm rather than act as part of the natural process in which all organic life lives and dies. Death became the Grim Reaper and the clergy of that era began insisting that Death was in league with the Devil and therefore an enemy of God. This is another of those things that must have sounded good over tankards of mead in the back chamber of a cathedral, but which doesn't stand up to logic. Not even to religious logic. If Death is the enemy of God and in league with the Devil, and all things die, then God is constantly losing to the Devil. Somehow the flaw in this syllogism was lost on them at the time. This is the same argument that urged that ghosts are actual evil spirits; that in fact all ghosts are evil. We could go off on a tangent about the Holy Spirit, about the visitation of dead saints and so on, but the flaws in that argument are pretty apparent to modern thinkers, no matter what their religious beliefs may be.

However, if the legends and tales of vengeance ghosts are to be believed, they are evil, malicious, or, at the very least, dangerous. And later in this chapter we'll meet some really nasty ones from various times and cultures.

POP-CULTURE POLTERGEISTS

Ghost stories are among the cornerstones of folklore. Our ancestors have been spinning ghost tales since they lived in caves, and we'll probably be spinning them when we've colonized the galaxy. Ghost stories appear in fiction and drama, and they also show up in religious, historical, and even legal records. The story of the Greenbrier Ghost from 1897, for example, tells of the spirit of a young woman who appeared to her mother in dreams to reveal the fact that she had been murdered rather than died as a result of a fall. The mother went to the county prosecutor in Greenbrier, West Virginia, and was so adamant about her vision that an exhu-

2. "Death Be Not Proud" by John Donne (1572–1631).

Exploring Local Legends in Storytelling

"My story 'Screaming Jenny,' from *Legends of the Mountain State*, made use of a West Virginia legend about a woman who was killed by a train after accidentally setting herself on fire in her hovel near the tracks. The challenge of that anthology was to use a legend instead of merely retelling it. I wrote a modern story that utilized elements of the legend in a way that the final tale wasn't even a fantasy but rather a straightforward crime caper. I have another (currently unpublished) story inspired by a legend from where I grew up called the Chaleur Phantom, a burning ghost ship that has been witnessed for decades in the waters of the Bay of Chaleur under certain meteorological conditions."
—Bev Vincent is the author of *The Road to the Dark Tower* (NAL, 2004) and contributing editor for *Cemetery Dance* magazine.

mation was ordered. An autopsy revealed the cause of death—strangulation—and the young woman's husband was put on trial for her murder. The mother gave testimony in the case, and her account of what her daughter's ghost told her became part of the court record. This is one of only a handful of cases in U.S. legal history where the testimony of a ghost was entered as evidence and led to a conviction. The jury—if not the actual court—believed the ghost's tale.[3]

Much of our most prized literature is rife with ghosts, from *Hamlet* to *A Christmas Carol* to *The Lovely Bones* (Picador, 2003). They're even showing up in mainstream novels that are not considered technically supernatural, such as *Burning Angel* by James Lee Burke; however, there are plenty of novels that focus directly on ghosts and hauntings. Some of our favorites that feature nasty ghosts include *Something Wicked This Way Comes* by Ray Bradbury, *The Haunting of Hill House* by Shirley Jackson, *Ghost Story*

3. A fictionalized account, "The Adventure of the Greenbrier Ghost" by Jonathan Maberry, appeared in the *Legends of the Mountain State 2* anthology, edited by Michael Knost (Woodside Press). Other cases include the Rebecca Cornell case of 1673 and the Billings trial of 1878.

The Ghosts of Edgar Allen Poe

 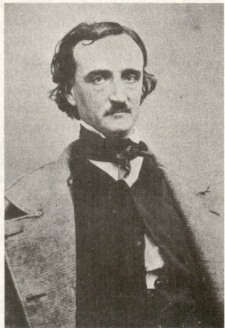

Ed Pettit

"From the very beginning of Edgar Allan Poe's writing career, he takes up the theme of a spirit menacing the living. His first published story, 'Metzengerstein,' opens with an epigraph that embodies the threat of the avenging revenant: 'Living I have been your plague, dying I shall be your death.' A reckless and wanton German aristocrat, Frederick Metzengerstein, is haunted by a fiery-colored horse, come to life from a tapestry in his ancient family chateau. In the end, as his home crackles and crumbles in flames, the 'Demon of the Tempest' horse arrives and carries away the doomed nobleman through a blaze of purifying fire. The horse in this story represents the most significant element of all Gothic tales, the burden of ancestral sins upon the living. However, the horse is also the first in a series of revenants that will haunt Poe's characters throughout his tales. In 'Morella,' the spirit of a deceased mother passes into her daughter to haunt the father. In 'Ligeia,' a widower remarries only to have his second wife die and resurrect, transformed into his first wife. In one of

Poe's most well-known tales, 'The Black Cat,' a man kills his cat, Pluto, in a drunken rage, only to have the animal come back from the dead. After the man murders his wife and bricks her body into his cellar, it is the cat whose shrieks alert the police to his crime. In Poe's stories, the dead rarely rest in peace, nor do the living." —Edward Pettit is a freelance writer and book reviewer who teaches writing at La Salle University, and lectures anywhere on Edgar Allan Poe.

---

by Peter Straub, *The Shining* and *Pet Semetery* by Stephen King, *Turn of the Screw* by Henry James, *Hell House* and *A Stir of Echoes* by Richard Matheson, *Nazareth Hill* by Ramsey Campbell, *Burnt Offerings* by Robert Marasco, *Ghosts* by Noel Hynd, *The House Next Door* by Anne Rivers Siddons, *The Green Man* by Kingsley Amis, *Revenant* by Melanie Tem, *Fog Heart* by Thomas Tessier, *Mystery Walk* by Robert McCammon, *The Woman in Black: A Ghost Story* by Susan Hill, *Haunted* by James Herbert, *Nightmare House* by Douglas Clegg, *The Devils of D-Day* by Graham Masterton, *The Manor* by Scott Nicholson, *The Taken* by Sarah Pinborough, *The Keeper* by Sarah Langan, *Dead Souls* by Michael Laimo, and *The Heart-Shaped Box* by Joe Hill.

Some truly classic ghost stories that are worth hunting down include: "The Apparition of Mrs. Veal" by Daniel Defoe, "Canon Alberic's Scrap-Book" by Montague Rhodes James, "The Haunted and the Haunters" by Edward Bulwer-Lytton, "The Phantom Rickshaw" by Rudyard Kipling, "The Damned Thing" by Ambrose Bierce, "The Abbot's Ghost" by Louisa May Alcott, "The Horla" by Guy De Maupassant, "De Profundis" by Arthur Conan Doyle, "Only a Dream" by H. Rider Haggard, "The Whistling Room" by William Hope Hodgson, "The Legend of Sleepy Hollow" by Washington Irving, "Doctor Feversham's Story" by Joseph Sheridan Le Fanu, "The Tell-Tale Heart" by Edgar Allen Poe, "The Yellow Wallpaper" by Charlotte Perkins Gilman, "The Monkey's Paw" by W. W. Jacobs, and "Green Tea" by J. Sheridan Le Fanu. These are just our favorites . . . a full list of truly great ghost stories would fill several thick volumes, which demonstrates how many storytelling possibilities exist within the realm of ghosts and hauntings.

When it comes to movies, however, there are a few good ones and a lot of mediocre or bad ones. Our choices for the must-see ghost flicks (excluding friendly ghosts) are: *The Old Dark House* (1932), *The Uninvited* (1944), *Dead of Night* (1945), *The Innocents* (1961), *The Haunting* (1963), *Kwaidan* (1964), *The Amityville Horror* (1979), *The Legend of Hell House* (1973), *The Turn of the Screw* (1974), *The Changeling* (1979), *The Fog* (1980), *The Shining* (1980), *Ghost Story* (1981), *The Entity* (1981), *Poltergeist* (1982), *Candyman* (1992), *The Crow* (1994), *The Kingdom* (1995), *Ringu* (1998), *The Blair Witch Project* (1999), *Stir of Echoes* (1999), *The Sixth Sense* (1999), *What Lies Beneath* (2000), *The Others* (2001), *The Eye* (2002), *Below* (2002), *The Ring* (2002), *Ju-On* (2003), *The Grudge* (2004), and *The Orphanage* (2007).[4]

Not all ghost films and fiction explore the vengeance theme—some mine the genre for tragedy, romance, comedy, and nonspecific horror—but vengeance and rage are most often the focus.

A DARKER SHADE OF PALE

Abbey Lubbers: Spiteful spirits who haunted the abbeys of fifteenth-century England and led otherwise devout monks into drunkenness and debauchery. These spirits have been variously interpreted as demons striving to destroy faith and devotion to God, or the ghosts of Muslims killed in the Crusades seeking vengeance, or pagan earth spirits trying to stop the spread of Christianity, or even the disgrtuntled ghosts of dead sinners who are sorting out their own spiritual issues by tormenting the living.

Apparition: A ghost appearing in human shape and in the form of someone familiar to the witness.

Asto Vidatu: The ancient Persians believed that when each person is born there is an invisible noose tied around their necks, placed

4. Of these, *The Haunting* is an easy call for the best ghost movie of all time; and *Below* gets our vote as the most criminally overlooked.

Folklore in Fiction

"I've used elements of folklore in several of my published short stories. 'What They Did to My Father' (*Black Gate*, Summer 2001) incorporates elements of African American folklore in the figure of the 'root man' whose use of roots, herbs, etcetera offer magic protection for one of the other characters. 'It Came Out of the Sky' (*North Carolina Literary Review* #10, 2001) is based on reported UFO sightings from the 1970s. 'Legacy' (*Lady Churchill's Rosebud Wristlet* #13, Nov. 2003) takes place in early twentieth-century Alabama but takes its premise from a footnote to the Bell Witch legend from nineteenth century Tennessee. Most recently, 'The Serpent and the Hatchet Gang' (*Black Gate* #2, Dec. 2007) draws on lore regarding nineteenth-century sightings of a 'sea serpent' off the Massachusetts coast. Folklore is a bottomless well of ideas and source material."
—F. Brett Cox's fiction, essays, and reviews have appeared in numerous publications. With Andy Duncan, he coedited *Crossroads: Tales of the Southern Literary Fantastic* (Tor, 2004).

there by a demonic death-spirit called Asto Vidatu. All through life Asto Vidatu tries to tug on the noose, but when a person's life energy is too strong, the demon cannot pull the noose tight enough to cut off air and blood. Only when a person has reached his or her appointed hour, in which the pull of death is greater than the pull of life, does the death demon close the noose and the person dies. Once the spiritual scales have tipped in Asto Vidatu's favor, there is no escape and death is certain.

Ays: Possession is a method of supernatural predation from which there is little initial defense. Since the possessing spirit is generally invisible and intangible, there are few warnings and therefore no practical defenses. Cures such as exorcism are the only recourse in such cases. In Armenian mythology the demonic spirit of the wind, called the Ays, comes hunting for vulnerable souls, stealing in through open bedroom windows, or seeping into a person while they lay asleep in a field or out in the open. The Ays is a blend of ghost and essential vampire, but instead of feeding on life force it

The Ays by Allen Koszowski

takes its sustenance from sanity. As it drives its victim mad, the Ays feeds on the intense psychic energy created by the fracturing mind. There are few monsters that do as much damage yet remain so completely hidden. It is nearly impossible to tell the difference between a person driven mad by this form of possession and a person who is mentally unstable because of emotional injury, physical damage, or chemical imbalance. The one clue available to the wise is that a person driven mad by an Ays experiences a very fast onset of insanity with little or no previous history of mental instability. In some rare cases the Ays takes over the person so completely that instead of just becoming insane, the victim actually undergoes a process of painful transformation that results in them becoming a demon themselves. The Ays can be driven out only through a long process of precisely followed religious rituals, prayers, and offerings. Even then, the outcome is seldom hopeful.

Banshee (also **Ban Sidhe**, **Bean-nighe**): A terrifying and deadly female ghost from Irish and Scottish folklore that foretells violent death with its chilling cry. The Banshee is seldom seen, but when

The Banshee by Mike Bohatch

A Ghost in Every House

Ghost stories are so common that at times it seems like every family has one. Here's an example from consultant and writer Ruth Heil: "No one ever talked about it, but by the time I was ten years old I realized that we were not the only ones living in our Pennsylvania home. We'd all hear heavy footsteps, see chairs rocking on their own, lights flashing. The dog saw them, too. Not often, but definitely there. It terrified me. Was it real or imagined? Did the ghost mean us harm or not? I'll never know, but either way, the fear was very, very real."

she is, observers either see a spectral figure floating on the night winds, or a strange hag with glaring eyes, a sharp single front tooth, a single large nostril, pendulous breasts, and great webbed feet. She is horrible to behold, and yet some intrepid adventurers have tried to find her because there is a legend that if someone were to suckle at the breast of a banshee they would be granted a single wish and would thereafter be protected by the creature.

Black Annis: A vengeance ghost from the Dane Hills in Leicestershire returned to earth in the form of a flesh-eating old hag with iron claws. The Black Annis lived in a cave and would hunt for children at night, cook them, and hang their skins on the walls of her cave. One popular folktale of the region has it that she was once a lovely young woman who was seduced by a lord of the manor. When she confessed to him that she had become pregnant, instead of marrying her, the lord had her beaten and driven off. Her baby was stillborn. After spying on the lord's children playing in the gardens, she was driven mad with grief and hatred and killed herself. The ghost that rose from the grave had an abiding hatred for all children and to this day is rumored to hunt in the Leicestershire hills.

Boggart: A spiteful ghost who sneaks into houses at night to physically abuse its victims by pinching, slapping, and biting them. Though often invisible, when they do become visible they are quite horrible to behold, with glaring eyes, sharp yellow teeth, and breath that reeks of sulfur and spoiled meat.

Bogie: A squat, hairy creature that has been variously described as a kind of seedy fairy or a disreputable-looking ghost. It stinks of methane and human waste, and it loves to terrify children, especially while they sleep.

Crossroad Ghosts: There are a variety of ghosts associated with crossroads, none of them pleasant. Some are the ghosts of criminals hanged at crossroads in centuries past, and these linger on to harass the living. Some are the lost souls of people who made unfortunate deals with the devil. They linger at the place where they sold their humanity and try to frighten away other humans from doing the same. Some crossroads ghosts are said to be the souls of people who tried unsuccessfully to astrally project and can no longer find their way back to their bodies. A few are the deranged ghosts of suicides who hanged themselves at the crossroads and now they eternally plague living travelers. And some wait for specific travelers so they can then conduct them to the underworld.

Doppelgänger: This is a German term meaning "double walker" or "double goer," and refers to a kind of shadow self that is bonded to every human. This other self is sometimes benign, but often is quite nasty, and the Doppelgänger is the basis for the phrase "evil twin." In the Doppelgänger a person's less savory qualities are exalted. Most often the Doppelgänger is invisible and lacks any real power; but in rare cases it can become the dominant half of a personality, and once empowered it can either influence the mortal self into doing evil or corrupt misdeeds or can separate itself (usually while the mortal body is asleep) and roam free to cause all manner of mischief.

Danag: Centuries ago the natives of the Philippines had forged an agreement with a group of spirits called the Danag. These otherworldly spirits were benign and friendly, and had such a deep knowledge of how to work the earth that they helped the Filipinos become excellent farmers. For generations the arrangement was idyllic, but a simple accident and an act of kindness changed everything for the worse.

One day, a woman cut her finger while farming and in an attempt to comfort her and soothe the wound a Danag licked it. The taste of the blood—something totally new to these ethereal creatures—was overwhelming and the Danag kept licking the wound, then started sucking it. Before anyone could do anything the Danag had drained every last drop of blood from the woman's body. Suddenly everything changed and from that moment on the Danag were not interested in helping the natives farm the land; now the only thing any of them wanted was fresh human blood. It was worse than any addiction, it became an undying obsession. The Danag have plagued and haunted the Filipinos ever since.

Dybbuk: The word "Dybbuk" comes from the Hebrew verb *ledavek*, "to cling," and refers to an evil spirit that possesses a sick or dying person, causing mental illness, irrationality, or aberrant behavior. It creates a separate personality for itself, and talks through the possessed person's mouth. The Dybbuk is drawn toward weakness, particularly when the body is so weakened by illness that the bond between spirit and flesh is in flux. This creates an opening for the Dybbuk to enter. In some cases the Dybbuk then invigorates the body and uses it as a vessel to do great acts of evil; in other cases it merely uses the voice of the sick person as a means of saying things to that person's relatives that cause them emotional harm. This suggests that the Dybbuk is either an essential vampire of some kind that feeds on pain and misery or merely spiteful and malicious.

Fetch: A ghost of Britain and Ireland that assumes the appearance of any person who has the misfortune to see it. If seen in the morning, the Fetch is an omen of a long and happy life, but if seen after twilight it's a sure sign of impending death—and a gruesome one at that.

Gable Ratches: Ghost dogs that travel with the Wild Hunt in Celtic folklore. They are occasionally used to hunt humans, chasing them so unrelentingly that the victims' hearts burst in their chests.

Gabriel Hounds: A variation of the Wild Hunt ghost dogs are the Gabriel Hounds, who have human faces and race across the sky while uttering blood-chilling howls.

Galley Beggar: A ferocious ghost from the North of England who appears as a rotted set of bones devoid of flesh and carrying its severed head under its arm. The Galley Beggar has a scream like a Banshee that can freeze the heart in a person's chest. It fears white dogs but can turn black dogs against their masters. Cats can sense it coming and will become alert and stare at a wall or door if this ghost is on the other side. In such cases it is important not to disturb or distract the cat because the Galley Beggar will not enter if a cat is watching. Like many predatory spirits, this ghost often waits for travelers at night on lonely roads.

Graveyard Ghosts: These range from the benign—lost spirits who don't know where or what they are and who are frightened of the living—to guardian spirits set to watch over certain graves or protect the whole graveyard against evil. In such cases the graveyard ghost often had a ghostly dog to help him, and together they could combat any form of evil short of Satan himself. However, in desanctified or nonsanctified graveyards, they often wait for the spirits of the newly buried to rise and then try to corrupt them into evil practices.

Guytrash (also **Gytrash**): The ghost of a huge cow from Northern England that is believed to be a death omen.

Hannya: In the rural villages of medieval Japan, mental illness or physical deformity was often regarded as proof of demonic possession, and when a deformed or disturbed person died, it was feared they would return to the world of the living as a corrupt and hideous ghost called a Hannya. These monsters have grotesque faces with wicked fangs, knobby chins, and sharp horns on their heads. Their eyes burn with an icy blue light and when the Hannya attacks it uses its powerful claws to catch and rend its prey.

Headless Ghosts: For many centuries there was such an abiding belief that all dead returned as ghosts if they went to the grave whole that it became a practice to lop off the head of a corpse while preparing the body for burial and to place the severed head between the knees before closing the casket. However, some of these spirits returned, sans head, to haunt the living. In other tales, the ghosts of people who were beheaded often returned to the

Exploring the Collective Unconscious

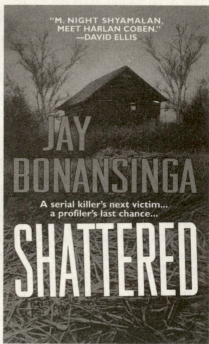

"M. NIGHT SHYAMALAN, MEET HARLAN COBEN."
—DAVID ELLIS

JAY BONANSINGA

A serial killer's next victim...
a profiler's last chance...

SHATTERED

Jay Bonansinga,
photo by Jim Newberry

"Folklore is a reflection of a culture's collective unconscious, but my own individual unconscious was formed—and perhaps twisted—by growing up Catholic. Hence, much of my work features the favorite monster of the Catholic Church: the unclean spirit, which is emblematic of our own dual nature."
—Jay Bonansinga is the internationally best-selling author of a dozen novels, including *Frozen*, *Shattered*, and *Perfect Victim* (all from Pinnacle Books).

mortal plane searching for their heads (which were not always buried with the body, especially during mass executions and after battles).

Headless Horsemen: There have been legends of Headless Horsemen for many centuries, and these ghosts have been reported worldwide. Usually these are soldiers who were decapitated while riding into battle; though some legends—particularly in Scandinavian countries and Mongolia—say that they are the headless spirits of great chieftains who lost their heads in battle and forever wander the earth looking for them.

Jack-in-Irons: A gigantic vengeance ghost from Yorkshire who is believed to be the spirit of a Viking killed in battle with the ancient British. Jack-in-Irons is draped in heavy chains and carries a fierce battle club. He wears a necklace from which are suspended the severed heads of the five toughest warriors he's killed—or, in some tales, the heads of the five people he's most recently killed. A variation of the legend is that Jack was a native of Yorkshire who was imprisoned for murder (fairly or unfairly, depending on which version of the story you hear, and at which pub it's told). He died in prison and now takes out his unending fury on anyone he can catch.

Jenny Green Teeth (also **Jinny Greenteeth**, **Ginny Greenteeth**, **Wicked Jenny**, **Peg o' Nell**, or **Jenny Burnt Tail**): A nasty cross between a mermaid and a ghost who haunts streams and rivers in Lancashire waiting for old people or children to pass by so she can drag them under the water and drown them. Greenteeth is a figure in English folklore. A river hag, similar to Peg Powler, she would pull children or the elderly into the water and drown them. She appears as a woman with green skin, jagged teeth, and long hair in which fish bones and moss are tangled. Jenny's got a lot of play in pop culture. Ridley Scott modeled his lake monster, Meg Mucklebones, after her for his 1985 film *Legend*; and she's been a character in *The Myth Hunters* (Spectra, 2007) by Christopher Golden and *The Wee Free Men* (HarperTeen, 2004) by Terry Pratchett, and appears in Jim Butcher's *Dresden Files* series as well as comics and even stand-up routines by British comics.

Lemure (also **Larvae**): According to Roman mythology, when the dead descended to the underworld, the souls were divided into two distinctly different groups: Manes and Lemure. The Manes, by far the largest group, were the honored spirits of dead ancestors. When a spirit received proper honors from his living relatives, and when

Pulp Folklore

  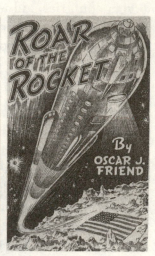

Oscar J. Friend

Pulp fiction (the genre, not the movie) emerged in the 1920s and brought a new vigor and excitement to fantastic storytelling. Known for high-concept fast-and-furious storytelling rather than deep literary merit,[5] pulp fiction encompassed fantasy/sword and sorcery, gangster, detective/mystery, science fiction, adventure, westerns, war, sports, railroad, men's adventure, romance, and horror/occult. Authors like Oscar Jerome Friend (1897–1963) helped bring scientific speculation into mainstream storytelling with tales of UFOs, invading aliens, interdimensional beings, as well as brand-new takes on classic monsters like vampires, werewolves, and mummies. Other key writers of the genre include Robert E. Howard, John D. MacDonald, Robert Bloch, Ray Bradbury, Edgar Rice Burroughs, Hugh B. Cave, Lester Dent, Emond Hamilton, Fritz Leiber, H. P. Lovecraft, Talbo Munday, and even H. G. Wells!

---

5. Though there's some truly wonderful bits of writing there. Try it . . . you'll surprise yourself!

certain holy rites had been performed, the Manes received permission to ascend from the underworld and serve as a spiritual guide and guardian to his descendants. However, those persons whose souls were tainted because they lived evil lives were sent back to haunt and torment the living as the Lemure.

Myling (also **Utburd**): A ghost from Scandinavian folklore that rises from the corpse of an abandoned, unbaptized, or murdered child. Mylings haunt remote areas and are prone to chasing lone travelers. They leap onto the traveler's back and demand to be carried to the nearest graveyard; but as the traveler hurries to obey, the Myling becomes larger and heavier. Theories abound, but a leading explanation is that the Myling absorbs life essence and mass from its victim—increasing as the victim becomes weaker. Another theory is that as it nears its own buried remains it takes on more of its physical form. In some stories the Myling became so heavy it drove its victim all the way into the graveyard soil. The creature seldom killed its victim unless the traveler was unable to bear it all the way to the cemetery. Its other nickname, "utburd," means "that which is taken outside," and refers to the practice of sometimes taking unwanted children to a remote spot and abandoning them there. The children left to die are filled with rage and return from death to seek vengeance on the cruel living. If a person finds the unburied remains of a Myling and then properly buries them in sanctified soil, the creature will find eternal rest.

Noggle: One of the many night-traveling spirits of Britain is the Noggle, whose exact nature is unknown but who generally takes the appearance of a gray horse with a saddle. If anyone makes the error of climbing into the saddle, the Noggle sprints away and throws itself into the nearest deep body of water, changing at once to its true form: a lethal cloud of burning blue light. The Noggle is like a gremlin in nature in that it enjoys making machines (particularly mills) malfunction, but it is afraid of sharp steel and the best way to chase it away from the machinery is to stick a slender knife blade into any open hole in the wheels.

Oni: Supernatural creatures of Japanese folklore, the Oni have been depicted with horns, sharp claws, and gaping mouths and wearing

Extreme Horror

"I think many people—myself not among them—enjoy the visceral response that comes with being terrified—in a safe environment. Movies give them the opportunity to experience the adrenaline rush of fear and the relief of knowing it's all make-believe." —Adrienne Barbeau starred in *The Fog* (1980), *Swamp Thing* (1982), and *Carnivale* (2003–05) and is the coauthor of *Vampyres of Hollywood* (Thomas Dunne, 2008).

Adrienne Barbeau

tiger skins. More than simply monsters, the Oni are the personification of the dark nature of man and can cause disease. The red- or green-bodied Oni of hell prowl the earth in search of sinners and deliver them by chariot to Enma Daiou, the god of hell, who judges them with the aid of two decapitated heads.

Onryō: This Japanese vengeance ghost is a staple of Kabuki,[6] and a prime example of the layered structure of the spirit world as viewed in Shinto culture. Our physical world exists at one side of death and on the other is Yoni, a dreadful underworld where the dead go to rot and suffer for eternity. Between these two extremes is a half-world purgatory that overlaps both sides of the veil. A variety of creatures are trapped there, usually because there is some wrong that needs to be redressed. Sometimes vengeance is sought fairly, and when justice is served against an evildoer the

6. A traditional form of Japanese theater known for highly stylized drama and the frequent mix of folkloric elements and actual historical characters.

Adapting *The Grudge*

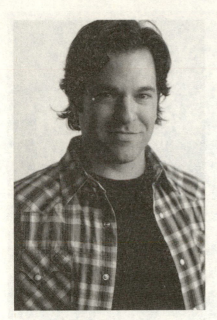

Stephen Susco

"The source material—the two original Ju-On videos (which together comprised about ninety minutes of story)—was unlike anything I'd seen before in the genre. Following multiple characters in multiple storylines, the narrative cut back and forth across time seemingly at random, without any of the usual cues to orient the viewer's perception. I had to watch them at least a half-dozen times before I could fully grasp what the writer/director (Takashi Shimizu) was trying to do. The irony is that when we finally met for the first time, he answered nearly all of my 'what did that mean?' questions with a wry smile, and one of two sentences: 'Well, I just don't know' and 'Does it really matter?' " —Stephen Susco is the screenwriter for *The Grudge* (2004), *Grudge 2* (2006), and *Red* (2008).

---

ghost passes on to a place of eternal rest or into another incarnation. Sometimes the monster will attack anyone—whether that person is the true author of their suffering or not. Pop-culture movies have gotten a lot of play out of these kinds of vengeance ghosts. Films like *Ringu* (*The Ring*), *Ju-On* (*The Grudge*), and others of the Japanese vengeance-ghost film genre have become enormously popular worldwide, both in their original versions and in big-budget American remakes.

Phantom Coaches: These ghostly vehicles are believed to be messengers of death who act like psychopomps to bear human souls to the afterlife. In many of the tales either the coachman or his horses

World Folklore

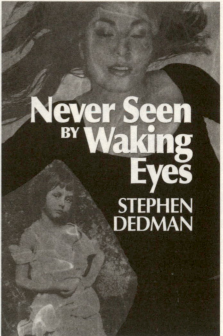

Stephen Dedman,
photo by Beth Gwinn

"In our modern age, with access to information and stories from all over the world, we authors have so many rich cultures from which to draw inspiration and story content. My novels *The Art of Arrow Cutting* and *Shadows Bite* and my short story 'A Single Shadow' were inspired by creatures from Japanese folklore; 'Watch.' 'Upon the Midnight Clear,' and 'A Sentiment Open to Doubt' by beings from Breton, Scottish, and Malaysian folklore respectively; 'The Dance that Everyone Must Do,' 'Waste Land,' and 'What You Wish For' by assorted European vampire myths; 'Probable Cause' and 'Dead of Winter' by the urban legend of the Phantom Hitchhiker, and ' 'Til Human Voices Wake Us' by older stories of La Llorona. I've also borrowed from Greek myth, Norse myth, voodoo, and Jewish folklore at various times, as well as using ghosts, dragons, and other ubiquitous paradigms when they suited my storytelling purpose. World folklore is a limitless well of ideas."

are headless (though no common explanation seems to exist in folklore for this), and everything—coach, driver, and horses—is black. When the coachman does have his head, he wears a fixed and skeletal grin. Phantom Coaches often appear out of nowhere and pass quickly without making a sound. Unlike psychopomps, these unnatural conveyances will sometimes go out of their way to pick up an unwilling passenger. If someone happens to stray into the path of a coach, their life is forfeit and down to the underworld they go.

Poltergeist: There are many kinds of ghosts and spirits in the vast world of the supernatural, ranging from the most benign of house-guests to pernicious creatures such as the vampire. At the mid-point between threat and nuisance is the poltergeist. The poltergeist is a mischievous and occasionally malevolent spirit that manifests its presence by making noises, moving objects, breaking things, and in some cases even assaulting people and animals. The term "poltergeist" comes from the German words poltern, "to knock," and geist, "spirit;" hence a "noisy spirit."

During the twentieth century there were quite a few scientific investigations into the nature of poltergeist phenomena, often yielding nonsupernatural causes such as houses settling on their foundations, seismic activities, sunspots, and other reasons. But many cases of suspected poltergeists remain unexplained despite extensive scientific investigation, and these may involve actual spirits.

The most famous American poltergeist story is that of the Bell Witch of Tennessee. John Bell and his family settled in Robertson County, Tennessee, in 1804 and lived peacefully for over a decade; then in 1817 Bell was walking in his cornfield and encountered a strange animal. It had the head of a rabbit but the body of a large dog. Bell, frightened of the creature, took a shot at it, and it fled into the corn. For reasons never fully explained, the incident kicked off a series of strange events such as the sound of gnawing and pounding and an assault on Bell's seventeen-year-old daughter, Betsy, by an invisible force. Bell himself suffered from facial seizures that often rendered him speechless. This vicious poltergeist was named "the Bell Witch," which is an unfair label since there was no actual witch involved. Maybe "Bell Ghost" didn't have the same ring.

When Bell died in 1820, his family found a small vial on his person that contained an unknown liquid that they presumed to be some kind of medicine; but when they gave a sample of it to the cat, the animal died at once. The rest of the contents were disposed of, and mourners claimed to hear the Bell Witch laughing during the funeral service. In 1883 Goodspeed Publishing released a book[7] containing the first written account of the incident, and it contained this description: "So great was the excitement that people came from hundreds of miles around to witness the manifestations of what was popularly known as the 'Bell Witch.' This witch was supposed to be some spiritual being having the voice and attributes of a woman. It was invisible to the eye, yet it would hold conversation and even shake hands with certain individuals. The feats it performed were wonderful and seemingly designed to annoy the family. It would take the sugar from the bowls, spill the milk, take the quilts from the beds, slap and pinch the children, and then laugh at the discomfiture of its victims. At first it was supposed to be a good spirit, but its subsequent acts, together with the curses with which it supplemented its remarks, proved the contrary."

Like most folktales, the story grew and changed in the telling. Writer and amateur folklorist Nancy Keim Conley shared this variation with us, which includes details that were added after the Bell story was over but which are not part of the most common versions told: "James Johnson, a friend of John Bell's came and spent the night at the request of his friend. When the usual disturbances began, Johnson engaged the phantom in conversation. After this, 'Kate,' as they called the entity, spoke often. She pried into everyone's life, and if she thought ill of someone, she immediately tattled. Kate loved going to prayer meetings and quoting scripture. One day the witch attended both Baptist and Methodist meetings. Confused, she later visited a still and returned to the Bell home drunk, swearing, slapping children, and filling the house with foul

7. The author is unknown.

breath. Many people, including Andrew Jackson, visited. The wheels of his carriage stopped as he approached and were only released after the witch spoke to him. The witch was fond of mother Lucy Bell but hated John Bell. When Lucy was ill, the witch gave her grapes and nuts. When John Bell died, the witch claimed that she killed him. Then the Bell Witch[8] left. As she foretold, she returned briefly after seven years."

Brent Monahan, author of *The Bell Witch/An American Haunting* (St. Martins, 2001), shared his views with us: "No poltergeist has been as celebrated as that of the Bell Witch, particularly because the talking spirit took credit for the death of the father of the bedeviled family. Since ghosts don't kill people, I researched the family diaries and the collected accounts of the neighbors. Although the literary evidence is circumstantial, a succession of facts convinced me that John Bell's murder was fostered by his crime of incest. This led me to write the novel *The Bell Witch/An American Haunting* in pseudo-diary form, and this in turn became the After Dark film *An American Haunting* (2005), starring Donald Sutherland and Sissy Spacek. The actual event quickly passed into regional folklore as locals embellished and exaggerated facts. Just a few examples are the unproven visit of Andrew Jackson, wherein his wagon was allegedly stuck to the earth by the mischievous poltergeist, by its ability to produce nuts and berries out of thin air to coax the ill Lucy Bell to eat, and by its feat of saving a child in a cave under the Bell property."

So what are the facts? No one really knows, but the legend of the Bell Witch lives on, even to the point of heavily influencing the creation of *The Blair Witch Project* (1999), a highly successful independent film that took advantage of early Internet viral marketing to foster the belief that the movie was a documentary about a real witch. While filming, the actors believed that the story was based on a real haunting, though they later discovered the truth during the film's release. The studio even listed the film's three

8. The full story of the Bell Witch is also chronicled in *An Authenticated History of the Famous Bell Witch* by Martin Van Buren Ingram (1894) and *Our Family Trouble: The Story of the Bell Witch* by Richard Williams Bell (1846).

actors as "missing, presumed dead" on their Internet Movie Database profiles. Even though the studio later openly admitted that it was all part of a prerelease advertising campaign, belief persists and there is an urban legend that the filmmakers were told to later claim that the movie was not based on fact.

This is how legends get started. Though some might argue, this is how real ghost stories work their way into the fabric of our everyday consciousness.

Will-o'-the-Wisp: The English-language name for a ghostly phenomenon found in belief systems around the world, the Latin name for Will-o'-the-Wisp is *Ignis Fatuus*, which means "foolish fire." It is also often referred to as a "corpse candle." Most often it appears as one or more fiery balls of light in the night sky that, if followed, will lead travelers from well-trodden paths into treacherous marshes, quicksand, or other dangers and dooms. Folklorists have always disagreed on the nature of the Will-o'-the-Wisp, arguing that it is a ghost, a faerie, a demon, or even a vampire. It is commonly agreed, however, that the Will-o'-the-Wisp is not a cute little forest sprite, but rather a malevolent spirit. The Will-o'-the-Wisp is also commonly believed to be a spirit (or somehow connected to a spirit) of a person who could not enter either heaven or hell, and is forever doomed to wander the earth. It is also frequently linked to funerals, or ghostly repetitions of funerals. Scientists, however, believe that the Will-o'-the-Wisp is an illusion formed by marsh gases. Under the right kinds of weather and environmental conditions, pockets of methane created by rotting vegetation can spontaneously ignite to form standing flames. Ball lightning is another natural phenomenon often blamed for sightings of the Will-o'-the-Wisp. UFO researchers claim that the Will-o'-the-Wisp is a form of intelligent alien life or an alien ship here to observe us. In recent reports of crop circles, glowing balls of light have been frequently filmed and reported. The Will-o'-the-Wisp is called by scores of different names across Europe: Joan the Wad (Cornwall and Somerset), (The Lantern Man) East Anglia, Peg-a-Lantern (Hertfordshire and East Anglia), the Hobby Lantern (Lancashire), Spunkies (Lowland Scotland), Will-o'-the-Wikes (Norfolk),

Using Old and New Folklore

Ramsey Campbell,
photo by J. K. Potter

"My 1993 novel, *The Long Lost*, takes a classic folklore notion—the sin-eater—and plants it in modern suburbia. I was never sure if I'd made it clear in the final line that sin-eating itself might be seen as the ultimate sin. My new novel, *Creatures of the Pool*, draws on Liverpool traditions—urban mysteries, received notions, sinister elements of its history. The narrator blurs the line between history and legend. Maybe in a city like Liverpool (and who knows how many others), where there are so many oral traditions, its life is as much in its tales as in its landscape."
—Ramsey Campbell is Britain's most celebrated living horror writer.

Jenny with the Lantern (North Yorkshire and Northumberland), Will the Smith[9] (Shropshire), Hinky Punk (Somerset and Devon), Jacky Lantern or Jack a Lantern (The West Country), Pwca or the Ellylldan (Wales), Hobbedy's Lantern (Warwickshire Gloucestershire), and Pinket[10] (Worcestershire).

Wraith: The ghost of a person who is about to die but which appears to them before the actual moment of death. Anyone seeing a wraith knows for sure that they are going to die very soon.

9. No relation to the actor.
10. No relation to that same actor's wife. Or . . . is there?

Yūrei: These are Japanese ghosts who have been kept from a peaceful afterlife by some need for vengeance or justice. The name comes from two kanji: *yuu*, meaning "faint" or "dim" and *rei*, meaning "soul" or "spirit." Variations on this include *Borei*, "ruined spirit" and Shiryo, "dead spirit."

6 THEY DEFILE
Hellfire and Demons

DEMONOLOGY 101

Whether or not one believes in the concept of hell, it's impossible not to acknowledge that the infernal depths have been in business for a few thousand years now and logically must be chock-full of the souls of not only just plain bad folks, but everyone who might disagree with someone else's beliefs—in other words, everybody who's not you.

With all of the sin and wickedness in the world today, it's easy to imagine that any and all conceptions of hell are clerical nightmares. What with all the constant coming and going of damned souls, there's hardly time for the odd smoke break. So, to each hell, its Department of Inhuman Resources—and a full staff of devoted demons and other fiery folk who see to it that the machinery of anguish is forever chugging along.

In some schools of thought, demons are unable to procreate, and have always been. Other beliefs have demonic beasties springing up from blasphemies, obscene acts, or even just the utterance of a few naughty words.

The amount of demons in the underworld has been the subject of some fiery debate. In Christian thought, which often leans toward hyperbole, the amount of angels in the universe is incalculable—and the ranks of fallen angels account for one third of that amount. So—that's a lot.

Fallen Angel by Vinessa J. Olp

If one also takes into consideration that "pagan" deities and their consorts (which compose every other belief in the world outside of Christianity) are also essentially demonic figures, then there's more demons prowling the cosmos than you can shake a stick at.

In his 1583 tome *Pseudomonarchia Daemonum*, the Dutch occultist Johann Weyer (1515–1558) wrote of a distinct hierarchy in the demon universe that rivals any similar system in our mortal one. He speculated that there are 666 legions of demons, each containing 6,666 faithful troops, and led by 66 grand dukes, princes and kings of hell—an army that totals 44,435,622. However, subsequent editions of the book played pretty fast and loose with these figures. The humble number one after 665 has suffered a bad rap since the days of Revelation.

Many of the "devils" of the world gained their infamy by stealing valuable gifts that the gods felt were "beneath" mankind to use and shrewdly passing them along. Depending on the religion, some of these items were a sense of self, fire, and the secrets of farming and fishing, as well as gifts a bit more arcane. And, boy, do they get punished for it.

Demons are free to do the five big no-no's in Judeo-Christian belief—that is, divination or sorcery; interpreting omens or practicing astrology; practicing witchcraft; acting as a medium in communication with the spirits; and necromancy.

In the New Testament, demons are said to be responsible for many of man's ills. Mental illnesses such as depression, self-mutilation, and suicide are perhaps the most notable. People also saw dark work in other states of the human condition and the sick. Those who were blind, deaf, mute, or who suffered from seizures, epilepsy, or autism were surely being tormented by demons.

The following pages present a compendium of these devoted servants of deviltry.

Lovecraft and the Cthulhu Mythos

Kenneth Hall and Yog Sothoth from *Halfway House*

The Great Old Ones, the terrifying and immensely powerful race of elder gods of H. P. Lovecraft's Cthulhu Mythos[1] have been tapped as source material for pop-culture fiction and film ostensibly about the struggle against demons. Lovecraft's story cycle deals with ancient races of monsters and gods that had been forced out of this plane of existence and who are constantly seeking ways to sneak back in and reclaim the world they feel is rightly theirs. Central to this mythos is a book called the *Necronomicon*,[2] which is a wholly fictional creation of Lovecraft but which was written of so often by the author and many of his peers and admirers (such as Robert Bloch, Robert E. Howard, August Derleth, and others) that it is widely believed by fans of

1. Also known as the Lovecraft Mythos, the phrase "Cthulhu Mythos" was actually coined by August Derleth.

2. The *Necronomicon* was supposedly written by "Mad Arab" Abdul Alhazred and was first mentioned in the 1924 short story "The Hound."

the genre to have once been an actual book. The *Necronomicon* and the legends of Cthulhu have become part of folklore in its truest sense in that people believe that these were once actual belief systems.

The influence of Lovecraft can hardly be understated and echoes of "elder gods" concepts that are very similar to his can be seen in pop culture from *Re-Animator* (1985) to *Hellboy* (2004) to the *Evil Dead* (1983) films. There have been hundreds of Lovecraftian short stories and scores of films that mine this rich faux mythology for story content. References to the Great Old Ones have appeared in TV's *Justice League*, *Babylon 5*, *Doctor Who*, *Teenage Mutant Ninja Turtles*, and even *The Simpsons*. The Mythos are referenced in dozens of video and role-playing games, including World of Warcraft, Chaos Gods, Dungeons & Dragons, Castlevania, and Quake.

DEMONS AND FALLEN ANGELS

Aamon: A demon that serves as an assistant to the great king of hell Astaroth, Aamon is the keeper of the knowledge of the future and the past. He may be a corruption of the Egyptian deity Amun, or of Ba'al Hammon, which is associated with ancient Carthage.

The American death metal band Deicide, formed in Tampa, Florida, in 1997 was originally called Amon, but was changed due to Roadrunner Records label mate King Diamond using the term for an old house in his concept album *Them* released the same year.

Abaddon: Another of the many terms that has become inter-changeably associated with the devil. In Revelation 9:11 he is the "King of the Grasshoppers" who will rise at the sounding of the fifth trumpet blast at the end of days. His name in Hebrew means destruction, but can also mean a place of destruction and is often associated with Sheol—a jewish concept of the afterlife.

Abathur: Though not a predator of any kind, Abathur is certainly involved in the influence the supernatural world has over matters

of living and dying. Abathur is—according to myths from ancient Iraq and Iran—the Judge of the Dead. He weighs and measures the souls of the recently deceased and based on their actions and character while alive determines if they are sent onward to paradise or downward to eternal torment. His position and nature are analogous in most ways with Thoth, lord of the scales in the Egyptian Book of the Dead, and St. Peter from Christian belief.

Demons and Christian Fundamentalism

"Having been a former Christian fundamentalist, I've also written about demons, such as in my novelette *This Body of Death*, and lots of mythology. I'm particularly fond of having the gods play unexpected roles within my stories, such as 'When Gods Die,' where Loki turns out to be a patient in the Intensive Care Unit of a neurosurgeon with a dark secret." —Maria Alexander has been publishing her dark fiction and poetry to some acclaim since 2000.

Abigor (also **Eligor, Eligos**): Demons are seldom direct killers, and instead act as manipulators of men who, in turn, commit the actual murders. Lesser demons may possess a single person and cause him to act irrationally and dangerously, whereas great demons could influence whole armies.

Abigor, a demon from the pre-Judeo-Christian era of beliefs, was one of the true elite of Hell and was the most senior demon of warfare and battle. He had the power of second sight and could see the future well enough to advise generals on how and where to attack in order to do the most damage to their enemies. If a human prince or general were to offer up his soul to Abigor, this Duke of Hell would buy it with secrets of how to win battles and conquer enemies. These secrets often led to the bloodiest victories in history.

Adramelech: A demon that is said to serve as the president of the Demonic Senate (which probably pales in comparison to the palpable evil that is the Senate of the United States). He is said to be the overseer of Satan's wardrobe. In art, he is often depicted as a centaur. In the modern age, Adramelech has made himself at home in the video game world in Final Fantasy Tactics: The War of the Lions (2007) as the dragon character of Adramelechk.

Aerial Demons: In medieval times, theologians placed all demons into six classes, including those that move through the air. These

Abigor, Duke of Hell

aerial demons are formless by nature but can adopt any appearance they choose. These demons are the evil counterpart of the far more benign spirits of the air such as faerie folk, elementals, and so on. Aerial demons are often invoked by sorcerers and used as weapons against their enemies. Being either formless or in a deceptive form, they make excellent tools of attack or revenge.

Agaliarept: A high-ranking demon and one of the great generals of hell and the commander of the second legion of demons. He is a direct servant—or perhaps advisor—to Lucifer. His areas of earthly dominion include Asia Minor and parts of Europe. His most potent weapon is his unnatural ability to sow distrust and discord between men, often resulting in outbreaks of violence or war.

Ahriman: To those who follow the religion known as Zoroastrianism, Ahriman is the central demonic figure and could be called its devil, ever battling against the god Ahura Mazda. Ahriman has since been invoked by wordslingers such as Philip K. Dick in *The Cosmic Puppets* (1957); Robert A. Heinlein's *Stranger in a Strange Land* (1961); Dean Koontz in *False Memory* (2000); Jacqueline Carey's *Kushiel's Avatar* (2003); Karl Friedrich May in *Im Reiche des silbernen Löwen* (1898); Philadelphia's own Ben Bova in *Orion* (series 1984–1995); and in David Zindell's *Lightstone* (2001). He's also been portrayed in video games as level bosses of varying ferocity battled Wonder Woman, and commanded chaos in *Warhammer 40k*.

Aim: Also called Aym or Harborym, Aim is a grand duke of hell and a master of destruction by fire. He is depicted as a man with three heads, that of a handsome youth with two stars upon his forehead, a serpent, and a calf. Aim is part of the Dungeons & Dragons gaming world and has also appeared in DC Comics—Sabbac is an enemy of Captain Marvel and the "a" in his name is in homage to the demon.

Demons in Art

"My favorites would have to be Vasilii Maksimov's *A Sorcerer Comes to a Peasant Wedding* and Mikhail Vrubel's many works based on Mikhail Lermontov's *Demon* and Goethe's *Faust*. I also enjoyed Stephen Gammell's illustrations in the Scary Stories series from which I derived much delight as a kid. He had a truly unique style and I still get chills looking at his illustrations."
—Dorian Townsend completed a PhD at the University of New South Wales on the Symbolism of the Vampire Myth in Russian literature.

Aitvara: In Lithuania there is a particularly nasty little spite demon called the Aitvara who makes a nest behind the stove in rural family homes. The Aitvara is never seen in its true form—whatever that may be—but instead shape-shifts into the form of a black cock or a black cat, though in either of these forms it can communicate either through ordinary speech or telepathically. The Aitvara is a trickster and offers deals to the unwary, offering marvelous treasures in exchange for their souls. All of these offered treasures are stolen, however, so the victims give away their most sacred possession in exchange for money or other goods whose very nature is tainted. The best method for keeping the Aitvara from even attempting to make such an offer is to leave offerings of food—well prepared, not table scraps—and a bowl of clean water. These simple offerings, frequently renewed, are apparently enough to keep the Aitvara from playing its devilish tricks.

Hell and Damnation by Allen Koszowski

Alastor: To the Greeks, Alastor is the personification of the lust of vengeance. His influence can make men kill and participate in long-running feuds. He also serves as the chief executioner of hell. Alastor's presence has also been seen in anime and in inspired media like *Devil May Cry* (2001), *Viewtiful Joe* (2003) and the *Castlevania* (1988) series of video games and in the character of Alastor "Mad Eye" Moody in J. K. Rowlings's Harry Potter books.

Aldinach: A demon of ancient Egypt said to be the cause of natural disasters such as floods and famine, as well as accidents at sea. He is often depicted in the form of a human female.

***Aldinach* by Mike Bohatch**

Amaymon: A prince in command of the western provinces of hell, he is said to possess poisonous breath. Anyone brave (or foolish) enough to conjure him had best stand firmly on his feet and be polite, for the demon is easily offended. Once a conjurer has invoked the creature's ire, the intended goal of the spell, for good or for ill, is doomed to failure.

Amaymon, Prince of Hell by Allen Koszowski

Amdusias: A demon whose voice can be heard in the booming of thunder. After he is invoked, he is followed by a blare of musical instruments heralding his coming. In art he is depicted as a man with the talons of a bird for his hands and feet. Another demon close to the hearts of video gamers, Amdusias plays a recurring role in the worlds of *Castlevania* and *Final Fantasy* and even in gamedom is said to be the most rockin' musician in all of hell.

And speaking of rocking, the Mexican aggrotech (a dark mixture of techno and industrial sounds) band Amduscia is also named for him.

Apaosa: The foul and powerful arch-demon Apaosa of ancient Persia led a great host of evil demons and wherever this horde went the land was broken and laid waste. Apaosa delighted in drying up water sources to create drought and in spreading famine and disease. He caused eclipses that blotted out the sun and reveled in the fear caused by even the smallest of his cruel acts. In the Great War between the demons of hell and the legions of heaven, Apaosa met his match in the person of the god of fertility and water, Tistrya, who met and defeated the arch-demon in a battle that shook the earth.

Asmodeus: Also called Aeshma or Aesma, Asmodeus was once viewed as the ruler of all demons. He figured prominently in the mythology of ancient Persia, as well as in the New Testament in the Book of Tobit. In the music world, Asmodeus is a death-metal act out of Australia, a Dutch psychobilly band, and undoubtedly a few thousand fledgling bands of all genres from around the world that haven't quite made it out of the garage. The character of Asmodeus Poisonteeth the adder is a staple in Brian Jacques's Redwall (1986) series of fantasy books. Don't let the talking rodentia on the cover fool you—these books are excellent, and fantasy readers of all ages are sure to dig them.

Astaroth: The figure generally regarded as the Grand Duke of hell, Astaroth was first referenced in the *Key of Solomon* (seventeenth century). In film, Astaroth has been all over the astral map, from the 1921 German silent film *The Golem: How He Came Into the World* to the 1971 Disney classic *Bedknobs and Broomsticks*, in which the "Star of Astaroth" is a potent magic totem that makes flying beds look like pulling so many rabbits out of a hat. Bet you'll never look at Angela Lansbury in the same way again. You're welcome. Demons of all sorts are close to the dark little hearts of metal bands everywhere and Astaroth is no exception. He has been invoked via power chord by Mercyful Fate (Denmark); Testament (USA); Black Widow (UK); Candlemass (Sweden); Behemoth (Poland); Thus Defiled (UK); Mägo de Oz (Spain); and scores of others. In the video game world, Astaroth is about as old school as a boss can get in the coin-op games *Ghosts n' Goblins* (1985), *Ghouls n' Ghosts* (1988), and in the PC game classic *Ultima V* (1988).

Azi Dahaka: Demons that serve as a symbol of ultimate destruction are common in mythology; and these monsters are the beings that will rise to power during an Armageddon (or Ragnarok, etcetera). One such monster is the Azi Dahaka from Iranian folklore, a three-headed, six-eyed serpent of immense size and power that is destined for a climactic battle with the warrior god Thraetaona during the final end-of-days battle called Fraso-Kereti. While biding his time for the end of the world, the Azi Dahaka amuses himself by slaughtering livestock, destroying farms, carrying off humans for snacks, and generally acting in a way consistent with an evil monster.

At some point in history, when events start shaping up toward the apocalypse, the heroic Thraetaona will overcome Azi Dahaka and imprison him on the top of the mountain Dermawend. Azi Dahaka will escape as the global situation disintegrates from bad to awful, and it will cause havoc and destruction throughout the land. However, the monster is fated to die in Ayohsust, the great river of fire that will burn its way through the land as time itself ends.

Baalberith: A demon who is the overseer of pacts and bargains made between demons and men. His seal appears on all contracts of an infernal nature (like there are any that aren't).

Beast of the Apocalypse: In the last book of the Christian New Testament, the apostle John records his visions of the End of Days. In his vision he encounters God, the Messiah, angels; and all manner of supernatural creatures, including the most frightening of all monsters—the Beast. This immensely powerful creature speaks with the voice of a dragon and bears on its horned head the mystical number 666, known as the "number of the beast." John writes: "And I stood upon the sand of the sea, and saw a beast rise

Classic Artists in Demonology

Claustrophobia by Diana Pasov

"I wouldn't really call William Blake a horror artist, yet there is no one else to have painted demons better than him. I'm also very much into the art of Luis Royo and Dorian Cleavenger for both amazing skill and originality." —Diana Pasov is a medical student and artist living in Bucharest, Romania.

up out of the sea, having seven heads and ten horns, and upon his horns ten crowns, and upon his heads the name of blasphemy."[3] The coming of the Beast, or Antichrist, has been predicted for over a thousand years, and diverse writers, scholars, and theologians have variously assumed it to be manifested in human form as one of the Caesars, Napoleon, Hitler, and others. None of these have, apparently, actually been the Antichrist, as evidenced by the continued existence of the world, tumultuous as it may be.

Belephegor (also **Baal-Peor**, **Chemosh**): This is a demon from ancient Assyria whose method of attack is to inspire unsavory sexual practices in persons otherwise chaste. To corrupt is the delight of this monster, and he has appeared in one form or another throughout history. His name is a corruption of the biblical name Baal-Peor, a god of the Moabites to whom the Israelites became attached in Shittim (also known as Abel-shittim). This was the last place in which the Israelites encamped before reaching the Holy Land following their Exodus from Egypt. During this early encounter with the Moabites, the women of Israel were supernaturally compelled to have illicit relations with the men of that land.[4] As punishment, Moses commanded that all of the Israelites who had sacrificed to Baal-Peor were to be killed, a slaughter that claimed 24,000 lives. Belphegor has been depicted in a number of lurid ways in religious (and even sacrilegious) artwork. In some he is a capering satyr, in others a more traditionally demonic black goat, and in others he is merely represented as a monstrous phallic symbol.

Buer: A duke of hell with fifty legions in his command, he can bestow knowledge of nature, philosophy, and herbology. He is often depicted like the Zodiac sign Sagittarius—an archer with the head and trunk of a man and the body of a horse. In video games, he is portrayed both as a many-winged bat in *Castlevania: Dawn of Sorrow* (2005) and as a demon surrounded by rings of flame in *Final Fantasy* (1987). He has also appeared in the comics *Hellblazer* (1998) and Alan Moore's *Promethea* (1999).

3. Revelation 13:1.
4. Numbers 25

Favorite Folklore Topics

Offerings to a Demon

"I've always liked demon stories, including non-Judeo-Christian concepts of similar kinds of beings. My family, who is both Irish and Italian, used to tell me stories of banshees and of leprechauns, and their Italian equivalent, whose name I can pronounce, but can't spell. Both countries have rich fairy tales and folklore, an abundance of superstition and beliefs, and I've always found those stories fascinating." —Mary SanGiovanni is the author of the Bram Stoker Award–nominated *The Hollower* (Leisure Books, 2007) and *Found You* (2008).

Eblis by Allen Koszowski

Eblis: In Islam, Eblis is one of the most important and deadly demonic figures. Eblis is said to have disobeyed the will of Allah and was exiled from heaven and cast into Jahannam (the hell of Islamic beliefs).

Enma Daiou: In Japanese tradition, hell is referred to as Jigoku, and Enma Daiou is its king. It is his charge to judge the souls of the wicked and send them to a fitting punishment. Not surprisingly, Enma Daiou appears often in Japanese popular culture, and has blended into our own through the success of manga, a Japanese style of comic book, and anime, the blanket term used (to the jeers of some fans) for Japanese-style animated films. Enma Daiou appears both in print and in such films as *Dragon Ball Z* (1985); *Avatar* (2005); *Spooky Kitaro 4* (1959); *Yu Yu Hakusho* (1990); and *Jigoku Shoujo: Girl from Hell.*

Erinyes: The Romans called these Greek-inspired winged women "the furies." They serve as the personification of the spirit of

Demons in Folklore

Steve Wedel

"My novella *Seven Days in Benevolence* uses folklore about ghosts and witches. In short fiction I've used several elements of folklore about snake gods, vampires, and demonic possession. I've also used things like ancient religions and recurring tabloid headlines about male pregnancy and such."—Steven E. Wedel is the author of dozens of short stories, hundreds of articles, and several books, most notably the books of the Werewolf Saga.

vengeance in the souls who had wrongly died. Despite their not-so-easy-on-the-eyes appearance, alternately depicted like a gorgon with a head full of writhing serpents or with a dog's body and a bat's wings, as demons go they are fairly neutral in their activities and tend to give balance rather than disrupt it.

Eurynome: This demon first appeared in Greek mythology as one of the Titans. In later conceptions of demonology, he became the prince of death and a devourer of carrion. He is depicted as being cloaked with a wolf's hide that is covered with oozing sores and rot. Fans of early black metal associate the stage name Euronymous with Øystein Aarseth (1968–1993), founder of the Norweigan band Mayhem. In this story there's less fame and more infamy because he was murdered by fellow musician "Varg" Vikernes, of the project band Burzum. Despite Euronymous's murder, or perhaps because of it, the black-metal scene thrived and bands invoking the snow-covered mountains and forests of Norway have since popped up in pretty much every climate the world has to offer.

Gong Gong (also **Kung-Kung**): There is a fierce black dragon in Chinese folklore who, like Lucifer, was a high official in heaven but tired of being a servant and challenged the god of fire, Zhu-Rong, to a battle. Their conflict lasted many days before the two gods, still locked in immortal combat, tumbled from heaven and fell like a burning comet to the earth. When they struck, Gong-Gong was dazed and weakened while Zhu-Rong rose up victorious and ascended again to heaven. Humiliated by his defeat, Gong-Gong attempted to kill himself by ramming his head against one of the Pillars of Heaven. Gong-Gong did manage to commit suicide, but at the same time tore a massive hole in the dimension wall between heaven and earth, a catastrophe that resulted in the Great Flood that covered the planet. The goddess Nu-Gua attempted to restore the balance, but the damage was so extensive that though the world was saved, heaven was forever slanted sideways, which explains why the Pole Star no longer sits in the center of the night sky.

Hecate: In Greek mythology she was the goddess of the wilderness and the patron of midwives and childbirth. Though this seems pretty innocuous, she was also the goddess of sorcery, which led to her being regarded as a demonic figure in Christian thought. In the *Buffy the Vampire Slayer* television series (1997–2001), the delightfully witchy Willow Rosenberg (Alyson Hannigan) often invoked her aid when working her spells, and on at least one occasion said, "For the love of Hecate, somebody stop me." In the equally bewitching WB series *Charmed* (1988–2006) Prudence, Piper, and Phoebe tangle with a risen, pissed-off, and gnarly looking Hecate, who's come to earth to find a boyfriend.

Lilith: Over time the Lilû story evolved into that of Lilith, and from there has been sewn into the cultural fabric of many nations.

Demons as New Folklore

Martin Treanor

"My novel *Drawn* originally started out as *Banshee*, the idea being that: 'What if most of our spookier folklore was based on real evil presences?' The main reckoning behind this was that demons and malicious spirits were masquerading behind a lore that encourages a certain amount of skepticism; their true nature and purpose can be masked by the very superstition they breed from. The idea didn't totally take root, but it formed an interesting basis for the story to develop."
—Martin Treanor is an Irish short-story writer and novelist of psychological horror and supernatural thrillers.

In the *Epic of Gilgamesh*, Lilith is a female demon who has taken up residence in the sacred Tree of Life that belongs to the Goddess Inanna, and her very presence stunts the growth of the tree. Gilgamesh manages to drive the demon out and frees the tree of other monsters (including a gigantic bird), and Lilith flees into the wilderness. Lilith's story doesn't end there. Her story is picked up again in Hebrew religious history, which mentions her as the first mate of Adam. She and Adam had the first case of irreconcilable differences and she was cast out of Eden by a couple of angels acting as celestial bouncers. Lilith, understandably, was royally pissed and supposedly went to the abode of demons, where she then gave birth to countless demon children. Some legends suggest that her offspring were the first vampires.

However, not everyone buys into this version of Lilith's history and even insist that she's the victim of sexist propaganda and disinformation. Today Lilith has a huge international following that regards her as one of the most potent feminist icons present in today's New Age and Wiccan cultures.

Lilû (also **Ardat Lili**): The Lilû (lit. "spirit") were a race of ancient elemental demons very similar to the Succubus who took human form in order to hunt. Most often they'd assume the form of a beautiful woman who exuded an irresistible sexual appeal that would make the suddenly sex-starved victim follow them to a secluded place when the creature would feed on sexual essence, life essence, breath, and even blood, leaving him desiccated and lifeless. The most ferocious of these creatures was Ardat Lili, who many scholars credit as the first of the "Old Hag" myths. Ardat

---

The Inspiration of Lilith

*"**Night Angel**, starring Linden Ashby and Karen Black, was based on the ancient Middle Eastern legend of Lilith, the prototypical sexual demon. The film was produced nine years before the first Lilith Fair brought knowledge of Lilith into the mainstream, and I'd been aware of the legend long before I wrote the script. Like Night of the Demons, the film was based on a spec script, originally titled Lilith. Part of my inspiration came from my personal history. In my wild younger days I was something of a sex addict, and very irresponsible in my dealings with the opposite sex. Luckily, my wildest phase ended before the advent of herpes and AIDS, but eventually karma kicked my ass, in the form of a dark-haired seductress who would have made a perfect Lilith if we'd have been casting the film when she entered my life. My brief affair with her destroyed a great relationship I'd been in, and turned my world upside down."* —Joe Augustyn created the horror-film franchise *Night of the Demons*, which was based on his original screenplay *The Halloween Party*, and is scheduled to be remade in 2008 with Shannon Elizabeth taking over the lead role of Angela.

Supernatural Predation

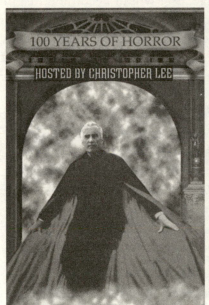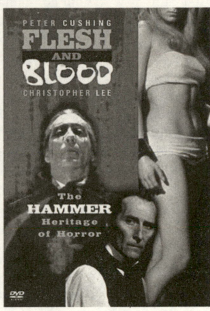

Horror documentaries by Ted Newsome

"Take the vampire idea: most cultures have an ur-myth of a demon or cursed human who drains the life from the living. That probably has a basis in primordial fears of losing control of the Self, of the psychological truth that some personalities can drain others, and the ancient practice of cannibalism and blood drinking still present in the Catholic Mass. But as similar in some ways as these ancient myths are—the succubus, Lilith, the strega, the Chinese tales of cats sucking life-breath from babies, etcetera—they are not the same 'monster,' nor do they follow the same rules of engagement." —Ted Newsom has directed and/or produced more than seventy documentaries, including *Flesh and Blood*, *The Hammer Heritage of Horror* (the last teaming of icons Peter Cushing and Christopher Lee), *100 Years of Horror* (also with Christopher Lee), and the 1950s parody *The Naked Monster*.

Lili's hunting technique was far subtler than those of the other Lilû. Though she often appeared as a very desirable woman it was in dreams that she did her damage. She would become pure spirit and enter into the sleeping mind of her victim and inspire intensely erotic dreams. It was believed that a nocturnal discharge of semen meant that a man had become the victim of Ardat Lili, and each time this happened he would be substantially weaker and less sexually potent.

Throughout the writings of the Sumerians there are references to similar beings—or possibly the same beings with different regional or historical spellings—such as Lulu, the spirit of reckless wantonness; and Limnu, the spirit of evil. As the Sumerian and Babylonian cultures blended, the stories of these Night Comers changed and evolved. During the time of the Hebrew Captivity in Babylon (600 B.C.E.), the Hebrews absorbed some of the Sumerian legends and in their folktales the Lilitu evolved into a new creature: Lilith.

Malphas: A demon depicted as a raven that can transform into a human. He takes great pleasure in knocking down human-built structures for the enemies of those that would dare conjure him. Another demonic staple of the video game world, Malphas throws series fireballs in several *Castlevania* games as well as in *Savage 2: A Tortured Soul* (2008).

Mammon: A demon for those that desire great wealth, and aren't too picky about stepping on a few heads to do it. His name even means "wealth" in Aramaic. In popular culture, he's on board with causes aplenty. In Mozilla net-speak, Mammon is used to refer to Microsoft's Internet Explorer software, which, considering the adversarial nature of the two companies is less than flattering. He's also made appearances in videogames like *Chrono Trigger* (1995), in films such as the Keanu Reeves film *Constantine* (2005), and in Todd McFarlane's bad-ass comic *Spawn* (1992).

Mejenkwaad (also **Mejenkwaar**): The Marshall Islands, known as the Pearl of the Pacific, is a group of more than twelve hundred islands and islets with some of the most beautiful beaches, trees, and scenery on Earth. They are also the home to a species of

Mephistopheles by Allen Koszowski

(mostly) female demons called the Mejenkwaad, who begin as ordinary human women but can inexplicably transform into monstrous cannibals. The process is simple but very strange. Among the natives of those islands it's customary for the husband of a pregnant woman to sail off in his boat to gather special foods and collect items of rare natural beauty—shells, etcetera—that would make appropriate birthing gifts. However, the husband is required to accomplish all this very quickly because if he is gone too long—more than a lunar month—his pregnant bride will suddenly transform from normal human to a homophagic[5] beast. She will first devour her own child, and then, when her husband returns, he'll be next on the menu.

5. Cannibalistic.

Mephistopheles: Though there is no direct mention of him in the Bible, Mephistopheles has nonetheless become one of the most commonly mentioned aspects of the Devil. It seems likely that he is a fictional character created by Renaissance-era Christians. In these stories, Mephistopheles was the first rebel angel to align with Lucifer and consequently the second to be cast into Hell afterward. Mephistopheles has appeared in the works of Christopher Marlowe, Goethe, Mikhail Bulgakov, Thomas Mann, Hector Berlioz, Franz Liszt, Washington Irving, and Charles Gounod. Many of these tales are reworkings or interpretations of the German legend of Faust[6]—the classic cautionary tale of a man who sells his soul to the devil in exchange for untold riches and pleasures. Mephistopheles is also a recurring supervillain in Marvel Comics.

Murmur: A duke of hell that is depicted as a man wearing a crown and riding a giant vulture. Those who invoke him do so to raise the dead so that they might answer any questions demanded of them. Murmur is also the alter ego of Dr. Michael Amar, a once successful and respected surgeon driven mad by the voices in his head in the DC Comics universe. Now a supervillain, he first did the deadly dance with The Flash in 2001.

Old Scratch: Scratch, or, Old Scratch, is one of the many nicknames given to the devil, and drawn from the old Scandinavian word for a goblin, *skratta*. In modern Scandinavian, *scratti* is used.

Orias: A duke of hell that can disclose the secrets of divination and the mysteries of the zodiac to those that would conjure him. In art, he is depicted as a lion with the tail of a serpent, or as a man riding a lion while holding a writhing snake in each clenched fist. In the Disney adaptation of C. S. Lewis's *The Lion, the Witch and the Wardrobe* (2005), a character called Orias plays lion-king Aslan's right-hand centaur—but that doesn't jibe with the book. We know it's tough for centaurs to get work in Hollywood—so we're cool with it.

---

6. In German "Faust" means "fist"; the Latin variation, Faustus, means "auspicious" or "lucky."

Old Scratch by Allen Koszowski

Pan: One of the most familiar images in Greek mythology, this god of lust, wine, and all around good times is portrayed as a faun, a man with the lower half of a goat, horns, and a beard. Religious ceremonies dealing with Pan were drunken orgies, with perhaps a few prayers thrown in for good measure. Later cultures reduced this old goat to a demonic figure.

Pazuzu: A powerful demon of the desert that was greatly feared by the people of ancient Mesopotamia. Depicted as a towering figure with a great spread of wings, the claws of a lion, the stinging tail of

The Influence of Demons

"One of my stories, 'Firebird,' which appeared in *Year's Best Horror* and *Best New Horror*, features an antagonist called a Drude, an arcane Germanic demon that invades the dreams of its victims. It's one of my finest efforts, and I feel that the Old-World folklore monster gave the story a sense of menace that could not have been achieved by a modern antagonist."
—J. L. Comeau is an award-winning short-story writer whose work has appeared in major horror anthologies including *Best New Horror*, *Year's Best Horror*, *Dark Visions*, *Borderlands*, and *Hot Blood*.

a scorpion, and a monstrously deformed head, Pazuzu was the personification of storm winds blowing from south to east; these were the winds that brought disease. The legends of Pazuzu were the basis for the novel and 1973 film *The Exorcist*. Fans of Matt Groening's spaced-out animated series *Futurama* (1999–2003) also know Pazuzu as the devoted gargoyle belonging to 160-year-young Professor Hubert J. Farnsworth, who returns once in the nick of time to save his life.

Rahu: The dragon-headed Hindu demon Rahu has the power to actually cause eclipses. He rides across the sky in a golden jewel-encrusted chariot pulled by a team of eight very fierce-looking horses, and is depicted with his mouth thrown wide, ready to devour the sun.

Rakshasa: The Rakshasa of India is very well known in that vast nation, and deeply feared. In different regions of India, the Rakshasa legend changes. In some areas it is a race of demonic females who use shape-shifting abilities to take the form of beautiful women in order to attack men. In other areas the Rakshasa can be either female or male, and uses theriomorphy to take whatever shape will allow it to hunt most effectively. In some of the oldest Rakshasa tales, the creatures bear no resemblance to humans at all and are just monstrous night hunters. In all cases, however, the

---

The Future of the Mystery Story

"I'm a mystery writer, and in this genre we're seeing a groundswell of stories that not only incorporate vampires and werewolves and demons but also offer these creatures as the heroes of the novels. It's a different world from Chandler and Hammett. Will it last? Only time will tell."
—William Kent Krueger writes the Cork O'Connor mystery series, set in the great Northwoods of Minnesota. His work has received a number of awards, including the Anthony Award for Best Novel in both 2005 and 2006

Rakshasa is a deadly monster who delights in slaughter. They will even prey on pregnant women and babies, slaughtering them and drinking their blood. Though the Rakshasa are smart and strong, they can be destroyed by fire. They are also one of the few species of monster against whom sunlight is an effective weapon, although forcing the creature out into the light of day is another matter.

The Rakshasa by Hervé Scott Flament

Shax: A great duke of hell that revels in being able to strike men deaf, dumb, and blind in one fell swoop. To add insult to injury, Shax will also steal your property and livestock. Shax has battled *Hellboy* (1993) in comic books and is a recurring character name in the work of American author Shirley Jackson (1916–1965) and the name of her beloved black cat. If you've never read "The Lottery," well, you should, and we mean right now.

Tieholtsodi: A Navajo water demon that was once a great enemy of mankind and caused the cataclysmic floods that destroyed an earlier version of the world. Over time, however, the Tieholtsodi has become more genial and has not attacked humanity as a whole in some time.

Ufir: A demon from Christian folklore of the Middle East who unlocks the secrets of human physiology by dissecting corpses in graveyards. He shares this knowledge with other demons so that they can cause sickness and infirmity.

Xaphan (also **Shafan**): A demon from Middle Eastern and Hebrew myth that ambitiously tried to set fire to heaven. When Lucifer fell, this arsonist-demon fell with him and now is charged with the task of keeping the fires of hell burning. In art he is depicted as carrying a massive bellows, but due to his punishment he must keep the flames stoked using his breath alone.

7 THEY DECEIVE
Tricksters and Seducers

Succubus by Bill Chancellor

WEIRD AND WICKED

As the saying goes, "you can catch more flies with honey than you can with vinegar." And plenty of supernatural predators have kept this concept close to their blackened little hearts. We've already talked about vampires and other creatures that feast on the blood of men—but there are other creatures of the night that require sustenance of a more personal variety. Some creatures require the potent sexual essence of men (and women) and take an extra dark delight in deflowering virgins, ruining marriages, and sowing general discord.

The etymology of the term "succubus" is twofold. While the word is derived from the Latin *succuba*, meaning adulterer, trollop, or prostitute, the term is created from sub (beneath) and cubo (I lie). So, the meaning of succubus is literally "one that lies beneath"—and its male counterpart is the incubus (the prefix "in" meaning on top). According to some theologies, succubae and incubi are locked in a hideous contract. The succubus will steal semen from men in nocturnal sexual encounters, and the incubus will use the cache to impregnate women with demonic offspring called cambion, who are often born deformed or with supernatural abilities, as these creatures do not have any other method of procreation. Among the more infamous cambions of folklore include the character of Caliban in Shakespeare's *The Tempest*. According to some takes on Arthurian legends, some speculate that the wizard Merlin was also a cambion. And to amp up the creepy factor a few notches, this dark union was purported to be between an incubus and a nun.

While the visages of the succubus range from the truly alluring to the truly revolting, but they are generally a combination of both. It is the classic folly of man to be beguiled by beauty to the detriment of his common sense, bank account, and social standing with his single buddies. As is often the case, the true nature of the succubus is discovered too late, and by then the victim is left a lifeless husk, the creature is stalking off through the cosmos in search of a new victim.

In modern parlance, "succubus" has come to mean a woman whose relationship changes the nature of a man (usually in the view of "the victim's" friends and family). As is the case with the legends, the man is generally blissfully unaware that any changes have taken place.

Like so many other tales of supernatural predators, concepts like succubae and incubi were paths to explain the unexplainable and wrap one's brain around the unthinkable. We now know that nocturnal emissions (wet dreams) are a healthy and normal part of growing up as a man. Even with this knowledge firmly in the psyche, there's a certain shock that comes from that first experience. If you add to this mix a healthy dose of Old Testament fire and damnation, then the experience becomes terrifying.

In those cases, it's almost preferable to believe that a man is visited by a night-spirit that's come to steal his sexual essence than to

Deadly Seduction by Kathy Gold

face the prospect that some ejaculations are beyond his control—especially among the "holy men" (from the Pope on down to the town priest) who had taken solemn vows of celibacy. While science has slain a few more supernatural predators in the last several decades, some seem to remain continually out of our reach.

Pop culture has seen its fair share of both succubae and incubi in films, television, and literature. Science fiction icon William Shatner has twice faced the fabled beastie—first in his pre-Starfleet days in the 1965 film *Incubus*, where he portrays the plaything of the beautiful succubus Kia (played by Allyson Ames).

Still, *Incubus* is more an art-house flick, with the dubious distinction in that dialogue is performed in Esperanto—a language created in the 1870s by Polish ophthalmologist Dr. Ludovic Lazarus Zamenhof (1859–1917). Happily, Shatner brings his over-acting abilities to even the world's youngest established language—mugging his way through the film in his classic, endearing style.

As Captain Kirk, he again faced a succubus-like creature in the "Obsession" episode of the original *Star Trek* series in 1967. In this case the creature is formless, a mysterious cloud that Kirk first faced in his youth. As is the case with many legends associated with the succubus, Kirk maintains his obsession with the creature while those around him are helpless to do anything but watch him slowly succumb to its will.

The Kenneth J. Hall b-movie *Nightmare Sisters* features the tag-team duo of the gorgeous Brinke Stevens and lovely Linnea Quigley in the entirely believable role of a pair of homely college girls who couldn't dig up a date in a cemetery with a backhoe. One night, a combination pajama party/demon-summoning ritual goes awry (as they often do) and as a result our heroines are transformed into sex-crazed demons. Apparently goldfish swallowing just doesn't cut it on the modern college campus anymore. Filmmaker Kenneth J. Hall shared this comment with us: "The original title of the film was *Sorority Succubus Sisters*, so, naturally, there was a succubus in it. Rather than stick to the legend where the demon seduces sleeping men, we had it possess three nerdy college girls during a séance, turning them into hotties who went around orally castrating frat guys. It was, after all, a camp comedy."

In 1982, the incubus finally got his due in *Satan's Mistress*, a

Lamia by Andy Jones

film featuring Lana Wood (younger sister of Natalie Wood who played the busty "Bond Girl" Plenty O'Toole), John Carradine, and Britt Ekland (Bond Girl "Holly Goodnight"). The incubus is portrayed by dashing Indian actor Kabir Bedi. The film never really wanders far from its schlock-exploitation roots.

In the 2007 film *Succubus: Hell Bent*, writer/director Kim Bass enlisted the help of Gary Busey, Lorenzo Lamas, and eye candy Kelly Hu to tell the story of a rich, womanizing playboy who unwittingly meets Lilith in the form of "Coors Light Girl" Natalie Denise Sperl. Unholy hijinks ensue.

Not even our children are safe from the wrath of the succubus— especially the children of the irreverent animated cable TV series *South Park* (1997–current), who have had their share of paranormal experiences. In the third-season episode "Succubus," Kyle, Stan, Cartman, and Kenny battle over the spirit of Chef (voiced by R&B legend Isaac Hayes, who sadly passed away in August 2008), who is entranced by a woman who is actually a hideous demon.

DEAD SEXY: SUCCUBI, INCUBI, AND THEIR ILK

Adzeekh: The Kitimat Indians of British Columbia have long held the belief that, after death, a person's soul is sometimes so resistant to passing on to the Land of the Dead that it clings to the soul of any living person around during the moment of transition. As a result, this stubborn soul—called an Adzeekh—can drag the souls of the living along with it. For this reason, the dying are often left alone at the moment of passing, or the proper transition from life to death is guaranteed by the singing of sacred songs and by prayers.

Baobhan Sith: In Scottish legend, the Baobhan Sith dwells in the dangerous highlands searching for victims. The creature appears as a beautiful woman with long hair wearing a green gown that hides the fact that she has the lower half of a goat. The creature feeds upon both blood and life essence. Both fire and cold can kill it, but it needs to be cornered and caught first, which is no easy feat.

Baobhan Sith by Vinessa J. Olp

Glaistig: This creature is very much like the Baobhan Sith, and also appears as a beautiful young woman wearing a long green skirt to conceal a cloven secret down below. Despite having two left goat feet, this creature does a seductive dance to attract the attention of men. Once under her spell, the men are compelled to dance with her—helpless to keep up the dance until they literally drop from exhaustion. Once in this state, the creatures turn deadly, throwing themselves upon their victims to tear out their throats and feast on the blood spurting from the wounds.

Lamia: In Greek mythology, Lamia was the daughter of Poseidon and Lybie. She was the queen of Libya and indeed the personification of the country itself. Like so many other beautiful women in Greek myth, she became yet another victim of Zeus's libido and Hera's jealous rage. In perhaps one of Zeus's wife's more cruel punishments, Lamia's children were taken from her. In her own motherly rage, Lamia was transformed into a creature that feasted upon the children of man. In later Greek culture, Lamia became a

Sirens by Hervé Scott Flament

"bogeywoman" of sorts, and misbehaving children were threatened with her wrath.

Sirens: These early femme fatales were just that: women whose nature was fatal to men. Depictions of the Sirens vary between the older Greek version of women with human heads and bodies of great birds and the more modern version of impossibly alluring (and normal-looking) women. In either case, their song was so compelling that men were driven mad and wrecked their ships on the rocks of the Sirens' island. The lucky sailors drowned; the unlucky ones got eaten. The Sirens were confronted by both Odysseus and by Jason and the Argonauts, and their escapes were very close calls. According to Ovid, the Sirens are a species of nymph, which is a class of female supernatural spirits found in various parts of nature.

Tokoloshe (also **Tikoloshe** and **Hili**): In Zulu mythology, there is a particularly vicious water demon called Tokoloshe, who is known and feared as a sexual predator as much as a flesh-eating monster. The creature is small, not much taller than a child, and has only one leg and one arm, but none of those deformities hinder it from being a rapacious monster. The Tokoloshe is a magic-user and can make itself invisible by swallowing an enchanted pebble. Unseen, it sneaks into the village and sexually assaults as many women as it can. If the women are protected or beyond reach, the hungers of the Tokoloshe turn to a different kind of violence and it challenges any man it can find to a fight. If the Tokoloshe wins, the man is often killed and the creature sucks out his blood and life energy; if the man should win, however, the Tokoloshe is obliged to teach the man secrets of magic for the space of a single night.

TRICKSTERS: JOKERS IN THE PACK

Anansi: To the Ashanti people of West Africa, Anansi is a trickster who brought brought rain from the sky to quench rampant wildfires and taught men the secrets of agriculture. There are many legends associated with Anansi, most notably when he cleverly used a "tar-baby" to trick the "Fairy Whom Men Never See." This

The Folklore Heritage

Tokoloshe Takes a Pebble by Michael Ian Bateson

"Despite being rooted in the traditions of past cultures, folklore is a constantly evolving system. As societies rise and fall, they usurp the beliefs and fears of other peoples. Today's artists and writers are the descendants of those souls who painted on walls or passed down tales to explain why the world was and how it came to be." —Michael Ian Bateson is an award-winning Web designer, artist, and illustrator.

concept became a staple in the lore legend of Africans, and eventually African Americans, in the form of tales of Uncle Remus, the clever Br'er Rabbit, the ever-duped Br'er Fox, and his somewhat slower companion Br'er Bear. These charming tales were brought to life in the 1946 Walt Disney film *Song of the South*—the film responsible for bringing "Zip-Ah-Dee-Do-Dah" into modern parlance. Bestselling novelist Neil Gaiman has done two takes on Anansi, first with the character of Mr. Nancy in *American Gods* (Harper Perennial, 2003) and then as the central focus of *Anansi Boys* (William Morrow, 2005). Other takes on Anansi have appeared in cartoons (in the Disney cartoon *Gargoyles*, Anansi was depicted as a giant spider in the episode "Mark Of The Panther"), children's TV shows (in the WB program *Static Shock*, the character Statis encounters an Anansi-like character in Africa), and the PBS series *Sesame Street* Anansi the Spider[1] read stories from African folklore. Anansi, true to his changeable nature, is known by a variety of names, including Annancy or Anancy, Anancyi, Ananansa, Ananse, Aunt Nancy, Hanansi, Kompa Nanzi, Compé Anansi, Kweku Anansi, and many others.

Anchanchu: Many of the demons of the Andes region of Chile in South America have both benevolent and evil aspects, and the Anchanchu is no exception. Among the Aymara people of Bolivia and Peru, the Anchanchu is a trickster monster that affects a genial guise and manner. Using friendly smiles, songs, jokes, and food treats he ingratiates himself into a community and then spreads virulent disease among the townsfolk. However, to the Puna Ayllinos, also a people of the Andes, the Anchanchu is a helpful spirit who helps miners search for gold. In some villages the Anchanchu is the name given only to this being's benevolent aspect while its evil aspect is called Tío Juaniquillo.

In both cases the Anchanchu appears in the form of a small manlike creature about a yard tall with brown skin and black hair. If the miners leave the Anchanchu offerings at night (coca, cigarettes, and alcohol are favored treats), the next morning there will be a golden sparkle in the rocks indicating the presence of gold.

The Tío Juaniquillo aspect does not look at all like one of the natives but appears as a smiling gringo with a crooked nose that is twisted sharply to the left. Tío Juaniquillo also uses the trick of

---

1. Voiced by the late, great Ossie Davis.

African American Folklore

Maurice Broaddus,
photo by Mel Bradley

"Much of my fiction is influenced by folklore. I feel doubly blessed as the product of two distinct traditions of oral story-telling. As an African American, I inherit a huge oral tradition of tales, stories passed on from generation to generation. My father's family passed along folktales and a legacy of stories handed down from the days of slavery that helped my family endure and carry on.

"My mother's family comes from Jamaica. They have stories for every occasion and a folklore life so rich that I feel like I have spent my entire life collecting stories. Take, for example, my story 'Family Business.' It is about a young man who returns to Jamaica to bury his grandfather, whom he knew very little about. The story is a tribute to not only the obeah culture (think: voodoo) but also the folktales that were so much a part of the daily fabric of life (including the creature known as the rollin' calf) which is slowly going away." —Maurice Broaddus has written dozens of short stories and articles appearing in places including *Apex Science Fiction and Horror Digest*, *Horror Literature Quarterly*, and Dark Dreams anthology series.

Terrifying Television

"The landscape of made-for-TV horror is mostly pretty arid and featureless, but for my money, among the scariest couple of seconds on film are in the 1990 TV miniseries *IT*, based on the novel by Stephen King. If, like me, you always thought clowns way more repellent than funny, the idea of a little kid crawling into a sewer and seeing a clown with a mouth full of teeth like razors is all you need to keep you up the rest of the night. And the next night, too. Tim Curry plays the clown, reaching for children out of storm drains and old photographs and calling to them from somewhere below the bathroom sink. For once, the flat, affectless landscape of TV-on-a-budget works for the horror, and Pennywise leaps out at the viewer from the colorless background and gets inside his skull. The movie itself doesn't always fire on all cylinders, but it has a hardworking cast of TV luminaries (look for a very young Seth Green as one of the terrified kids), and Pennywise the Clown genuinely haunts the movie and earns a place in the pantheon of Things with Teeth."
—Dennis Tafoya is the author of *Dope Thief* (St. Martins Minotaur, 2009).

affability to ingratiate himself with the locals—usually miners—and at first, his presence seems to bring good fortune to everyone. But the longer he lingers, the more the miners become prone to a variety of wasting diseases. As the miners die off, they are reborn as horned devils and are forever forced to labor in the mines for Tío Juaniquillo, using their horns to gouge gold out of the living rock.

Bolla (also **Kulshedra**): Generally in the folklore of monsters, transformations tend to involve a person assuming an animal or insect shape, or a monster taking human form in order to deceive its prey. However, the Bolla[2] of Albanian legend actually goes through a metamorphosis from one kind of monster to an even fiercer and more deadly beast. In the early part of its life cycle, the Bolla is a kind of coiling dragon (more along the lines of the serpentine Chi-

2. In southern Albania, it is spelled Buller.

nese dragon than the sauropod-like European version). It has four small legs and vestigial wings, and it cannot move very fast. As a result the Bolla is not a very active predator, sleeping through most of the year in a hidden grotto far from where humans are likely to wander. However on Saint George's Day it wakes up and comes out of its lair. Anyone unlucky enough to see the Bolla will be literally frightened to death and will be instantly devoured by the monster.

The Bolla only ventures forth on that one day of the year and the rest of the time it remains hidden away, asleep. It repeats this cycle for twelve years, and during its last year of sleep the Bolla undergoes a great transformation from a simple (though dangerous) dragon into a far more frightening creature with nine whiplike tongues and the ability to breathe fire. During this time the monster, now known as a Kulshedra, also develops much greater wings and with them it takes to the air to hunt men and livestock.

Coyote: The role of the trickster is perhaps most prominent in the mythology of Native American tribes. The Indians associated the role of the trickster spirit with various animals such as the crow and the raccoon. But perhaps the most devious of all of the tricksters is the clever Coyote. Coyote plays a role in the very creation of Indians themselves. The Pomos of Northern California believe Coyote gave birth to humanity and captured the sun to get his charges warm. The Sioux of the Dakotas believe Coyote created the horse as a gift to its people. The Navajo regard Coyote as a symbol of evil and imbalance.

One legend tells of a time before man lived on earth. A giant monster stalked the earth, devouring everything in its path. Soon, only Coyote remained, and he was angry at the loss of all of his forest-dwelling friends. So, Coyote climbed the highest mountain and called down to the monster in challenge.

The monster drew in a great breath, hoping the wind would pull Coyote down from the mountain. Fortunately, sly Coyote had tied himself down. The monster tried many ways to reach Coyote, but failed each time. Realizing that Coyote's wit might be too much for him, the monster devised a plan. He would befriend Coyote and invite him to stay in its home. Coyote agreed, but only under the condition that he could venture into the belly of the beast to

**Digital artist Jason Beam and model Amanda Palmer
created the character of Cryptessa, a living-dead vixen.
Fans of the horror genre responded with immediate
enthusiasm for this new sexy supernatural seductress.**

visit with his friends. In its frustration and confusion, the monster
agreed. Once inside the monster, Coyote cut out its heart and set
fire to its insides, killing the beast and freeing his friends. Coyote
decided to create a new animal and flung pieces of the monster in
all directions. Wherever a piece landed, a new tribe of Indians
emerged. He used the blood on his hands to create the Nez Percé,
a tribe of Indians in the Pacific Northwest that existed ten thousand years before the arrival of white explorers in the New World.

Full Moon by Mahmood Tariq al Khaja

Erlik: The Altaic Tartars of Siberia have ancient legends of a supernatural spirit called Erlik who was formed out of a piece of muddy flotsam by the high god Ulgan. It was the high god's intention to make a brother god out of Erlik, but this new immortal had corruption at the heart of his being and snubbed this friendship of Ulgan. Disappointed and angry, Ulgan banished Erlik to the land of the dead and there Erlik fully embraced his nature to become the god of evil. Erlik is a shape-shifter who most commonly takes the form of a gigantic and remarkably foul-tempered bear.

Eshu: A trickster god of the Yoruba people of West Africa, Eshu is the patron of travelers and overseer of roads and byways. He also serves as a conduit between the spirit world and man. He is associated with the number three and the colors black, white, and red and is often portrayed as a traveler carrying a cane and smoking a pipe. In one legend, Eshu walked across a village wearing a cap that was red on one side and black on the other. The villagers on each side nearly came to blows over the issue of what color hat Eshu was wearing. On his return trip, it became obvious that the hat had two colors, and viewing it was merely a matter of one's perception, a valuable lesson indeed. The legends of Eshu made their way to the New World with the slave trade, and he also became a fixture in Santeria, where he was associated with St. Anthony and St. Michael.

Fox Spirits: Fox myths abound in the folklore of many nations, and often overlap with the stories of faerie folk. It is fair to say that the Fox spirit in Asian cultures occupies virtually the same place in their stories as the faeries do in Western mythology. These creatures are often very beautiful, whether appearing as foxes or while taking human form. They are tricksters, however, and are elusive, vindictive, and often quite nasty despite their beauty.

The majority of fox spirits in world myths are female, and gen-

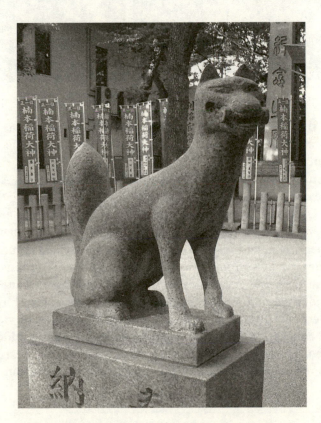

An ancient statue of a fox spirit in Inari, Japan.

The Origin of the Spider in Greek Myth

Arachne, the Spider Goddess by Chad Savage

"The Ancient Greeks had a story to explain the origins of the spider, and why it spins a web. The short version is that a woman named Arachne, who wove tapestries, boasted that she was better at weaving than the gods. Athena challenged Arachne to a weaving contest. Athena created a tapestry depicting the glories of Olympus; Arachne created one showing the folly and less-than-divine escapades of the gods. Outraged at her insolence and disrespect, Athena turned Arachne into a spider and commanded that she and her children would weave forever. Obviously this is where the term 'Arachnid' originates. I find the idea and image of a spider/woman hybrid simultaneously attractive and hideous, and every few years I paint a different interpretation or variation on the concept." —Chad Savage's Sinister Visions provides Web design, print design, illustration, sound design, font design, and more for the horror, Halloween, and haunted attraction industries.

erally appear as women of such compelling beauty that their male victims are instantly captivated. When fox spirits appear as men, they are often handsome, but their defining characteristic is their great wisdom. The one sure way to discover whether a person is a fox spirit in human form is to get them undressed, because although they mimic the human form fairly well, they cannot get rid of their tails.

Most fox spirits are essential vampires of one kind or another, often bordering on the Succubus or Incubus in nature. They feed off life energy or sexual essence. When they select a victim, they cultivate a relationship with this person that may last for weeks, months, or even years, depending on the degree of hunger in the fox and the level of stamina in the victim. The end result is often the same in that the victim is ultimately drained past the point of recovery and then dies. When killed, a fox spirit reverts back to its animal form.

Huehuecoyotl: The Aztec god of music and song was also a trickster much in keeping with Coyote. His pranks were as often played on other gods as on men, and usually a great (though subtle) lesson was to be learned at the end of all the goings-on. If a person fell prey to one of Huehuecoyotl's pranks—which was usually the case when some element of greed was in the mix—it typically turned out that it was the person's fault for letting his own baser instincts rule his judgment.

Iktomi: To the Lakota tribe of the Dakota, the Iktomi is a trickster god who often appears in the form of a spider. He can transform into human form and meddle in the affairs of men. He can also concoct potions that allow him to control the actions of gods and men alike.

Khanzab: Sometimes it is difficult to determine whether a demon or spirit is evil or whether its actions, however malevolent they appear, may actually be serving man's greater good. One such example is the Khanzab, a demon from among the beliefs of Islam. On one hand, the demon appears to be harmful because it appears at times of prayer, often as a whispering voice in the mind of a person praying, and the things it whispers cause doubt in God and

Jaguar Spirits

"As the largest cat species and most ferocious predator of Mesoamerica, the jaguar played a major role in the religion and spiritual cycles of the Olmecs, Aztecs, and especially the Mayans. Jaguar ears, paws, and pelts are common in depictions of Mayan gods and rulers, marking the jaguar as a symbol of authority. Jaguars are also used in the design of thrones, such as the jade-studded throne in the inner chamber of the main pyramid in Chichen Itza.

"Other ancient carvings of jaguars reveal a connection with fertility and water. Since jaguars are nocturnal, hunting and active in darkness, they are associated with the underworld, which Mayans considered to be the origin of plants and water. Freshwater for the Mayans accumulated in large limestone pools called *cenotes*, where members of the community were occasionally sacrificed, further associating the jaguar with the cycles of life and death. The jaguar is said to have the ability to cross between worlds—night and day, life and spirit—much like its natural ability to hunt in both trees and water in its search for prey." —Katy Diana is a writer and editor from Philadelphia.

in His teachings. On the other hand, the presence of doubt often leads a person to seek answers and find ways to deepen his faith, so the creature may actually be a divine form of the trickster.

Kitsune: The Japanese word for fox and also a common feature in Shinto mythology. Rather than appearing as a normal fox, kitsune can have multiple tails. It is said that the more tails a kitsune has, the older and wiser it is. The creature is also a shape-shifter and can transform into a human. They are said to serve as consorts and messengers of the Shinto deity Inari, the god of fertility and agriculture. Kitsune are known to play tricks on the arrogant to take them down a peg, or lead travelers astray by the use of *kitsune-bi* or "foxfire."

Loki: In the mythology of the Norse, the source of the mischief was the god Loki. He was a shape-shifting creature that could transform into either sex, or into many sorts of animals, in order to best create chaos. Among his more innocent pranks was an impromptu haircut of the goddess Sif's beautiful blond hair. Among the more serious of these acts was when, disguised as a giantess, he fooled the blind god Höðr into throwing a dart made of mistletoe at his brother Balder. While this might seem innocent, mistletoe was the only substance that could harm Balder, and when pierced with the dart he consequently died. To add insult to injury, Loki was the only being that refused to weep for Balder's death, thus ensuring that he would never return from Hel, the Norse underworld.

Manannan Mac Lir: The god of the sea to the ancient Celts, and the patron of the Isle of Man. He is the protector of sailors and can ensure a bountiful catch for fishermen. Among his more helpful pranks is the creation of an illusion of a fleet of powerful warships to frighten off potential invaders.

Neza (also **Nata**): A feature of both Chinese and Japanese mythology, Nezha is often depicted as a man with many arms, a flaming wheel beneath each foot. He is truly a child in a man's body; his mother waited for more than three years to deliver him into the world. This so enraged his father that he split the newborn with his sword, and Nezha emerged—fully grown, but with a child's mind.

Prometheus: In Greek mythology, it was Prometheus who stole fire from Zeus and brought it down to earth for man's use. However pivotal to the history of the Greeks, he paid a hefty price for his indiscretion. Zeus had Prometheus chained to a boulder in Caucasus, an area that is now the land that lies between Europe and Asia. Each day his liver would be devoured by a predatory bird, and each night it would grow back, only to be feasted upon the next day. Some time later, Heracles slew the bird and released Prometheus from his bondage—probably not soon enough, we imagine.

Raven: Native American tribes of the Northwest envisioned the spirit of the raven as a greedy trickster—forever hungry and lying in wait to deceive. However, it was the raven that stole the moon and placed it in the night sky to aid mankind.

The Modern Prometheus

Deborah LeBlanc

"One way to breathe life into a monster paradigm is to do just that . . . breathe life into it, the way Mary Shelley did with Frankenstein. She gave her 'monster' human traits and emotions we could relate to (i.e., rejection, fear, and confusion), which, in my opinion, is what firmly plants the character in a reader's mind. Today's monsters appear to be two-dimensional, and our creation of them too dependent on major doses of blood, guts, and gore. We might do a decent job of grossing people out, but is that the same as weaving three-dimensional characters into a chilling story that truly evokes fear?" —Deborah LeBlanc is a past president of the Horror Writers Association, president of the Writers' Guild of Acadiana, and president of Mystery Writers of America's Southwest Chapter.

Saci-Pererê: One of the most notable characters in Brazilian folklore, Saci is portayed as a one-legged man with holes in his palms who smokes a pipe and wears a magical red hat. As pranksters go, the Saci is more of a minor annoyance, and prefers to release farm animals, spill salt, or cause chicken eggs not to hatch as opposed to more harmful mischeif.

If one is pursued by a Saci, he need only look for a source of running water, which the creature is unable to cross. The spirit can also be stopped by dropping a knotted rope on the ground, which the Saci will be helplessly compelled to untie—so, the more knots, the better. And in case you're wondering, the Saci is a nimble creature, so the missing leg is no hindrance to it.

Tikbalang: Living in the deepest swamps of the Philippines there is a very strange creature called the Tikbalang with a humanoid body topped by the head of a horse. The Tikbalang is a vile trickster who delights in leading travelers astray so that they become hopelessly lost. For some inexplicable reason the lost person can find his way back by simply wearing his shirt inside out.

Ti Malice: In the practice of Voodoo, the gods are referred to as "loa" and have various powers and abilities. Ti Malice was a trickster who often played his pranks upon Uncle Bouki, a character that is still an important part of Haitian folklore. In fact, the children's song "Frère Jacques" has a Vodoun version, "Uncle Bouki, Uncle Bouki. Are you sleeping, are you sleeping? Get up to play the drum, get up and play the drum. Ding, ding, dong."

In one such legend, Ti Malice tells Uncle Bouki that he can fertilize his field of yams by killing a pig, cooking it, and burying it in the field. The deed done, Ti Malice returned to the field, unearthed both the pig and the yams, and had a marvelous feast. When Uncle Bouki returned and saw his ruined crops, he sought out Ti Malice with revenge on his mind. When he finally came upon him, Ti Malice feigned sickness from eating the pig and Uncle Bouki left, his vengeance satisfied.

Tyanak (also **Chanak**): Mating between humans and demons seldom ends well, especially if there are offspring. In the Philippines, if a woman mates with a demon, her child is often born as an evil Tyanak, whose main delight in life is to cause hardship and mischief. The creature often looks like a normal baby by daylight, but at night its skin shifts in color of an unhealthy bruised red, all of its hair vanishes, and its eyes glow with a hellish light. The Tyanak is a predator and hunter, but generally it wounds more often than it kills, taking great bites out of people and animals. In

Campfire Tales

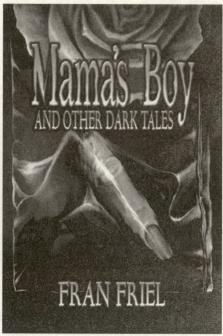

Fran Friel, photo by Paul Friel

"I love that 'around the campfire' feeling I get when I read a good story woven with folklore." —Fran Friel is a Bram Stoker–nominated author, residing by the Cthulhu-riddled sea in rural New England with her husband and a mad dog.

some tales, the Tyanak is created when a woman attempts to abort the fetus she's carrying—especially after a rape or other violent crime, or if she has been unfaithful and fears that the child she's carrying is not her husband's. The aborted fetus rises from wherever it has been buried or hidden away and begins haunting the night as a meat-eating monster that also taints every house it enters with enduring bad luck.

Veles: The Slavic god of the underworld, livestock, music, commerce, and trickery, Veles was worshipped by the ancient peoples of Russia and Poland. After the advent of Christianity, his image was warped into that of a demonic figure and he is often associated with the devil himself. He has traits similar to a cat and to other trickster figures such as Hermes, Pan, Hades, and Cernunnos.

Immortal Seductress by Kevin Breaux

8 THEY KILL

A Miscellany of Monsters

The Hydra by Caniglia

JUST PLAIN WEIRD

We've always believed in monsters. Always. Some of our monsters are supernatural beasties that probably never actually walked the earth. Some were animals that were all too real, and as our ancestors came carefully down from the trees and out of the caves they encountered ferocious creatures—saber-toothed cats, dire wolves, giant bears, mammoths, crocodiles—beasts that were the match of just about anything the imagination could conjure.

And yet, with all the natural predators around us, we still extended our beliefs to encompass more of them: demons from hell dimensions, brutes that raced across the heavens or stood guard to the underworld, invisible specters, giants, ogres, trolls, and djinn. We filled all of the shadowy corners of our world with jaws that bite and claws that catch.

Monsters vary in type and intent. There are quite a few monsters from folklore and myth that bear no apparent ill will toward humans, and a fair few who are overtly helpful. But we are concerned here with those monsters who either possess enough intelligence to deliberately target humans or whose appetites are such that humans seem like a good source of protein and fiber.

In this chapter we'll encounter some very weird and definitely dangerous beasts. Step carefully . . . for here there be dragons. And other things that bite!

Here There Be Dragons by Andy Jones

MONSTERS IN STORYTELLING

It's fair to say that storytelling and the belief in monsters evolved together. Consider cave paintings, the earliest recorded stories, dating back thirty-two thousand years. These illustrations didn't just chronicle daily life but instead told of complex cosmologies—gods and demons—and of fantastic creatures. So far, scientists, researchers, and in some cases ordinary folks[1] have discovered nearly 350 sets of cave paintings, some of which show ordinary things like horses and beasts of burden typical of the place and time when the paintings were created. Some appear to be attempts by the artist to depict something that was (at least to him and his cronies) new and wondrous, such as a giraffe or a buffalo. Yet some show animal-headed men and creatures unknown to science.

We see similar things painted on the walls of ancient temples and carved into rocks. Occasionally scientists encounter an anachronism—an animal unknown to the region in which the painting or carving was made, or a creature out of synch with the timing of that culture and the creation of the art. A prime example is the Dragon of the Ishtar Gate. When German archaeologist Robert Koldewey excavated the city of Babylon in 1902, he discovered the legendary Ishtar Gate, which was the eighth gate to the inner city and which King Nebuchadnezzar II had ordered built circa 575 B.C.E. in homage to the goddess Ishtar. The Ishtar Gate is magnificent; it is made from blue tiles and set with a variety of bas-reliefs of animals both real and mythological. Among the marvelously detailed bas-reliefs are two creatures of particular interest to cryptozoologists. The first and least interesting of the two is the Re'em (also called Rimi), a species of cattle known to be extinct (though not at the time of the construction of the gate); and the other, the Sirrush,[2] which is a close approximation of a dinosaur.

This "dragon," as it was known, has a long reptilian body complete with tail, but its hind feet are like those of a bird. This brings up a number of disturbing problems. The first of which is the

1. The Lascaux caves in southwestern France were discovered in 1940 by four teenagers.
2. Derived from an Akkadian word loosely translated "splendor serpent."

strangeness of a dinosaur being accurately depicted sixty-five million years after they'd become extinct, and many centuries before the science of paleontology began piecing together their bones and roughing out what the monsters looked like. Then there's the fact that the concept of dinosaurs being related to birds was not made until well into the twentieth century. And yet there was a dinosaur with birdlike qualities right on that ancient wall.

In the Apocrypha[3] there is an account of the prophet Daniel's encounter with King Nebuchadnezzar and the dragon he kept in the temple of the god Bel:

> Therefore the king slew them, and delivered Bel into Daniel's power, who destroyed him and his temple. And in that same place there was a great dragon, which they of Babylon worshipped . . . And the king said unto Daniel, Wilt thou also say that this is of brass? Lo! he liveth, he eateth and drinketh; thou canst not say that he is no living god: therefore worship him. Then said Daniel unto the king, I will worship the Lord my God: for he is the living God. But give me leave, O king, and I shall slay this dragon without sword or staff. The king said, I give thee leave. Then Daniel took pitch, and fat, and hair, and did seethe them together, and made lumps thereof: this he put in the dragon's mouth, and so the dragon burst in sunder; and Daniel said, Lo, these are the gods ye worship.[4]

So what was the Dragon of Bel's temple? Was it a theropod, perhaps a Coelurosaur, held over from the Cretaceous Age? Was it a creature disguised by the king of Babylon to fool Daniel? If so, what did he use as a model for his monster? Or was it just the working of a stonemason's imagination?

Koldewey, the gate's discoverer, believed that the animal was real; his argument was that the Sirrush was depicted alongside actual animals of the era. Noted folklorist Adrienne Mayor[5] has

---

3. The collection of stories claimed by some to be excised sections of the Bible. Most major religions, such as the Catholic Church, and many biblical scholars dispute the authenticity of these stories.

4. The Apocrypha; The Book of Bel and the Dragon, Chapter 1, verses 22–27.

5. She is the author of *The First Fossil Hunters: Paleontology in Greek and Roman Times*, Princeton University Press, 2001.

suggested that the Babylonians may have excavated dinosaur fossils while building their temples and assembled them into a rough approximation of the original animal and based their art on that. After all, to them the concept of ancient bones probably equaled "from a few hundred or thousand years ago;" they would not have been capable of conceiving of life from tens of millions of years ago.

Between those two viewpoints is a vast gray area. Lots of theories have been put forth, but no one actually knows, and we probably will never know. This is where myth, folklore, and belief come in. We're allowed to believe, and sometimes we believe the most outrageous things that are later revealed as true or possible. That covers everything from the discovery of the giant squid to man walking on the moon.

The Dragon of the Isthtar Gate is by no means a singular incident. Other anomalous creatures have appeared in art and legend, such as the Monster of Troy, a tale first told by Homer in the eighth century B.C.E. The monster was a bizarre sea creature that suddenly appeared on the Trojan coast after a flood and began chomping on the farmers in the neighborhood of Sigeum. Hesione, daughter of the king, was sent as a sacrifice to the monster, but according to the legend, Heracles[6] arrives in time to kill it. Illustrations of the Monster of Troy do not clearly match any animal known to have ever lived, though the shape of the skull bears some superficial resemblance to the Samotherium, a giant giraffe of the Miocene epoch. Again . . . we'll probably never know quite what it is. Too many ancient writings, languages, and crucial relics are lost to time, the destruction from constant warfare, tomb robbers, natural disaster, and the growth of new civilizations that have been built on the rubble of the old.

Epic storytelling is filled with gods, heroes, and monsters. Many, many monsters. And these monster tales underpin all of human society and learning. These include[7] the *Epic of Gilgamesh* and *Atrahasis* (Mesopotamian mythology); *Enuma Elish* (Babylonian);

6. Hercules is his Roman name.
7. This list is a tiny fragment of world myth captured in epic poems and other writings.

the *Iliad*, the *Odyssey*, *Aeneid* and *Works and Days* (Greek and Roman); *Jaya*, *Bharata*, and the *Mahabharata* (Hindu); The Old Testament (Judaism/Christianity); *Buddhacarita*, *Kumaārasam-bhava*, *Raghuvamsa*, and *Saundaranandakavya* (Indian); *Beowulf* (Anglo-Saxon); *Waldere* (Old English); *David of Sasun* (Armenian); *Bhagavata Purana* (Sanskrit); *Shahnameh* (Persian); *Poetic Edda* (Norse); *Digenis Akritas* (Byzantine); *La Chanson de Roland* (French); *Epic of King Gesar* (Tibetan); *Epic of Manas* (Kyrgyz); the Arthurian legends (Middle English); *Der Nibelungenlied* (Germanic); the *Divine Comedy* (Italian); the *Mukashibanashi* (Japan); and so on. Hundreds of thousands of stories with countless variations are inextricably tied to the histories of ancient cultures so that myth and truth become indistinct and overlapping concepts.

And everywhere you look there are monsters. The trend has by no means slowed down. Rather, the reverse is true, because as folklore merged into fiction and film, new monsters and mythologies emerged. Our movie monsters have become so much a part of our culture that some people believe that flesh-eating zombies, Godzilla, and other purely fictional creatures are based on folklore. The modern storyteller has stepped into the role of the bard or traveling storyteller of yore. Urban myths abound, some of which (like the choking Doberman) are based on folktales from Europe but which have been told and retold so many times, often in the oral storytelling style (which we now just call word of mouth), that those people who believe in these myths believe them to have happened in the United States. A familiar tale becomes our tale. To a kid of our generation the Jedi and Sith are as real as the vampires were to kids two hundred years ago. If you doubt that, consider that on the 2001 census so many people claimed "Jedi" as their declared religion that the governments of Great Britain, New Zealand, and the United States were forced to accept it as a recognized religion. Sure, most of it was done as a joke, but it's now part of our culture. And there are at least three actual churches based on the Jedi religion. In two hundred years, when archaeologists poke through our records and relics, what will they think that we believe?

Modern storytelling is all about monsters. *Dracula* is the most frequently filmed novel, and the character appears in every kind

Comics and Folklore

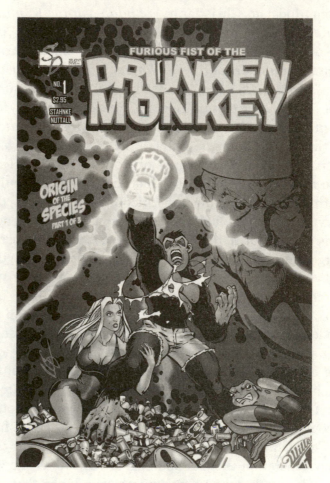

Furious Fist of the Drunken Monkey, No. 1

"Zombie, vampires, and other monsters sometimes lose their bite, but comic creators can bring back a particular type of monster or genre to give it a fresh spin. For example, Robert Kirkman's *The Walking Dead* is a human drama as profound as George Romero's films. Writer Steve Niles and artist Ben Templesmith tackled the vampire story and brought those creatures back into the fold as something to be genuinely feared."
—Rich Stahnke is creator of *Furious Fist of the Drunken Monkey* (Silent Devil Productions, 2006).

Classic Monsters as New Folklore

"Nicholson, like Stephen King, has a true talent for terror."
—BENTLEY LITTLE

THEY
HUNGER

SCOTT
NICHOLSON

(Scott Nicholson photo by Marie Freeman)

"Movies pushed those tropes to all the extremes and now they've entered the public consciousness. Frankenstein's monster and Dracula were intended to be frightening and strange but then went through the extreme of becoming comedy fodder. They lost their last shred of terror when they were cast as Frankenberry and Count Chocula on cereal boxes—it had devolved to kiddie fare. It takes passion and imagination to put meat on the bones and make them scary again for modern audiences."

—Scott Nicholson is the author of seven supernatural thrillers set in the Southern Appalachian mountains. He's also a screenwriter and journalist and has published over sixty stories.

of pop culture, from breakfast cereal to toys to theme parks. Frankenstein has been not only filmed repeatedly but also reinterpreted in a thousand ways, with the story elements assigned to new characters and with different outcomes.[8] The story itself has become a symbol for science run amok. The concept of a monstrous other self presented in Robert Louis Stevenson's *The Strange Case of Dr Jekyll and Mr. Hyde* (1886) has influenced so many stories that it's impossible to compile a list, but obvious examples include Angel/Angelus on the Joss Whedon TV shows *Buffy the Vampire Slayer* and *Angel*; Marvel Comics' *Incredible Hulk*, created by Stan Lee and Jack Kirby in 1962; and, of course, *Batman*. We'll always have monsters.

THE BESTIARY

Ballybog (also **Bogles**, **Bolliwogs**, **Peat Faeries**, **Mudbogs**, **Bor-a-boos**, **Boggies**): The Ballybog is an Earth Elemental (see listing for Elementals in this chapter) who favors marshes and bogs (hence the name), and is usually seen smeared from head to foot in mud.

Basilisk (also **Basilcock**): The name Basilisk is from the Greek *basilieus* and means "little king" or "king of snakes." In truth, this creature is huge and is certainly a king among monsters. The Basilisk is believed to be the physical incarnation of the God of Death. The Basilisk appears in the form of a vast serpent, though some accounts refer to it as a dragon. It is born from a chicken egg that has been brooded over by a snake,[9] and even from infancy it has deadly powers. The Basilisk's stare is lethal and, unlike the Gorgon, who can be looked at in a reflection, even the reflected gaze of the Basilisk will kill. This works both ways, for if the Basilisk beheld itself in a mirror it would burst apart in fear of its own appearance.

8. Check out *Young Frankenstein* on Broadway or the DVD collection of The *Munsters* and you'll get the point.
9. A concept first put forth by the Venerable Bede (672 to 735), the noted scholar and author of *Historia ecclesiastica gentis Anglorum* (The Ecclesiastical History of the English People), which gained him the title "The father of English history."

Many tales of the Basilisk overlap with those of the Cockatrice, which shares a number of similar qualities. The Cockatrice, however, generally is depicted as having the head of a rooster, or in some cases, a dragon. Some images of the Basilisk show it with great wings (either birdlike or batlike), but not all. Strangely, the diminutive weasel somehow possesses the power to overcome the Basilisk, and the crow of the rooster is fatal to the beast.

The oldest legends of the Basilisk described a much smaller creature, and either it has grown over the centuries or, more likely, the natural exaggeration of the storyteller has made the beast into a giant. Chaucer mentioned the creature in his *Canterbury Tales*, though he blended the two monsters into one and called it a "Basilicock."

One of the pioneers of zoology, Edward Topsell,[10] described it thus:

> The King of Serpents, not for his magnitude or greatnesse: For there are many Serpents bigger than he, as there are many fourefooted Beastes bigger than the Lyon, but, because of his stately pace, and magnanimous mind: for he creepeth not on the earth like other Serpents, but goeth half upright, for which all other serpents avoyde his sight.

The basilisk was brought into modern consciousness largely because of the novel *Harry Potter and the Chamber of Secrets* by J. K. Rowling, in which the monster haunts the wizarding school Hogwarts. Basilisks also feature in the role-playing game *Dungeons & Dragons*.

Cailleac Bhuer (also the **Blue Hag**, **Black Annis**, the **Stone Woman**): A vile member of the fairy folk, the Cailleac Bhuer goes about disguised as an old woman who totters along, leaning on a holly staff that is topped with the skull of a carrion crow. A live crow perches on her left shoulder. Like many spirits, she is easily offended and quick to retaliate, but stories vary as to whether she bears deliberate ill will or is perhaps the victim of a smear campaign. The Cailleac Bhuer is probably one of the representations of the Celtic

---

10. Topsell (1572–1625), was an English cleric and author best known for his bestiary, or *Bestiarum vocabulum*, a significant early text on zoology.

Crone Goddess, and that the nasty habits attributed to her may have been deliberate disinformation on the part of the early Christian church. The Crone Goddess is one of the many aspects of what scholar and poet Robert Graves (1895–1985) called the Triple Goddess, whose other aspects include Diana and Hecate. It wouldn't be the first time an old god was given a makeover to suit early Christian expansionism. For example, Ēostre was an Anglo-Saxon goddess whose feast day was "borrowed" to create Easter—now the most holy day in the Christian calendar.

Celtic Mythology

Novels by Louise Bohmer

"I take quite a bit of my inspiration from old myths, mostly Celtic in origin. Some basic nature-spirit archetypes appear in my fiction often—Pan, Cernunnos, the Green Woman in various forms. I really like to play with the concept of nature as a sentient organism, something that interacts with us constantly, in ways so subtle, sometimes we barely perceive the interaction, but we are still touched, changed, in some way. I very much like to work with the concept of being faerie-or pixie-led, or the idea of the 'enchantment' woven by nature beings, commonly referred to as Fae." —Louise Bohmer is the editor-in-chief for Lachesis Publishing, and she also freelances for other small press companies. Her debut novel, *The Black Act*, was published in 2009.

The Cailleac Bhuer's most popular alternate name is Black Annis, and several pop-culture writers have worked her into their stories. One fascinating take on her appears in DC's *Doom Patrol* comic by Grant Morrison, in which the character Crazy Jane—who suffers from multiple personality disorder—manifests one aspect as Black Annis. Black Annis also made a brief appearance in the comic *2000 AD*, in the issue "London Falling" written by writer Simon Spurrier. A creature called the Annis Hag appears in the game *Dungeons & Dragons*, and a similar monster, Black Arliss, is a character in the Discworld novels by Terry Pratchett.

Centaur: In the older Greek myths the half-human, half-horse Centaurs were not as charming as they've often been portrayed in later centuries. Centaurs were known to kidnap human women and savagely rape them. They were flesh eaters who were not above putting humans on their menus. It is because of these baser qualities that Centaurs—like Satyrs—have come to symbolize the animalistic appetites, such as lust and rage, that taint the soul of men.

The female version, called Centaurides, did not factor in Greek mythology and didn't emerge (or at least we have no records of them) prior to fourth-century Macedonia, and even then mostly on pottery. From the few pieces of ancient writing on the subject we can suppose that their natures were a bit less beastly, as suggested by Philostratus the Elder (b. 190 C.E.) in this excerpt from his commentary on painting in Neapolis (in northern Naples).

> How beautiful the Centaurides are, even where they are horses; for some grow out of white mares, others are attached to chestnut mares, and the coats of others are dappled, but they glisten like those of horses that are well cared for. There is also a white female Centaur that grows out of a black mare, and the very opposition of the colors helps to produce the united beauty of the whole.

In the more recent tales, and particularly in fiction, the Centaur was shown in a different light. Still violent, foul-tempered, and dangerous, the revised Centaur was a mystic devoted to astrology and other forms of divination. Though possessed of great intellect, their animal natures are constantly present. Centaurs take offense easily and react badly. J. K. Rowling got a lot of mileage out of this with the herd of centaur mystics in her Harry Potter novels. They also appear in the Narnia novels and movies, in Eoin Colfer's Artemis Fowl series, and in Disney's *Fantasia* (1940). Regular and mutant centaurs appear in the video games *Tomb Raider 1* (2001) and *Tomb Raider Anniversary* (2007). Motaro, a key character in the *Mortal Kombat* game (1992), is a centaur king.

Charun (also **Charon**, **Cheron**): The pathway to the underworld has many guardians in many cultures. For the Etruscans, the guardian was the hammer-wielding Charun, a strange being with great dark wings, ears that rise to spiked points, and the beak of a vulture. In the stories, Charun was both a guardian of the doorway to hell and one of the principal tormentors of the damned. He also made sure that anyone approaching the doorway to the underworld was truly dead, a task he accomplished by smashing his hammer down on the head of anyone who got within reach. It was even popularly believed that Charun appeared on the floor of the Roman circus using his hammer to smash the heads of the fallen to ensure that they were dead and therefore his to usher below.

In Etruscan funeral ceremonies the priests would tap (not smash) the dead on the head in a way symbolic of what they could expect from Charun. Even nowadays, in the modern funeral rites as performed in the Vatican, the dead are tapped on the head with a small silver hammer to test whether they are truly dead. Charun has appeared in artwork for many centuries, notably in early Christian artwork, and is always shown with his hammer. The artist Giotto, a master during the Renaissance, depicted both Satan and Judas with hammers, and it is likely he based this representation on earlier paintings showing Charun. Charun was modeled after Charon, the Styx ferryman from Greek mythology who ushered the dead across the waters to the gates of Hell.

Cockatrice: Another aspect of the Basilisk, spoken of in the Bible in Isaiah and Jeremiah. The creature has the head of a rooster and the body of a serpent and is hatched from a chicken egg that has been tended for nine years by a toad. The voice of the Cockatrice is lethal, as is its breath. If someone is unwise enough to stab a Cockatrice, its poisonous blood will travel up the blade and kill the attacker. The Cockatrice has two enemies: the weasel, who is immune to its poison, and the crow of a rooster. However it can be killed instantly if it catches sight of its own reflection. Author Walter Wangerin, Jr., uses the cockatrice as his villain in his National Book Award–winning novel *The Book of the Dun-Cow* (Harper and Row, 1978). The novel was adapted as a musical by Mark St. Germain and Randy Courts and produced as an off-Broadway show in 2006 by The Prospect Theater Company.

Cuco: A pumpkin-headed ghost from Portugal used as a boogey-man to frighten children into obedience. The Cuco is the male version, the Coco is the female. The creature is similar to the jack-o'lantern, though whereas the Celtic and American carved pumpkins were used to scare bad things away, Cuco is itself the big nasty thing in the dark. The Cuco legend spread throughout Portugal and Spain and then jumped the Atlantic with explorers and settlers. When Vasco da Gama's sailors first encountered palm trees, they thought the big hairy fruit looked like the female version of their homegrown monster . . . and so they named it the coconut.

Cucuy (also **El Cucuy**, **Chucho**, and **Chamuco**): This is the Latin American version of the Cuco. It is a dark and frightening being that hides in closets or under beds and preys on children who don't say their prayers at night.

Dalhan: Both on the mainland in the deserts and on the islands that dot the seas near the Middle East, there are tales of a carnivorous demon called the Dalhan. The creature is vaguely human in appearance, but its skin is nearly black and covered with filthy rags through which coarse hair sprouts. The creature's face has a sloped brow and flat nose and a wide gash of a mouth filled with sharp but rotting teeth. Its body reeks of filth and decay.

The Dalhan is a flesh-eating monster who preys on travelers wandering in lonely places, or in some cases unfortunates who have been shipwrecked on desert islands. The creature rides a beast of burden very like an ostrich, but this ostrich has fiery red eyes and can run faster than any horse. When the Dalhan chases its

The Dalhan by Allen Koszowski

prey, the demon attacks the rider while the bird-creature uses talons like those of a velociraptor to slash the throat of the victim's horse or camel. Once the quarry has been brought down, both rider and mount begin to feed.

Dragon: These are among the oldest monsters in our bestiary; they come in all shapes and sizes and appear in virtually every culture. On the whole, they're either reptilian, serpentine, or a blend of both. The European dragon more closely resembles a dinosaur, with a large and ponderous body, armored scales, four very strong legs, and batlike wings. Usually European dragons could breathe fire, a fact that turned many an intrepid knight in shining armor into a heat-and-serve meal in a lunchbox.

Asian dragons tend to be more serpentine, with a writhing body, a headful of horns, and five dreadful claws. They rarely have wings, although they possess the power of flight. While European dragons were almost always evil, the Chinese dragon more often existed as

Dragonfire by Allen Koszowski

either an elemental force associated with rain and water or as a symbol for yang, the male aspect of universal duality. In fact, many Chinese refer to themselves as "Descendants of the Dragon" as a way to establish their ethnic identity.

Every culture that has dragons has dragon legends. Fictional dragons abound: Sua, the fire-breathing monster who fights Beowulf to the death in the Old English saga; Smaug from J. R. R. Tolkien's *The Hobbit* (1937) and Ancalagon the Black in *The Silmarillion* (1977); Avatre and several others in the Dragon Jousters series by Mercedes Lackey; the genetically engineered Dragons of Pern from Anne McCaffrey's many novels; Norbert and various other species of dragon in the Harry Potter books by J. K. Rowling; the dragons in *Eragon* (Knopf, 2003), *Eldest* (2005), and *Brisingr* (2008) by Christopher Paolini; the dragons in Gordon R. Dickson's the Dragon Knight series; and countless others. And dragons have been given the big-screen treatment in films like *Dragonheart*

(1996), *Dragonslayer* (1981), *Reign of Fire* (2002), *Shrek* (2001), *The Neverending Story* (1984), *Ghidorah, the Three-Headed Monster* (1964), *The 7th Voyage of Sinbad* (1958), and a few dozen others. They're also one of the most common elements in video games, role-playing games, and collectible card games.

Elder Gods: H. P. Lovecraft did not invent the concept of races of gods for his Cthulhu stories, though he certainly brought them into the era of modern storytelling. Most pantheons of gods in world myth and religion have stories of even older beings, such as the Titans who preceded the Olympians of ancient Greece. In Greek mythology, the Titanomachy, or War of the Titans, was a series of battles fought between the older and younger races of gods before the existence of mankind. At the outset there were twelve Titans (males were known as Titanes, and the females Titanides). The upstart Olympians eventually cast down the Titans and imprisoned them in Tartarus—an abyss within Hades. The Titans, though defeated, were not destroyed, and there was a belief that one day they would find a way to regain control of the universe.

The Elder Gods by Allen Koszowski

Visions of the Elder Gods

After the Hunt by Hervé Scott Flament

"For *After the Hunt* I wanted to create a menacing and bloody atmosphere presaging something dark and undefined in uncontrollable and slow gestation . . . the death of the great goddess Nature. In a palace bedecked with giant and repulsive Guardian Gods, some soldiers are bringing to their Lord a huge beast fished in the lagoon where it is reflecting the full moon. The animal does not move anymore, it's all dead and leaving bloody tracks on the marble floor where it has been dragged along. The prey, still shackled, is torn by flesh-eating birds. It is not so well armed with the usual big teeth and claws. By contrast, the soldiers are showing self-assurance while a lady and her young daughter are rushing to contemplate their catch . . . And so under the blind-eyed statues made of ivory—a much sought-after organic matter to adorn a so-called 'civilization'—a free and wild Creature, different by nature, died for the pride and joy of 'The Chosen Species,' the gregarious tribe, the king of predators: *Homo sapiens.*"

This scenario is played out over and over again in world religion, as seen in tales of the struggles between the Æsir and Vanir in Scandinavian mythology and in the Babylonian epic Enuma Elish, the Hittite Kingship in Heaven narrative, and even the rebellion of Lucifer against heaven. What makes all of these stories (or beliefs, if you prefer) so compelling is that there is always the promise of something vastly old and powerful that is constantly and tirelessly working to break into our world, and that once it does this we will suffer the torments of the damned as payment for the suffering of these elder beings. Lovecraft and his many followers connected with this idea and, through the Cthulhu Mythos and other similar cosmological story cycles, have managed to scare the bejesus out of us for years.

Elementals: These are spirits believed by many cultures to embody specific aspects of nature—air, water, earth, fire—and for the most part they are either benign or totally indifferent toward humans. However, some elementals (such as the Ballybog) have earned a reputation for being spiteful. They're cunning rather than smart, and are easily offended. Once they've taken offense at a human, they will do everything in their power to harm that person, usually by leading them into dangerous terrain full of quicksand, bogs, and deadfalls. Some cultures view the elementals as the source for many of the world's tricksters, incubi and succubi, and malicious imps; in other cultures they are regarded more as poltergeists. No one has yet managed to clearly define the nature and powers of the elementals.

Ga-Gorib: The Xhosa people of South Africa and the Khoikhoi tribes of southwestern Africa both share a common demon: Ga-Gorib, whose name means "thrower down." The name is apt, because Ga-Gorib's chief delight, it seems, is to perch on the edge of a pit and when someone walks by, he grabs them and throws them down into the pit. He also thought throwing stones at passersby was quite fun.

Dangerous and demonic as Ga-Gorib was, he was not the sharpest knife in the supernatural drawer and more often than not the stones he threw rebounded and whacked him in the head, causing him to fall into his own pit.

Elemental Art

Elemental by Scott Grimando

"Most of my work is inspired by folklore and mythological themes. These often overlap in the artist's experience. I've been obsessed with the fairy and the green man. They can sometimes be cast as mischievous tricksters, but mostly I think I enjoy them because they represent guardians of the natural world. They are the part of us that we have lost as we become more separated from nature. I try to work that theme into my fine-art work to give the viewer a new connection to the natural world through the narrative of the painting."—Scott Grimando is a New York artist whose work includes the cover of John Maddox Robert's novel *Hannibal's Children* (Ace, 2002).

A variety of legends surrounding Ga-Gorib exist, and in some he was defeated by a great hero. Heitsi-eibib tricked the monster (in itself no legendary feat) and knocked him into the pit. Another more energetic story described how Ga-Gorib chased Heitsi-eibib around the edge of the pit and then lost his balance and fell in. A third story—by far the most dynamic—describes a fierce wrestling match between Ga-Gorib and Heitsi-eibib which went on for many hours, with each combatant giving and taking grievous blows, before the hero overbalanced the demon and sent him tumbling to his death.

Giants: Enormous humanlike creatures. Often violent, they strike fear into any humans who run across them. In Greek and Roman story cycles, the giants were often turbulent and violent creatures that were frequently in conflict with the gods. This is certainly true not only in the myths of the Greeks, the Romans, and the Norse but also in other beliefs. In Hinduism, for example, the Daityas were a race of giants who fought against the gods because they were jealous of their Deva half brothers. The Norse giants, who come in different varieties—frost giants (*hrímpursar*) fire giants (*eldjötnar*), and mountain giants (*bergrisar*)—are predicted to be successful in their campaign against the gods and the legend of Ragnarok ("Twilight of the Gods") tells of their triumph and the fall of Asgard.

Most giants have a dimmer future, and legends present them as an elder race whose time on earth is waning, or in some cases, has passed, which adds an element of tragedy to their story and may explain some of their rage. It's hard to stay even-tempered when you know that your existence is about to become a footnote in history. Or, perhaps, the giants were never noble and don't deserve much sympathy. Consider this entry from Genesis 6:4–5: "There were giants in the earth in those days; and also after that, when the sons of God came in unto the daughters of men, and they bear children to them, the same became mighty men which were of old, men of renown. And God saw that the wickedness of man was great in the earth, and that every imagination of the thoughts of his heart was only evil continually."

Many of the giant stories in religion, folklore, myth, and heroic fiction use the threat of a giant as a way of demonstrating how clever and resourceful a human can be. Classic examples include the biblical adventure of David and Goliath (told in 1 Samuel, chapter 17) and Ulysses's encounter with the Polyphemus the Cyclops. Storytellers have always loved this kind of tale, because it's the ultimate underdog story. It doesn't matter whether the giant is smart or dumb as a box of hammers: he's a giant and that's all the threat necessary to create real dramatic tension.

There were stories during the crusades of Moorish giants who were eventually overthrown by the forces of Christendom. However, in Ireland the giants were more often heroes than villains, particularly Fionn mac Cumhaill (Finn McCool or Fingal) who used his massive strength in a series of hilarious adventures. The American giant Paul Bunyan, created by storyteller James MacGillivray, is almost certainly a variation on Fionn mac Cumhaill.

The race of giants factor into the wonderful series of Thomas Covenant the Unbeliever. Stephen R. Donaldson shows them as capable of nobility and treachery according to their own personal nature. This is only partly the case in the last few books of the Harry Potter series, which clearly shows that most giants are quite nasty.

Glycon (also **Glykon**): There are many ways in which predation is played out, both on the spiritual level and the human level. A case in point is the creation of a false god that is used to strike fear and awe into the population in a way that coerces them into obedience. The predator is the person behind the deception, the prey is the masses of the faithful, and the meat of the hunt is power. Alexander of Abonutichus, a Greek prophet of the second century C. E., wanted to create a new religion that would allow him to be revered as its chief cleric, a position of great power. Alexander claimed that a new god had been born that was a serpent with the head of a man, and that the snake-god was a new incarnation of Asclepius.[11] Alexander's cult grew fast and it grew strong and even

11. A legendary Greek physician who later became the god of medicine; reputedly the son of Apollo and Coronis.

outlived the false prophet. The historian Lucian of Samosaota revealed the truth of this scam in his writings, stating that Glycon was just a snake with a puppet head attached through which Alexander or one of his cronies would speak. Belief in the monster persisted, however.

Glycon was revered as a healer and it was widely believed at the time that the snake-god, with Asclepius acting through him from Heaven, protected the people from the terrible plague of the late 160s. Alexander/Glycon's protective spell can be found on an inscription from Antioch, the capital of ancient Syria, and translates as: "Long-tressed Phoebus shall dispel the plague-cloud." This spell is also mentioned in Lucian's writings. One could argue that despite his hunger for power Alexander and his pseudo-god, Glycon, actually managed to do some good. The plague was stopped—by whatever means—and throughout those dark times the people felt comforted. The end result may have been benign, but the intent was not, just as similar religious frauds today prey on the need and faith of those seeking spiritual comfort to allay their fears and doubts. Does the end justify the means? That argument has raged since Lucian wrote his exposé on the sham behind the snake nearly eighteen hundred years ago.

The noted graphic novelist Alan Moore, creator of *Watchmen* (comic book, 1986–1987; film adaptation, 2009), *V for Vendetta* (comic, 1991–1996; film, 2001), and *From Hell* (comic, 1982–1988; film 2006), recently admitted that he was a worshipper of Glycon, though he candidly admits the absurdity of worshipping a probable fraud. Moore is writing a book, *The Moon and Serpent Bumper Book of Magic*.[12] which will chronicle the history of magic as well as a detailed biography of Glycon.

Gorgon: A race of supernatural monsters from Greek myth. The Gorgons were female and each had a writhing tangle of serpents for hair and a face that was so hideous that any human who looked at it would be turned to stone. Though the Greek myths and histories tell of many Gorgons living in and around Greece, by far the

12. Scheduled for release in 2010 by Top Shelf Productions.

most famous were the three sisters Medusa, Stheno, and Eluryah, who were the daughters of the sea gods Phorcys and Ceto. Two of the sisters, Stheno and Eluryah, were immortals, but Medusa was not—she had once been a normal woman whose real beauty was unsurpassed. Sadly she was a bit too vain about her beauty and claimed that she was even more lovely than the goddess Athena. This vanity was also taken as a challenge by some of the male gods. One day, when Medusa was visiting the temple of Athena, she was brutally attacked and raped by Neptune. Instead of inter-

The Gorgon by Mike Bohatch

ceding on her behalf, Athena blamed Medusa for the rape—claiming that her vanity was at fault—which made Medusa doubly a victim. The Greek gods were seldom moral or fair-minded.

Outraged by the violence committed in her temple, Athena cursed Medusa and twisted her into a monstrous parody of her former self. Her exquisiteness became a lethal ugliness and her long shiny hair became a tangle of poisonous snakes. In time Medusa, embittered by this curse and by being snubbed by the goddess in whose temple she had been violated while attempting to pray, became a monster in nature as well as form and took joy in the destruction of handsome men whom she could not possess and who were repulsed by her.

Medusa's ultimate ruination came at the hand of the gallant Perseus, who was on a quest to save his mother Danae from the clutches of King Polydictes. Perseus was forced to complete a quest, and one of the tasks assigned to him was to retrieve Medusa's head. Perseus was able to accomplish this with some assistance from the still bitter and spiteful Athena, and from the god Hermes. He was given enchanted weapons—a mirrored shield and a magical sword—and used the mirror to look only at Medusa's reflection (which was not as lethal as a direct eye contact). Thus protected against Medusa's primary power, he was able to attack her with the magic sword and cut her head off.

Carvings of the Gorgon were used on Greek homes as proofs against evil, much as gargoyles were used elsewhere in Europe. Soldiers would also paint the face of Medusa on their shields to ward off the Keres (see listing in Vampires), who were evil spirits that hovered over battlefields and attacked the dying and wounded.

Griffen (also **Gryphon**): Many cultures throughout the Mediterranean, India, and the Middle East have legends of the mighty Griffin, a creature with the head, beak, and wings of an eagle, the body of a lion, and (occasionally) the tail of a serpent or scorpion. The creature has claws so long and strong that folks of that region used them to make drinking flagons. These drinking cups possessed a magic that enabled the drinker to detect poison before taking a sip. The Griffin was attracted by gold and would mine it or, when

Gargoyle by Alan F. Beck

"This gargoyle is based on the one at Notre Dame Cathedral in Paris. I live in Brooklyn, known as the borough of churches, and I see a lot of gargoyles. They are all over the place and I think late at night, they all gather in some dark area in a park and have a grand old time." —Alan F. Beck is an award-winning artist and illustrator.

more convenient, take it by force from humans, and then use the gold to line its nest. Naturally, this made their nests very appealing to hunters and adventurers, who sought them, hoping to steal the gold while the Griffin was out hunting. More often than not,

The Gryphon by Andrew McKiernan

the hunters became the meal, occasionally being portioned out to hatchlings nestled there among all that gold.

Milton, in his *Paradise Lost*, Book II, wrote:

As when a Gryphon through the wilderness,
With winged course, o'er hill and moory dale,
Pursues the Arimaspian who by stealth
Hath from his wakeful custody purloined
His guarded gold.

Harpy: This monstrous winged female monster from Greek myth delights in attacking travelers and gleefully tearing them to shreds with its brass talons. Oddly, some Harpies have also been known to act as vengeance monsters, killing those persons who have committed some great crime against the innocent, or savaging heretics. The tricky part is knowing ahead of time which way the Harpy's moods will swing. Harpies are the offspring of the sea god Thaus-mas and Electra. There were probably a great number of Harpies, though only three are named in mythology: Aello ("storm"), Ocypete ("swift-flier"), and Podarge ("swift-foot"). The most detailed account of the Harpies was the story of Jason and the Argonauts, in which Jason rescues the blind Phineas from the deadly creatures.

Hobgoblin: A mischievous magical creature frequently found in Western European folklore, the hobgoblin is an abbreviation of "Robin Goodfellow," better known as "Puck," a pre-Christian pagan trickster. In many of the older tales the hobgoblin is neither good nor bad but acts simply as a trickster, with the moral consequences of his actions often falling in one way or another on the human it tricks. Over the centuries the name has been slurred to Robin Goblin and hobgoblin; however as the name changed the nature of the creature seems to have changed as well and over the last few centuries the word "hobgoblin" has come to refer to a malicious spirit rather than a prankish one. In modern times the name is fairly interchangeable with "bogeyman," "bugaboo," and "bugbear," among others.

Puck/Robin Goodfellow is a character in William Shakespeare's play *A Midsummer Night's Dream;* other literary appearances include Ben Jonson's seventeenth-century ballad "The Mad Merry Pranks of Robin Goodfellow," John Milton's *L'Allegro*, Goethe's *Faust*, and Rudyard Kipling's "Puck of Pook's Hill."

Hydra: The fearsome Hydra was one of the most terrifying creatures from Greek myth—a gigantic beast with the thrashing body of a serpent and nine heads.[13] The Hydra lived deep in the swamps near the city of Lerna, in Argolis, and was a sibling to the Nemean lion, both of them being the offspring of the hundred-headed Typhon and Echidna, a half-woman, half-snake.[14] Aside from its bulk, its speed, and the tooth-filled mouths of its many heads, the

13. This number actually varies in different stories, though nine is the most commonly applied number.
14. Again, stories differ and some accounts credit Styx and the Titan Pallas as the parents of the monsters.

Hydra also had the extra combative advantage of becoming more powerful each time it was injured. If a head was lopped off, two more would instantly grow from the stump.

As part of his fabled Labors, Hercules was ordered to go and rescue the citizens of Lerna from the voracious appetites of the monsters, and the heroic demigod was quick to answer. He jumped into his enchanted chariot and along with Iolaus, his faithful charioteer, raced to Lerna to confront the beast. They used flaming arrows to lure the Hydra out of its cave and then Hercules waded in, blade flashing, and began cutting off heads. This proved to be a poor tactical choice, however, and Hercules fell back to reconsider. Then he ordered Iolaus to grab a torch and follow him, and this time as he cut off a head, the charioteer thrust the torch at the stump, cauterizing it. Hercules picked up a club and began smashing at the beast to finish it off. Once the monster was dead, Her-

The Hydra by Kevin Breaux

"Digital art allows modern artists to create photo-real interpretations of mythological monsters. It helps us imagine what our ancestors believed and feared."

cules dipped his arrows in the creature's poisonous blood, which gave the hero another weapon in his ongoing labors.

Illuyankas: Dragons are a staple element of heroic folklore. They are generally presented as evil or greedy, and the slaying of one is frequently used as a defining act to show that an adventurer is truly a hero. This is as true in Europe of recent centuries as it was with the Hittites of antiquity. In their myths, the Illuyankas was a particularly powerful and foul-tempered creature who had an appetite for eating townspeople or, when denied villagers, their herds of livestock. Teshub, god of sky and storm, took it upon himself to rid the region of the dragon, but that did not work out as well as expected and the dragon continued living, eating the locals, and breeding equally foul-tempered little baby dragons. Teshub then consults with Inara, the goddess who acted as the protector of all wildlife except, apparently, dragons, and she comes up with the idea of bringing in wagonloads of wine barrels to get the dragon drunk. Once the monster is thoroughly inebriated, Teshub and some of his fellow gods tie it up and then kill it.

In a later retelling of the tale, Teshub still loses the initial battle, but this time the great dragon takes the god's heart and eyes. Being a god, Teshub survives this and even goes on to sire children. His son, Sarruma, eventually marries the daughter of Illuyankas. As a wedding gift, Teshub asks his son to appeal to Illuyankas for the return of the purloined eyes and heart, which the dragon agrees to give back. Whole again, and a bit wiser for his experience, Teshub sets out once more to slay the dragon. This time he has the edge and at the moment when he is about to deliver the killing blow, his son, having just realized that his father had supported the bizarre marriage for the sole purpose of regaining his missing organs, steps in, gives his father an ultimatum, saying that if Teshub wants to kill Illuyankas, then he has to kill him as well, which Teshub does without even a flicker of regret. Gods of all kinds move in mysterious ways.

Iya: This is a nightmare monster from the story cycles of the Sioux peoples of the Dakotas. The Iya is nearly pure spiritual energy, though it often manifests itself as a great storm and lays waste to farms and villages. To the Sioux, the Iya is a terrible monster who

Kasha by Allen Koszowski

personifies evil and corruption and who also spreads disease among men and livestock alike.

Kasha: The Kasha is a Japanese ghoul that feeds by stealing recently buried corpses from their graves or taking bodies laid out in preparation for cremation. It is a small creature, about the size of a large dog, but immensely strong. When cornered, it has the power to kill several large men at once. It can easily run at full speed while carrying a corpse, and can leap over ten-foot-high walls. The Kasha are unpleasant, smell like rotting fish, and are exceedingly foul tempered. They have just enough human intelligence to take offense at the slightest insult, and sometimes listen at doors to see if someone is speaking ill of them. If so, they will intentionally despoil the graves of that person's family, urinate in the flower and vegetable gardens, and sometimes slaughter the family's pets and livestock.

The creature can be defeated by fire, and various Shinto tales featuring Samurai suggest that steel can harm the Kasha. It is not known whether gunfire will harm them, although it seems likely.

The surest way to defeat the Kasha is to adhere to proper burial rites so it cannot obtain any sustenance. With the proper religious rituals used, and the body guarded before burial and then protected by a strongly sealed coffin, the Kasha will become frustrated and skulk off in search of easier prey.

Kul: A water demon found in the Inuit culture, the Kul generally enjoys helping humans by locating fish in the frozen Arctic waters. A smart fisherman will toss some of the fish back to the Kul, which is enough to keep the creatures happy. A less clever fisherman will keep the entire catch for himself, and as a result the Kul will get furious and will bring all manner of harm against him and his village, including causing avalanches, cracking the ice under their feet, or sinking kayaks.

Liho (also **Likho**): The Russian and Slavic legend of the Liho is a strange nearly scene-for-scene retelling of the Cyclops legend from

Inuit Legends

"My novel, *Xombies* (Berkley, 2004), most definitely has a large element of folklore—mainly Inuit legends, which I found perfect because so many of the myths center around witchcraft and female power. Since my book was about a plague that turns women into 'monsters' (turning the tables on masculine assumptions of superiority), this was ideal. But I also touched on the Greek tradition, for instance by calling my plague Maenad Cytosis, which refers to the terrifying women who go berserk worshipping the god Dionysus. I think they all tap into subconscious fears of the unknown. Folklore is like religion (actually religion *is* folklore) in that it's an attempt to explain the mysteries of life in stark, emotional terms, as opposed to the perceived dryness of science. Words like 'anemia' and 'tuberculosis' are meaningless, but a vampire attack—that's something we can understand . . . and guard against. It appeals to the child in us."
—Walter Greatshell is the author of two as-yet-unpublished novels, *The Leaf-Blower* and *Terminal Island*.

the *Odyssey*. By nature, the Liho is the personification of evil misfortune. Some anthropologists suggest that the Liho legend may date back to Neolithic times. If so, then the older legends were then somehow blended with the Greek epic stories to form the modern take on the towering one-eyed monster.

The Liho is most often seen as a skinny old woman dressed in black, usually wearing a hood to hid the fact that she has only one eye. The Liho appears in a variety of folktales, and these stories reveal it to have a very deceptive and clever nature. For example, it often uses disguises in order to get close to potential victims. In the older stories, the Liho, like Polyphemus, the Cyclops of the *Odyssey*, is a man-eating monster who will eat human flesh without a qualm.

Mangkukulam (also **Bruha**): In the Philippines there are various good and bad magic users, and one of the worst, the Mangkukulam, serves as a strange kind of supernatural hit man. The Mangkukulam is a sorceress of the darkest arts. She makes a study of revenge and how to exact it through magic, and she sells these services to anyone who can meet her price. When hired to exact revenge, the Mangkukulam have been known to magically insert all sorts of deadly items into the victim's body, ranging from poisonous bugs to sharp needles and even broken glass.

Manticore: Asia has produced some of the most ferocious monsters in history and the Manticore is certainly in the front ranks. Believed to inhabit the forests of India, Indonesia, and Malaysia, the Manticore is a fearless predator with the powerful body of a red lion, the head of a human with piercing blue eyes, and a scaly tail that ends in a knot of poisonous spikes. When it opens its mouth, there are rows of teeth not unlike a shark's, and its claws can slash through the strongest armor. The Manticore's preferred method of attack is to whip its tail in a way that releases a rain of darts that will either paralyze or kill. Given that the Manticore then sets to devouring its victim at once, death is preferable to paralysis. When the Manticore is finished eating, there is not one scrap of flesh, bone, or clothing left behind.

Novelist Rick Riordan used a manticore as the villain in his

Folklore in Fiction

Holly Black, photo by D. Williford

"Almost all of my work has been inspired by folklore, specifically from Celtic and Scandinavian faery folklore, but also faery folklore from around the world. I have an interest in other stories, but my primary work has been with those. I'm drawn to faerie folklore, because, unlike vampires or werewolves, they are entirely alien. They have customs that are inhuman and strange. Also, because despite the fact that people often think of them as tiny, glittery girls with wings, in folklore they are capricious and dangerous beings, as likely to steal a baby and replace it with a changeling or blight crops.

"These archetypes are so enduring for the same reason that there is some form of animal transformation story and some form of vampire myth in almost every area of the world. These creatures speak to deep fears and deep desires: living forever, unleashing our animal selves, uncontrollable hunger, hurting the people that we love." —Holly Black is a best-selling writer of contemporary fantasy novels for kids, teens, and anyone willing to read them. Her books include the Modern Faerie Tale series: *Tithe* (Simon Pulse, 2004), *Valiant* (2006), *Ironside* (2008), *The Spiderwick Chronicles*, and the graphic novel series, *Good Neighbors* (Graphix, 2008).

young adult novel *The Titan's Curse* (Hyperion, 2007); a character from Salman Rushdie's controversial novel *The Satanic Verses* (Viking, 1988) encounters a manticore in the streets of the Arabian town Jahilia; the monster appears in Piers Anthony's first Xanth novel, *A Spell for Chameleon* (Ballantine, 1977); and a variation of the manticore appears in the novels of Holly Black's Spiderwick universe.

Minotaur: One of the greatest of the Greek myths is the story of Daedalus, the master architect, and his hot-headed son, Icarus, and of the building of the Labyrinth for Minos, the King of Crete. Prior to building that vast maze, however, Daedalus was given a less savory commission by Pasiphae, Minos's rather addled wife. Minos had been given a great bull by the sea god, Poseidon, which was intended as a sacrifice, but Minos being the shifty character that he was, decided to keep the bull as a pet. Infuriated, Poseidon[15] punished the king by casting a spell that made Pasiphae fall insanely in love with the bull.

Desperate to mate with the bull, Pasiphae forced Daedalus to construct a device that more or less made her look like a cow. The bull, being a typical bull, mated with the "cow," and Pasiphae became pregnant. The child of this bizarre and unsavory mating was a monster with the body of a man but the head of a bull.

Minos had Daedalus then build the Labyrinth to confine the creature, and every nine years seven young maidens and seven young men were brought from Athens and forced into the maze. The hybrid monster, known as the Minotaur, hunted them, abused them, and eventually ate them. Minos's daughter, Ariadne, helped hatch a plan for Theseus, the hero of Athens, to enter the maze and confront the bull. They fought a fierce and bloody battle, but Theseus eventually killed the Minotaur and escaped the Labyrinth.

Ogre: Ogre is a general name given to many of the world's hulking, foul-tempered monsters who have low I.Q.'s, tragically unappealing looks, and immense strength. The name is derived from the Latin "Orcus," a god of the underworld. In many of the stories in which Ogres appear, they are almost a metaphor for "bully," since they

15. In some versions of the story it was Aphrodite who did this.

are at first very strong and threatening, but when challenged prove to be cowards. Ogres are closely related to the Trolls of Scandinavian legend, and are very likely the same creature filtered through the folklore of different culture. Though Ogres are tremendously strong, they are also stupendously stupid, and many of the best

Ogre by Kelly Everaert

"Folklore monsters have been around for so long in our stories and old yarns handed down from generation after generation . . . and they're still scary. But quite frankly it's human beings who scare me more than anything out of myth or legend."
—Kelly Everaert lives and works as a freelance artist in Vancouver, B.C., Canada.

The New Mythology of Middle Earth

Gandalf the Gray by Jonathan Maberry

J. R. R. Tolkien is the Homer of our era. His books *The Hobbit* and the Lord of the Rings trilogy have become so iconic and so universally regarded that whole genres and subgenres have sprung up as a result. Certainly no other author (except possibly Homer) has had such a profound effect on fantasy storytelling. His versions of wizards (like Gandalf and Sauruman), elves, orcs, trolls, and dwarves have become the standard and so many authors copy the Tolkien versions of these beings under the misapprehension that Tolkien himself used them as he found them in folklore. He didn't. He changed them to suit his story in much the same way that Bram Stoker changed the nature and powers of the vampire to suit his novel *Dracula*. And this isn't a "damage done" effect: both Stoker and Tolkien have forever enriched and enlivened the world of storytelling.

ogre tales are built around a clever human pulling the wool over this monster's eyes.

Orc (also **Ork**): A gigantic and ferocious monster that has appeared in stories and tales from everyone from Ariosto to Tolkien. In the aforementioned tales the Orc is a man-eating sea monster; however in Beowulf, the Orc-néas, describes the race of monsters to which Grendel belongs. The name "Orc" is drawn from the same source as "Ogre": the name of a Roman god of the underworld, more or less interchangeable with Pluto, Hades, and Dis Pater. One of the oldest references to the creature was Pliny the Elder's description of the orca (killer whale), which he believed to be a supernatural monster and which he aptly described as a huge creature that was "armed with teeth."

In Tolkien's Lord of the Rings trilogy the Orcs take a new form, as mutated and ruined elves that serve the powers of darkness. In this form they are cannibalistic, ugly, but about the same basic size and strength as a human (though this varies among species, as you'll find when you read the books). Because of the popularity of the Rings, most people now consider this version of the Orc to be the official one, and the older and larger monster is largely forgotten. Among the high elves in Middle Earth, the orcs are also called goblins.

Ördög (also **Udug**, **Urdung**): The Ördög is a monstrous demonic being from Hungarian mythology whose very existence personifies darkness, evil, and malevolence. Its name translates as "lord of carrion," and it is the Satan figure in that culture.

Patupaiarehe: In the world of faeries and similar beings it is often difficult to establish whether their actions are "evil" or merely guided by a completely different set of values and laws in much the same way that historians are given the moral dilemma of determining whether the settlers of the New World were innocent immigrants or conquerors. Case in point is the faerie species known as the Patupaiarehe from the beliefs of the Maori peoples of New Zealand. Generally the Patupaiarehe are peaceful beings that can sometimes be called upon to reveal secrets or render aid to those who know the proper rituals needed to attract them. However, the Patupaiarehe have been known to steal humans away as mates.

Faerie **by Scott Grimando**

    In the folklore of the Patupaiarehe, the creatures are known to have very poor memories and (perhaps) limited intelligence. They often forget that they have a mate and simply go out and fetch another one, seeing no wrong in what they are doing according to whatever set of values operates in a community of magical beings. Even in the Maori beliefs, this is not necessarily seen as either rape or kidnapping, but as something in keeping with the nature of magical creatures. It is, essentially, just something they do, which makes it part of the overall balance of the universe.

This is not to say that the Maori do nothing about it. Lightning strikes may be part of nature as well, but the Maori don't stand under trees during a storm. So, in order to keep the Patupaiarehe from sneaking in and stealing a new husband or wife, the clever Maori use charms to fend them off. The Patupaiarehe cannot abide the color red, so lintels and window frames painted with red will seal a house against intrusion. Likewise the Patupaiarehe fear fire and ash, and protective fires will keep them at bay; nor will they steal food that has been cooked over a fire, though they will openly take uncooked food, especially fish, left untended.

The Patupaiarehe do not resemble the Maori at all. The faeries are tall, pale-skinned, and red-haired, and when they mate with a human the child is more often than not an albino. Patupaiarehe are cautious creatures, preferring to move in the dark or inside a rolling fog. They are great fishermen and there is an old folktale that tells of a human man who stealthily joined a Patupaiarehe fishing party and worked through the night with them to catch fish. Once the Patupaiarehe realized a man was working among them, they began arguing as to what to do with him, and the dispute lasted so long the sun rose and frightened them off. The man was left with their entire catch, and during the night he had learned the secret of how to make good fishing nets (something new to the Maori). He escaped with his life, the fish, and the lore of net-making. Maori storytellers cite this incident as the reason the Maori are so masterful at fishing.

Troll: A hulking, man-eating humanoid monster from Scandinavian legends probably related to Ogres. Trolls live in caves, under bridges, in the dungeons of castles, or deep in the shadows of ancient mountain strongholds. They differ from ogres in that they have at least marginal intelligence (though no supernatural Einsteins have emerged from this demographic), and they use what wits they have to amass great hoards of gold and jewels. Treasure, of course, lures treasure-hunters, and most of the best troll stories feature an intrepid (and equally greedy) hero who wants to sepa-

Trolls with a Twist

Troll by Allen Koszowski

"My short story 'The Stone Bridge Troll' (in the collection *Little Creatures*, Sam's Dot Publishing, 2008) and the poem 'The Troll of Madison County' (in the collection *Attack of the Two-Headed Poetry Monster*, cowritten with Mark McLaughlin, Skullvines Press, 2009) were inspired by the folklore of trolls. I've always had a fascination with trolls since I was a kid. Some of my favorite trolls were in J. R. R. Tolkien's *The Hobbit* and Terry Pratchett's *Men at Arms* and such movies as Stephen King's *Cat's Eye* and those loveable but cheesy '80s flicks *Troll* and *Troll 2*. Trolls can be ugly and adorable at the same time. 'The Troll of Madison County' is my troll satire of Robert James Waller's *The Bridges of Madison County*."
—Bram Stoker Finalist Michael McCarty is the author of ten horror and science fiction books.

rate the troll from his trove. Trickery is a must because no human could defeat a troll in a fair fight, but their immense strength is matched only by their meagerness of wits, and the resourceful hero usually wins out. J. R. R. Tolkien used trolls to good effect in the Lord of the Rings trilogy, and in the film versions they were depicted as huge, gray, slow-witted monsters—which seems like a pretty fair interpretation.

Wyvern: A monster very similar in many respects to both a dragon (though smaller and incapable of breathing fire) and a cockatrice, the Wyvern has great leathery wings, a reptilian body, and has only two legs and the hindquarters of a serpent. In medieval heraldry it was used to represent conquest, though it was also used as a symbol for pestilence. There are a number of subspecies, such as the fist-tailed Sea-Wyvern and the Lindworm, which has no legs. The Wyvern was often used as a familiar by sorcerers in the Middle Ages, and is said to have a catlike nature and disposition

Yatu-Dhana (also **Hatu-Dhana**)**:** The Rakshasa, vicious monsters of India, are messy eaters, and when they leave a bloody mess behind them at the scene of their kills, there is a parasitic fiend who feeds on these grisly leavings. Known as the Yatu-Dhana, these ghouls are actually sorcerers and they worship the fierce Rakshasa and are sometimes thought to be a lesser species of those monsters. Anyone who acts in a strange or unwholesome manner in Indian society may be suspected of being a Yatu-Dhana in disguise, which has led to the tradition of a person who wants to establish his humanity, generosity, or other virtuous qualities saying: "May I die today, if I am a Yatu-Dhana."

Zombies: There are two distinct types of zombies, real and fake, but the fake ones are far more well-known. Here's the skinny: prior to 1968 most people who had heard about zombies equated them with a living-dead person associated somehow with the Haitian religion of voodoo. The ethnobotanist Dr. Wade Davis, author of the nonfiction books *The Serpent and the Rainbow*[16] and *Passage*

---

16. *The Serpent and the Rainbow*, 1985, Simon & Schuster; *Passage of Darkness: The Ethnobiology of the Haitian Zombie*, 1988, The University of North Carolina Press

of Darkness, is one of the world's great experts on the subject. "The zombie, by Haitian belief," he told us, "is an individual who has lost their soul and been cast into purgatory. By that view, the act of making a zombie is a magical act. The victims have lost their animus—their true personality—and their conscious control. In my books, *Serpent and the Rainbow* and, more specifically, *Passage of Darkness*, I discuss how this is accomplished partly through what's called 'zombie powder,' a concoction made from toad skin and the chemical tetrodotoxin,[17] which is harvested from a species of puffer fish, which is the same order of fish as the Japanese fugu fish. A zombie of the vodoun kind is created in part by zombie powder and partly by the structure of the culture. Believing that becoming a zombie is possible helps to make it possible. It has a clear chemical base, but the creation of a zombie is a social event with a spiritual, political, and sociological basis."

But that kind of zombie is far less well-known these days, and the other kind of zombie is an example of how pop culture is now the substance generator for the new folklore. As mentioned in Part 1, in 1968 George A. Romero and John Russo wrote a screenplay for a cheapo little independent film called *Night of the Living Dead*, inspired in a large way by the vampire novel *I Am Legend* by Richard Matheson. Romero, who also directed, created a new kind of movie monster: a flesh-eating ghoul without consciousness or intelligence. It was as dangerous as a swarm of sharks, and as unreasoning.

Romero did not create a mythology for them, relying instead on oblique references to possible sources: radiation from a returning space probe or perhaps a disease. In the second film of the series, *Dawn of the Dead*, there's a sly reference to Macumba[18] and a hint at a possible spiritual cause, nicely summed up in what has since become the most iconic statement in the zombie genre: "When there's no more room in hell, the dead will walk the earth."[19]

17. Tetrodotoxin (anhydrotetrodotoxin 4-epitetrodotoxin, tetrodonic acid, or TTX) is a potent neurotoxin.
18. Brazilian slang for voodoo/vodoun used by nonpractitioners of that faith.
19. From the screenplay for *Dawn of the Dead* by George A. Romero. A line echoed in the 2004 Zack Snyder remake . . . both lines delivered by actor Ken Foree playing different roles.

With zombies we suddenly had a new kind of horror story-telling, and the genre has continued to expand and diversify, giving us both slow and fast zombies, mindless and intelligent zombies, terrifying and hilarious zombies, and other tweaks. The genre has also opened itself up to a variety of causes for zombies. The radiation concept was never strongly rooted in science and by the second film in Romero's series (at this writing he's done five of them) the emphasis was clearly on a disease of some unknown kind. Most zombie films take the disease route as a cause, mainly because it's not that far of a stretch outside of reality.[20] Other popular "causes" for the zombie outbreak include toxic spills, parasites, and demonic possession.

The zombie genre has been shambling along for over forty years, with blockbuster films like *Resident Evil* (2002), *28 Days Later* (2002), and *Shaun of the Dead* (2004), and plenty of sequels and new films coming out on a regular basis. Zombie fiction gave the genre a tremendous boost with bestsellers like Max Brooks's *Zombie Survival Guide* (Three Rivers Press, 2003) and *World War Z* (Crown, 2006); Brian Keene's *The Rising* (Leisure, 2004) and *City of the Dead* (2005); David Wellington's trilogy *Monster Island* (Thunder's Mouth, 2006), *Monster Nation* (2006) and *Monster Planet* (2007), Joe McKinney's *Dead City* (Pinnacle, 2006), and Stephen King's *The Cell* (Scribner, 2006). And even zombie comics became huge sellers, notably two series by Robert Kirkman—*The Walking Dead*, which is regarded by most critics as being on a par with the tone and social complexity of Romero's early films; and *Marvel Zombies*, in which all of the superheroes, from Spider-Man to Iron Man to the X-Men, become flesh-eating ghouls.

Comic book writer Robert Kirkman agrees: "Zombies play on our worst fear—death. It's something we can all relate to. Zombie stories are merely a metaphor for life. We're surrounded by death all day every day . . . no matter how slow it moves, it's always after us, and there is no escape. In the end, we all die."

Max Brooks had another take on it: "Because they scare me. No

20. For a lot of creepy reasons why zombies are *almost* medically possible, check out *Zombie CSU: The Forensics of the Living Dead* by Jonathan Maberry, 2008.

The Living Dead

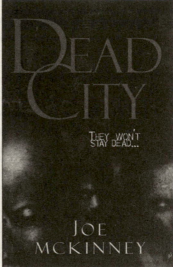

Joe McKinney,
photo by Alexander Devora
(Still Life Photography)

It seems everyone likes stories about dead people, which sounds weird and probably is weird. Joe McKinney shared his insights on this with us: "We've all seen death in one form or another these days. Thanks to the explosion of videos on the Internet and the nightly news and reality TV, it is statistically unlikely that any of us have managed to avoid seeing dead bodies. The networks are all too eager to show them to us, because they know that we just can't look away. So why is that? I think the main reason is because the dead on our TVs speak to our own fears of mortality. The Bible tells us that all flesh is grass. We all know that we're each going to meet our own final exit. You can't escape it. But knowing it as a logical proposition and really grasping it as a concrete fact are two very different things. Our fear of the dead, and our morbid fascination with them, stems from this two-tiered level of understanding. When confronted with the dead, we cannot help but feel the same emotions that our most primitive ancestors felt: The dead are our enemy, and they want nothing more than to carry us away with them.

"Modern literature and film have capitalized on this fear and given it a face with the zombie. Revenants like the zombie have been used as metaphors for every kind of social ill, as the supporting cast in apocalyptic wish-fulfillment tales of the last man on Earth, and even as the butts of dark humor about the futility of our mundane existence. And yet, for all of that, we haven't exhausted their potential. Like the best examples of folklore, they allow us a vehicle to discuss the hard truths of our lives while at the same time maintaining a narrative aloofness from those truths. I don't think this is seen any more clearly than in apocalyptic fiction. Zombies are, really, the apocalypse personified. Stories of the apocalypse deal with the end of the world. Generally speaking, apocalyptic stories show us a glimpse of the before, the world as it is now, and then spin off to terrifying visions of the aftermath of catastrophe. It's not a great stretch at all to see the zombie as a single-serving version of the apocalypse. We see the living person prior to their death, and this equates to the world before the apocalypse. We see the living person's death, and this equates to the cataclysmic event that precipitates the apocalypse. And finally, we see the shambling corpse wandering in search of prey, and this equates to the postapocalyptic world that is feeding off its own death. So, really, is it so strange that we take a certain comfort from zombie stories? They are so immediate, such personal representations of the dangers of our world, that we can't help but see ourselves in them."

—Joe McKinney is a police detective and the author of *Dead City* (Pinnacle Books, 2006).

---

seriously, they break every rule of horror. You have to go find most other monsters, but zombies come to you."

In his book *Danse Macabre* (Dodd Mead, 1983), Stephen King suggests that zombies have become a new horror paradigm, as complete and valid as vampires, ghosts, demons, and the rest. We agree, and apparently so does the entire horror world—fans, creators, critics. Zombies have become part of our current mythology and are sustained by the storytelling forces of our age: movies, books, and comics.

Zombie Comics

John Reppion   Leah Moore

"When Dynamite Entertainment came to us with the idea of doing a zombie series, we were overjoyed and embraced the project wholeheartedly. With *Raise the Dead*, we decided to hit the ground running and have our characters in the thick of a zombie outbreak right from the first page. Being zombie nerds, it was essential to both of us that the zombies in the story behaved a certain way; they are slow moving, of very low intelligence, cannot use tools or learn, retain nothing of their previous memories, cannot speak, and so on. In other words they had to be that blank 'other,' that thing which is like a human but is not a human and can stand for so much more as a consequence."
—Leah Moore and John Reppion are the creators of *Raise the Dead*; artwork by Huge Petrus.

Does that make them actual folkloric monsters? Do people really believe in them? The answer to that surprised us. We did some surveys of people—a large but random cross-section of society that included both genders; kids, teens and adults; folks with various education levels; homegrown folks and immigrants; and as many races as we could manage. forty-three percent of the people said zombies (of the *Night of the Living Dead* variety) are ancient monsters like werewolves and vampires. Twenty-seven percent said that these zombies are the same as the ones in voodoo. Six percent said that they believe that zombies either exist now, or may have existed at some point in history.

Those numbers hover somewhere between funny and scary. A little over four decades have passed and something that started as pure cinema fiction is now clearly creeping into our belief systems. It's the kind of effect we usually only see in cryptids. If these numbers fairly represent beliefs in this monster now . . . what will the numbers be forty years hence? Or four hundred? Will the next generations look back at zombies—and at other classic monsters of our modern storytelling age, such as Godzilla, Frankenstein, Jason Vorhees, and a hundred others—and think that's what we believed? And will they be correct?

We believe so.

More to the point . . . what do you believe?

Connect with Us

Visit us online at
KensingtonBooks.com
to read more from your favorite authors, see books
by series, view reading group guides, and more.

for sneak peeks, chances to win books and prize packs,
and to share your thoughts with other readers.

facebook.com/kensingtonpublishing
twitter.com/kensingtonbooks

Tell us what you think!

To share your thoughts, submit a review,
or sign up for our eNewsletters, please visit:
KensingtonBooks.com/TellUs.